THE LANDLORD'S LEGAL GUIDE IN MASSACHUSETTS

Second Edition

Joseph P. DiBlasi
Mark Warda
Attorneys at Law

SPHINX® PUBLISHING
AN IMPRINT OF SOURCEBOOKS, INC.®
NAPERVILLE, ILLINOIS

Second Edition, 2004

Published by: **Sphinx® Publishing, An Imprint of Sourcebooks, Inc.®**

Naperville Office
P.O. Box 4410
Naperville, Illinois 60567-4410
630-961-3900
Fax: 630-961-2168
http://www.sourcebooks.com
http://www.sphinxlegal.com

This publication is designed to provide accurate and authoritative information in regard to the subject matter covered. It is sold with the understanding that the publisher is not engaged in rendering legal, accounting, or other professional service. If legal advice or other expert assistance is required, the services of a competent professional person should be sought.

From a Declaration of Principles Jointly Adopted by a Committee of the
American Bar Association and a Committee of Publishers and Associations

This product is not a substitute for legal advice.

Disclaimer required by Texas statutes.

Library of Congress Cataloging-in-Publication Data
DiBlasi, Joseph P.
  The landlord's legal guide in Massachusetts / by Joseph DiBlasi and
Mark Warda.-- 2nd ed.
      p. cm.
  Includes index.
  ISBN 1-57248-398-9 (alk. paper)
  1. Landlord and tenant--Massachusetts--Popular works. 2.
Leases--Massachusetts--Popular works. 3. Landlord and
tenant--Massachusetts--Forms. 4. Leases--Massachusetts--Forms. I.
Warda, Mark. II. Title.
KFM2517.Z9 D528 2004
346.74404'34--dc22
                                        2004024496

To Laura,

Who came into my life from a far land and brought with her— love, happiness, and a beautiful smile. She is my present from God.

Acknowledgments

First and foremost, I wish to thank my parents, Joseph and Lucille DiBlasi, for their unyielding love and support in this and in all of my endeavors.

I wish to convey my love to my brother, Jim, and his wife, Silvana, and thank them for their support.

Thank you to attorney Christopher P. Hodgens and his wife, Deborah, for their dear friendship and their great assistance in the research and editing of this book.

Thank you to Daniel and Barbara Peterson of Peterson Real Estate in Saugus for their professional insight, helpful advice and suggestions, and for their friendship.

Thank you to my aunt, Elaine Puglisi, of Brad Hutchinson Real Estate in Melrose for her expertise and gracious assistance.

Finally, I would like to salute the thousands of honest and hard-working landlords in Massachusetts who persevere despite the obstacles.

Joseph P. DiBlasi

CONTENTS

USING SELF-HELP LAW BOOKS

Before using a self-help law book, you should realize the advantages and disadvantages of doing your own legal work and understand the challenges and diligence that this requires.

The Growing Trend

Rest assured that you won't be the first or only person handling your own legal matter. For example, in some states, more than seventy-five percent of the people in divorces and other cases represent themselves. Because of the high cost of legal services, this is a major trend and many courts are struggling to make it easier for people to represent themselves. However, some courts are not happy with people who do not use attorneys and refuse to help them in any way. For some, the attitude is, "Go to the law library and figure it out for yourself."

We write and publish self-help law books to give people an alternative to the often complicated and confusing legal books found in most law libraries. We have made the explanations of the law as simple and easy to understand as possible. Of course, unlike an attorney advising an individual client, we cannot cover every conceivable possibility.

Cost/Value Analysis

Whenever you shop for a product or service, you are faced with various levels of quality and price. In deciding what product or service to buy, you make a cost/value analysis on the basis of your willingness to pay and the quality you desire.

When buying a car, you decide whether you want transportation, comfort, status, or sex appeal. Accordingly, you decide among such choices as a Neon, a Lincoln, a Rolls Royce, or a Porsche. Before making a decision, you usually weigh the merits of each option against the cost.

When you get a headache, you can take a pain reliever (such as aspirin) or visit a medical specialist for a neurological examination. Given this choice, most people, of course, take a pain reliever, since it costs only pennies; whereas a medical examination costs hundreds of dollars and takes a lot of time. This is usually a logical choice because it is rare to need anything more than a pain reliever for a headache. But in some cases, a headache may indicate a brain tumor and failing to see a specialist right away can result in complications. Should everyone with a headache go to a specialist? Of course not, but people treating their own illnesses must realize that they are betting on the basis of their cost/value analysis of the situation. They are taking the most logical option.

The same cost/value analysis must be made when deciding to do one's own legal work. Many legal situations are very straight forward, requiring a simple form and no complicated analysis. Anyone with a little intelligence and a book of instructions can handle the matter without outside help.

But there is always the chance that complications are involved that only an attorney would notice. To simplify the law into a book like this, several legal cases often must be condensed into a single sentence or paragraph. Otherwise, the book would be several hundred pages long and too complicated for most people. However, this simplification necessarily leaves out many details and nuances that would apply to special or unusual situations. Also, there are many ways to interpret most legal questions. Your case may come before a judge who disagrees with the analysis of our authors.

Therefore, in deciding to use a self-help law book and to do your own legal work, you must realize that you are making a cost/value analysis. You have decided that the money you will save in doing it yourself outweighs the chance that your case will not turn out to your satisfaction. Most people handling their own simple legal matters never have a problem, but occasionally people find that it ended up costing them more to have an attorney straighten out the situation than it would have if they had hired an attorney in the beginning. Keep this in mind while handling your case, and be sure to consult an attorney if you feel you might need further guidance.

Local Rules The next thing to remember is that a book which covers the law for the entire nation, or even for an entire state, cannot possibly include every procedural difference of every jurisdiction. Whenever possible, we provide the exact form needed; however, in some areas, each county, or even each judge, may require unique forms and procedures. In our state books, our forms usually cover the majority of counties in the state, or provide examples of the type of form which will be required. In our national books, our forms are sometimes even more general in nature but are designed to give a good idea of the type of form that will be needed in most locations. Nonetheless, keep in mind that your state, county, or judge may have a requirement, or use a form, that is not included in this book.

You should not necessarily expect to be able to get all of the information and resources you need solely from within the pages of this book. This book will serve as your guide, giving you specific information whenever possible and helping you to find out what else you will need to know. This is just like if you decided to build your own backyard deck. You might purchase a book on how to build decks. However, such a book would not include the building codes and permit requirements of every city, town, county, and township in the nation; nor would it include the lumber, nails, saws, hammers, and other materials and tools you would need to actually build the deck. You would use the book as your guide, and then do some work and research involving such matters as whether you need a permit of some kind, what type and grade of wood are available in your area, whether to use hand tools or power tools, and how to use those tools.

Before using the forms in a book like this, you should check with your court clerk to see if there are any local rules of which you should be aware, or local forms you will need to use. Often, such forms will require the same information as the forms in the book but are merely laid out differently or use slightly different language. They will sometimes require additional information.

Changes in the Law Besides being subject to local rules and practices, the law is subject to change at any time. The courts and the legislatures of all fifty states are constantly revising the laws. It is possible that while you are reading this book, some aspect of the law is being changed.

In most cases, the change will be of minimal significance. A form will be redesigned, additional information will be required, or a waiting period will be extended. As a result, you might need to revise a form, file an extra form, or wait out a longer time period; these types of changes will not usually affect the outcome of your case. On the other hand, sometimes a major part of the law is changed, the entire law in a particular area is rewritten, or a case that was the basis of a central legal point is overruled. In such instances, your entire ability to pursue your case may be impaired.

Again, you should weigh the value of your case against the cost of an attorney and make a decision as to what you believe is in your best interest.

INTRODUCTION

Massachusetts' landlord/tenant laws are like a double-edged sword. If a landlord does not know about them, or ignores them, he or she can lose thousands of dollars in lost rent, penalties, and attorney's fees. However, a landlord who knows the law can use the procedures to simplify life and to save money. Knowledge is power and knowing the laws governing rentals will give you the power to protect your rights and to deal with problems effectively.

Laws are written to be precise, not to be easily readable. This book explains the law in simple language so that Massachusetts landlords can know what is required of them and know their rights under the law. If you would like more details about a law you can check the statutes in Appendix A or research the court cases as explained in Chapter 1.

Nearly every year the Massachusetts legislature passes new laws regulating landlord/tenant relations and the courts of the state write more opinions defining the rights of landlords and tenants. No book of this type can be expected to cover every situation that may arise. Laws change and different judges have different interpretations of what the laws mean. Only your lawyer can review the unique characteristics of your situation and give you an opinion of how the laws apply to your case. Nonetheless, this book can give you the legal framework to avoid costly mistakes.

The first ten chapters of the book are designed to follow the landlord/tenant relationship chronologically, from before the inception of the tenancy through termination of the tenancy and the court eviction process. Chapter 1 provides you with the framework to understand what laws govern rental property and where these laws can be found and researched. Chapter 2 discusses some very important tasks landlords need to complete and matters they need to consider prior to renting their unit.

Next, in Chapter 3, a review and comparison of the various options from which a landlord has to choose for the contractual agreement with a tenant are explored. Security deposits may be the single most misunderstood area for landlords. Chapter 4 provides the exact procedures the landlord needs to follow when taking both the security deposit and the last month's rent deposit.

Invariably, after the tenancy starts, tenants make requests for certain repairs. Chapter 5 details the responsibilities of the landlord and of the tenant. While rental property can be a lucrative investment, owners are vulnerable to insurance claims and lawsuits for various reasons. Chapter 6 examines for what reasons a landlord may be sued, the standards a court uses to determine if the landlord is at fault, and suggestions as to how a landlord can better protect him- or herself.

At some point during the tenancy, either the landlord or the tenant may request to change some term of the tenancy. The tenant may want to sublease the unit or the landlord may want to raise the rent. Chapter 7 discusses how various typical events will affect the tenancy relationship as well as how to correctly proceed to execute these changes. Chapter 8 identifies and provides analysis for some potential problem areas that occur during the tenancy, such as a landlord's need to gain access to the rental unit, the tenant leaving the unit in the middle of the lease, and the destruction of the premises either intentionally by the tenant or by mother nature.

At some point, all tenancies come to an end, either by the terms of the agreement or by one of the parties' affirmative act. Chapter 9 discusses the various ways a tenancy terminates and details what the landlord needs to do to terminate it correctly. The court eviction process is the only method by which a landlord can remove a tenant from the premises. Chapter 10 consists of an in-depth, step-by-step process of the court procedure along with defenses and counterclaims a landlord can expect the tenant to assert.

Self-storage facilities have become increasingly popular. Chapter 11 discusses the specific laws as they pertain to this type of rental property. And, finally, Chapter 12 is dedicated to those landlords of mobile homes and mobile parks.

When following the procedures in this book, keep in mind that different courts have different customs and some judges have their own way of doing things. The requirements in your area may differ somewhat from those outlined in this book. Clerks and court personnel cannot give you legal advice, but often they can tell you what is required in order for your case to proceed. Before filing any forms, ask if your court provides its own forms or has any special requirements.

I

LAWS THAT GOVERN RENTAL PROPERTY

Massachusetts landlord/tenant laws consist of both statutes passed by the legislature, regulations adopted by an agency of government such as the Department of Public Health, and legal opinions written by judges. The statutes and regulations usually address specific issues that have come up repeatedly in landlord/tenant relations. The judicial opinions interpret the statutes and regulations and decide what the law is in areas not specifically covered by statutes.

The most useful statutes and regulations are included in Appendices A and B of this book. Summaries of some cases, which explain what the law is, are included throughout the book. As explained later in this chapter, you can read the entire case if you believe it will be useful or you can look up other cases.

When reading the law contained in judges' opinions, be sure to note from which court the opinion originated. The written court decisions will state at or near the top the name of the court where it was rendered. If it is not from your district, it might not be binding on your case. Supreme Judicial Court of Massachusetts opinions apply to all areas of Massachusetts, but Appellate Division of the District Court opinions only apply to the district in which they sit.

Massachusetts Statutes

In Massachusetts, the statutes are called the Massachusetts General Laws and are abbreviated as "Mass. Gen. Laws" or "M.G.L." In this book, they will be abbreviated "Mass. Gen. Laws." This designation is followed by the Chapter and Section number. For example, the notation "Mass. Gen. Laws, Ch. 93, Sec. 40A" refers to Massachusetts General Laws, Chapter 93, Section 40A.

Massachusetts landlord/tenant laws are contained in different parts of the statutes. The following are the most important statutes that apply to landlord/tenant relationships:

- ✪ Mass. Gen. Laws, Ch. 186, "Estates for years and at Will";

- ✪ Mass. Gen. Laws, Ch. 239, "Summary Process for Possession of Land";

- ✪ Mass. Gen. Laws, Ch. 111, "Lead Paint";

- ✪ Mass. Gen. Laws, Ch. 105A, "Self Storage Units"; and,

- ✪ Mass. Gen. Laws, Ch. 140, Sections 32A-32S, "Mobile Home Parks."

Massachusetts Regulations

Regulations are laws that are written, not by the state legislature, but rather by a particular state agency, such as the Department of Public Health, pursuant to the authority given to it by a statute. Regulations are much more specific and detailed than statutes. The most important Massachusetts regulation for rental property is the Sanitary Code. It is found in Chapter 105 of the Massachusetts Code of Regulations, beginning at Section 410.0. The citation for this section is Mass. Code Reg., Ch. 105, Sec. 410.0.

Local Laws

Local governments in some areas have passed various rules regulating landlords. Be sure to check with your local city or town for any local laws that may apply to the renting of real property. For example, some cities and towns in

Massachusetts require the landlord to have a *certificate of occupancy* prior to renting the unit. The city (town) clerk at city (town) hall can often give you a copy of the laws with which you must comply.

Federal Laws

Federal laws that apply to the rental of real estate include discrimination laws such as the Civil Rights Act, the Americans with Disabilities Act, and lead-based paint rules of the Environmental Protection Agency. These laws are explained in Chapter 2 of this book.

The United States Department of Housing and Urban Development (HUD) has a handbook that explains the rules applicable to public housing and other HUD programs.

Legal Research

This book contains a summary of some important court cases. Appendix A includes the most important statutes that affect landlord/tenant laws. However, you may want to research your situation further by reading other statute sections or court cases.

Court cases referred to in this book are noted by the little book symbol 📖. Case citations include the name of the case, the volume and page of the reporter, and the court and year.

Example 1:   *Whittaker v. Saraceno*, 635 N.E.2d 1185 (1994), means that the case titled *Whittaker v. Saraceno* is found in Volume 635 of the *Northeast Reporter, Second Series*, at page 1185, and that it is a 1994 case.

Example 2:   The case *Tuchinsky v. Beacon Property Management*, 45 Mass. App. Ct. 469 (1998), is in Volume 45 of the *Massachusetts Appellate Reports* at page 469, and is a 1998 case.

2 | CREATING THE LANDLORD/TENANT RELATIONSHIP

After deciding to rent a residential unit with the hope of earning extra rental income, you must now take the all-important preliminary steps to ensure against potential problems down the road. These steps are like the foundation of a house, which must be strong and secure to support and protect the dwelling against potential hazards.

Certificate of Occupancy

Once you decide to rent a unit, you must first find out if it is capable of being rented and occupied. In order to find out, you must have the unit and its building inspected by the appropriate municipal officials. In most cases, the local building department and fire department are responsible for inspecting the building. Upon your application for a *certificate of occupancy* from the building department, these departments will inspect the unit for compliance with the state building code, the state fire code, and the applicable *zoning laws*. Zoning laws are the local city or town laws that govern where various types of houses and buildings can be located.

There is normally an application fee for the certificate of occupancy, as it requires considerable time on the part of the various officials and inspectors. Your town will not grant you a certificate of occupancy for a rental unit if it is in violation of a code provision or one of the zoning laws. Once your city or town issues a certificate of occupancy, you now have the town's official *O.K.* that you have a valid rental unit. Furthermore, if you have a multi-unit building, the certificate of occupancy will state how many legal units your building contains.

Health Inspection and Certificate

Upon your request, the local board of health (or inspectional services department) may conduct a separate *pre-inspection* of the individual unit to determine if it complies with another set of regulations—the Massachusetts Sanitary Code (discussed further in Chapter 5).

As with the application for the certificate of occupancy, a fee is charged for this pre-inspection, which is usually around $25 depending on the city or town.

Following a successful inspection, the board of health will issue a *certificate of compliance*. All rental units must be in good condition at the time they are rented. This certificate will help to prove compliance with the requirements of the Sanitary Code at the inception of the tenancy.

> *Landlord Tip:* Invest the time and money to get the unit pre-inspected and obtain the certificate of compliance before each new tenant moves into the unit. This is the cheapest and most effective form of insurance for any landlord.

Be sure to apply for the certificate of occupancy and certificate of compliance, as both are very effective tools to ensure against future allegations of unfitness by your tenants. Once obtained, keep them in a safe place with your other important documents.

Lead Paint

Prior to 1978, house paints contained lead metals. Unsupervised toddlers and small children would pick at flaking paint on the walls and eat the chips of paint. These children would often be diagnosed with neurological disorders that physicians linked to lead poisoning.

Massachusetts Law

In Massachusetts, there are strict laws governing lead paint in residential dwellings and the landlord's duty with respect to it. There are five *triggering events* that require compliance with the lead paint laws.

1. *Request for Inspection.* If the occupant of the unit requests that the lead poisoning control director (Massachusetts Department of Public Health) conduct an inspection and a lead hazard is found, the owner will be ordered to remedy the hazard and comply with the law.

2. *Lead Poisoning Case.* Upon being informed of a lead poisoning case, the poisoning control director must inspect the premises of the victim. If a lead hazard is found, the owner will be ordered to remedy the hazard.

3. *Occupancy by Child under Age Six.* If a child under six years of age resides in the premises built before 1978, the owner must have the home inspected for lead. If paint, plaster, soil, or other accessible materials are determined to contain dangerous levels of lead, the owner must take remedial action.

4. *Change of Ownership.* When there is a change of ownership of the premises and a child under six years of age resides in the premises, the buyer must remedy the problem.

5. *Determination of Discrimination.* If a court or the Massachusetts Commission Against Discrimination determines that discrimination has occurred regarding the occupancy of the premises, the provisions of the lead paint law apply.

The Owner's Duties. A landlord of housing units built before 1978 must *delead* (remove or lawfully cover all required surfaces containing lead-based paint) any unit when he or she rents to a family with at least one child under the age of six. Refusal to rent to families with a child or children under age six is not an option. This is deemed illegal in Massachusetts as it discriminates against families with young children. Delead the unit prior to accepting any rental applications.

The law has specific instructions as to what lead hazards must be removed or covered. Although the lead paint law, like all laws, may be amended, the following are the present requirements.

✪ *Loose Paint.* All loose lead paint, plaster, putty, or other accessible material on both exterior and interior surfaces and fixtures shall be removed or adequately contained, or the fixture or surface replaced. However, paint on metal surfaces and fixtures other than window sills, hand rails, and railing caps need only be made intact.

✪ *Intact Paint on Windows with Sills Less than Five Feet High.* Intact lead paint or putty on windows with sills five feet or less from the floor or ground shall be removed from all surfaces that are either movable or come in contact with movable surfaces. These surfaces include:

- interior and exterior sashes, including muntins;

- mullions;

- the interior sill and the portion of the sill between the storm window and the window unit, including window wells;

- exterior sills that constitute accessible, mouthable surfaces;

- parting beads; and,

- the entire interior and exterior inner and top sides of the window casing that come in contact with the sash.

If the window surfaces are metal and the paint is intact, only the sills need to be replaced. Alternatively, the law now allows these surfaces to be contained where feasible or the window and sill may be replaced.

✪ *Intact Paint on Other Surfaces.* Intact paint, plaster, putty, or other leaded material shall be removed on accessible, mouthable surfaces below five feet and four inches from all edges. These areas and surfaces include:

- doors, door jambs, and casings;

- exterior window sills;

- the face and outer sides of window casings;

- stair rails, balusters and treads from the tread to the lip and to the riser below;

- cabinets;

- porch railings; and,

- balusters.

If the areas and surfaces are made of metal, then all of the following items must be removed:

- window sills;

- handrails and railing caps, including handrails and railing caps on fire escapes (when used as porches); and,

- all other exterior and interior surfaces or fixtures that may be readily mouthable by children.

The law allows these surfaces and fixtures to be contained or replaced.

Costs. The cost of deleading varies depending on the amount of lead hazard involved and the difficulty of removing or covering. The biggest expense is replacing windows that contain and spread lead dust. During the deleading process, no person or pet may occupy the premises. Occupancy may not resume until the premises have been cleaned and found to be in compliance. Furthermore, Massachusetts courts have required that the owner pay the relocation costs for the tenants who are forced to move out during the deleading process.

Courts usually award $100–$300 per day to compensate tenants for relocating. Therefore, although the cost of deleading is high, if it is incurred prior to renting the unit, you eliminate the possibility of facing a costly discrimination battle, a lead paint poisoning lawsuit, Sanitary Code penalties ($500 per day), punitive damages, or the additional expense of paying to relocate your tenants during deleading.

Encapsulation. Since an amendment to the lead paint law allowing containment instead of removal where feasible, a process called *encapsulation* has become a popular alternative to deleading. Encapsulation is the name of the process in which a thick, white glue-like substance is applied over the leaded surfaces. This covers the lead paint so it cannot be touched and so no dangerous dust is produced. The actual encapsulation process is significantly cheaper than removal, and, upon approval by the Department of Public Health, the landlord is able to do the process him- or herself.

However, before you are able to encapsulate, the area must be tested by a licensed lead inspector to determine if the encapsulant will take to the surface. This testing obviously adds to the cost of the process.

Landlords can do some limited, *low-risk* deleading work themselves. The Massachusetts Department of Public Health will provide you with a list of authorized inspectors, a complete deleading and encapsulation package, and a step-by-step guide explaining the low-risk deleading options. They can be reached at:

Massachusetts Department of Public Health
Childhood Lead Poisoning Prevention Program
305 South Street
Jamaica Plain, MA 02130
800-532-9571

Notification and Certification. Landlords of tenants who live in units built before 1978 must give their tenants two copies of the **TENANT LEAD LAW NOTIFICATION**. (see form 2, p.197.) They must also give tenants two copies of the **TENANT CERTIFICATION FORM**. (see form 3, p.201.) These forms serve to inform tenants about the hazards of lead paint and about their rights as tenants in a unit containing lead. The **TENANT CERTIFICATION FORM** is to be signed by both the landlord and the tenant to indicate that the notification procedure was followed. Also, landlords are required to provide their tenants with copies of any existing lead status documents such as lead inspection reports, risk assessment reports, a compliance letter, or a letter of interim control.

Federal Law   The *Environmental Protection Agency* (EPA) and the *Department of Housing and Urban Development* (HUD) require notices to be given to tenants of rental housing built before 1978 that there may be lead-based paint present and that it could pose a health hazard to children. This requirement applies to all housing except housing for the elderly or zero-bedroom units (efficiencies, studio apartments, etc.).

The regulations of the agencies also require that a pamphlet about lead-based paint, titled "Protect Your Family From Lead in Your Home," be given to prospective tenants. However, since the Massachusetts lead law is stricter than the federal law, the EPA and HUD have agreed that using the Massachusetts forms will be sufficient and that the federal form is not needed in Massachusetts.

Application Process

The next preliminary matters are the advertisement of the unit and the acceptance of applications from prospective tenants. Your main concern at this point is to effectively market your unit to obtain quality tenants.

Real Estate Agents   At this stage, you have an option. You may market the unit and screen prospective tenants on your own or you may hire a *real estate agent* to oversee this process for you. Although the agent may seek compensation from the prospective tenant directly, Massachusetts law prohibits the landlord from collecting money from the tenant in reimbursement for the agent's fee. If the landlord pays, the typical fee is fifty to one hundred percent of the new tenant's first month's rent.

The benefits of obtaining an agent include having someone else do the following:

✪   show the unit;

✪   incur the advertising costs;

✪   gather information and applications from potential tenants; and,

✪   conduct credit and reference checks.

Some landlords choose to do all of these steps themselves. This way, they save the expense of the commission and feel reassured by meeting and speaking with the potential tenants.

If you choose to use an agent, you must realize that the agent's sole job is to market your unit and locate potential tenants. The agent does not guarantee the character or creditworthiness of tenants—that responsibility is yours. If you do retain the services of a real estate agent, be aware that you, as the landlord, are primarily concerned with obtaining the best-qualified tenant. The agent, however, is paid as soon as he or she finds a tenant that is accepted. Nondiligent agents will *sell* you one of the first applicants, even though they may not be well-qualified, in order to quickly collect their commission. Problems caused by these *less-than-qualified* tenants often take a few months to materialize—long after the agent is paid and out of the picture.

> *Landlord Tip:* Do not solely rely on your agent's characterization of the prospective tenant. Review the application materials collected by your agent to arrive at your own determination.

Rental Application

Before you agree to rent a unit to a tenant, you must make sure that you have evaluated the person and feel comfortable about him or her. After all, you are allowing a person into your property or home to live. Once the tenant is in, it is not always easy to get him or her out of your property.

The simplest way to size up your prospective tenant is to have him or her fill out a **RENTAL APPLICATION**. (see form 1, p.195.) This is a simple procedure, yet many landlords, especially small, nonprofessional ones, rent to tenants without even knowing their last name or employment status.

You should see to it that your prospective tenant completes the **RENTAL APPLICATION** in full. Due to housing laws, you cannot ask for any information from the tenant relating to race, color, national origin, religion, sex, sexual orientation, marital status, age, ancestry, or handicap status. This information is not permitted to be asked of potential tenants because housing cannot be denied for any of these reasons. Instead, you should be sure to obtain the individual's name, address, employment status, income, and rental history. For future reference, the applicant's social security number should also be included.

A separate application should be completed for each adult cotenant. An incomplete application may indicate an unwillingness on the part of the applicant to disclose some telling information. If this occurs, proceed with caution with that applicant. Furthermore, any applicant who is not willing to complete the application should not be considered as a possible tenant. Have the applicant sign his or her name to the application and save it to compare with other applications.

An applicant may embellish on the **RENTAL APPLICATION**, so it is up to you to determine an applicant's truthfulness. One good way to learn more about the prospective tenant is to obtain references from his or her present employer and past and present landlords. All requests for employment and previous rental information should be made in writing and should ask for written replies.

When contacting the employer, verify the applicant's job status and salary. When contacting his or her present landlord, ask about the applicant's payment history and what kind of tenant he or she has been.

Although it is good practice to contact the present landlord, you may not receive a very truthful or accurate report. A landlord of a problem tenant may say anything in order to get rid of the tenant, even if it means lying to you. Therefore, be sure to check with the applicant's prior landlords as well. Refer to the **PRIOR LANDLORD AND CREDIT REPORT AUTHORIZATION** for this. (see form 4, p.203.) Be aware that in response to your request for their landlord contact information, some undesirable tenants may provide you with the name and/or telephone number of a friend or relative who will impersonate the applicant's landlord. You should verify your applicant's former address from their driver's license or utility bills and then independently confirm the name, address, and telephone number of the owner or property manager of that address.

The extra-cautious landlord will also ask the tenant to produce, as part of the application, receipts for rent payment for the last year or two. Finally, you should also contact personal references furnished by the applicant.

> *Landlord Tip:* When checking an applicant's references, always check with and give more weight to the previous landlord's reference rather than the current one.

Credit Check
The **RENTAL APPLICATION** serves as a good tool to judge the applicant's character and reputation. It is not, however, a fail-safe tool to judge his or her credit and past history as a tenant. The cautious landlord will also have the applicant sign a **PRIOR LANDLORD AND CREDIT REPORT AUTHORIZATION LETTER** for authorization allowing access to the applicant's credit report. (see form 4, p.203.) With this authorization, you are now able to request the latest credit report of your applicant from one of a few large credit bureaus such as TRW, Transunion, or Equifax.

A credit report will provide information regarding the individual's payment history with creditors. You can locate these companies by referring to your local Yellow Pages directory under *Credit Reporting Agencies*. The charge for this report, usually $30 to $40, is minimal given its usefulness. It is a safe bet that a person who has a poor credit history will be lax in his or her payment obligations with you.

In addition to learning about the credit status, some credit reporting companies can provide information about an individual's prior tenant history, as well as any criminal record. *The National Tenant Network* (978-858-0756) provides this specific information for a reasonable fee. However, in deference to the potential tenant, you may want to request his or her explanation or version of any questionable history. A person who refuses access to credit information is not a person you want as your tenant.

Discrimination

Since Congress passed the *Civil Rights Act of 1968*, it has been a federal crime for a landlord to discriminate in the rental or sale of property on the basis of race, religion, sex, or national origin. In addition, Massachusetts has its own antidiscrimination law, which is stricter than the federal law and is described later in this chapter on page 18. In 1988, the United States Congress passed an amendment to the Civil Rights Act that bans discrimination against both the handicapped and families with children. Except for apartment complexes that fall into certain special exceptions, all rentals must allow children in all units.

Civil Rights Act of 1968   Under the *Civil Rights Act of 1968*, any policy that has a discriminatory effect is illegal. (see United States Code, Title 42, Sections 3601-17 (42 U.S.C. Secs. 3601-17).)

Penalty. A victim of discrimination under this Act can file a civil suit, a HUD complaint, or request the U.S. Attorney General to prosecute. Damages can include *actual losses* and *punitive damages* of up to $1,000. Actual losses are monetary damages suffered by the victims that directly flow from the discriminatory act. Punitive damages are damages not related to losses the victim sustained, but are assessed against the wrongdoer purely as punishment, so as to deter discrimination. Failure to attend a hearing or to produce records can subject you to up to a year in prison or a $1,000 fine.

Limitation. The complaint must be brought within 180 days.

Exemptions. This federal law does not apply to the sale or rental of single family homes if:

- ✪ the owner of the single family house does not own more than three such single family houses at one time;

- ✪ the owner did not sell another single-family house within the prior twenty-four months; and,

- ✪ no real estate broker and no discriminatory advertisement is used in the sale process.

It also does not apply to a property that the owner lives in if it has four or less units.

Coercion or Intimidation. Where coercion or intimidation is used to effectuate discrimination, there is no limit to when the action can be brought or the amount of damages.

Civil Rights Act Sec. 1982

The *Civil Rights Act, Section 1982*, is similar to the *Civil Rights Act of 1968*. But, where the 1968 Act applies to any policy that has a *discriminatory effect*, Section 1982 applies only where it can be proved that the person had an intent to discriminate. (42 U.S.C. Sec. 1982.)

Penalty. A person can get actual damages plus unlimited punitive damages.

    📖 In 1992, a jury in Washington, D.C., awarded civil rights groups $850,000 damages against a developer who only used Caucasian models in rental advertising. The Washington Post now requires that twenty-five percent of the models in ads it accepts must be African-American to reflect the percentage of African-Americans in the Washington area.

Limitation. There is no time period in which the complaint must be brought.

Exemptions. Anyone discriminated against can bring suit.

Civil Rights Act 1988 Amendment

The 1988 amendment to the *Civil Rights Act* bans discrimination against the handicapped and families with children. (42 U.S.C. Sec. 3601.) Unless a property falls into an exemption, it is illegal under this law to refuse to rent to persons because of age or to refuse to rent to people with children.

The exemptions are for two types of housing.

1. Where the units are rented solely by persons sixty-two or older.

2. Where eighty percent of the units are rented to persons fifty-five or older.

Families with children. While landlords may be justified in feeling that children cause damage to their property, Congress has ruled that the right of families to find housing is more important than the rights of landlords to protect the condition of their property.

Disabled persons. Regarding the disabled, the law allows them to remodel the unit to suit their needs as long as they return it to the original condition upon leaving. It also requires new buildings of four units or more to have electrical facilities and common areas accessible to the disabled. In late 1995, the law was amended so that the property as offered does not need to have special facilities for such persons' needs.

Penalty. A landlord will pay $10,000 for first offense, $25,000 for second violation within five years, and up to $50,000 for three or more violations within seven years. He or she may have to pay unlimited punitive damages in *private actions*. Private actions are civil suits brought against the wrongdoer, not by the government, but by the victim.

Limitation. The complaint must be brought within two years for private actions.

Exemptions. This law does not apply to single family homes if:

⊛ the owner owns three or less;

⊛ there is no more than one sale within twenty-four months;

⊛ the person does not own any interest in more than three at one time; and,

⊛ no real estate agent or discriminatory advertisement is used. (A condominium unit is not a single-family home, so it is not exempt.)

It also does not apply to a property that the owner lives in if it has four or less units.

Additionally, there are exemptions for:

✪ dwellings in state and federal programs for the elderly;

✪ complexes that are solely used by persons sixty-two or older;

✪ complexes used solely by persons fifty-five or over if there are substantial facilities designed for the elderly;

✪ religious housing; and,

✪ private clubs.

Americans with Disabilities Act

In 1992, the *Americans with Disabilities Act* (ADA) took effect. This law requires that *reasonable accommodations* be made to provide access to commercial premises for the disabled and it forbids discrimination against them. This means that the disabled must be able to get to, to enter, and to use the facilities in commercial premises. It requires that if access is *readily available* without *undue burden* or *undue hardship*, changes must be made to the property to make it accessible.

If any commercial premises are remodeled, the remodeling must include modifications that make the premises accessible. All new construction must also be made accessible.

The law does not clearly define terms like *reasonable accommodations*, *readily available*, *undue burden*, or *undue hardship*, and does not even explain exactly who will qualify as *handicapped*. The law includes people with emotional illnesses, AIDS, dyslexia, past alcohol or drug addictions, as well as hearing, sight, and mobility impairments.

What is *reasonable* will usually depend on the size of the business. Small businesses will not have to make major alterations to their premises if the expense would be an undue hardship. Even large businesses would not have to have shelving low enough for people in wheelchairs to reach as long as there was an employee to assist the person. There are tax credits for businesses with fewer than thirty employees and less than one million dollars in sales. For more information on these credits obtain IRS forms 8826 and 3800 and their instructions.

Some of the changes that must be made to property to make it more accessible to the disabled are:

✪ installing ramps;

✪ widening doorways;

✪ making curb cuts in sidewalks;

✪ repositioning shelves;

✪ repositioning telephones;

✪ removing high pile, low density carpeting; and,

✪ installing a full-length bathroom mirror.

Both the landlord (the owner of the premises) and the commercial tenant (as the owner of the business occupying the premises) can be liable if the changes are not made to the premises. Most likely the landlord would be liable for common areas and the tenant for the area under his or her control.

Penalty. Violators may pay injunctions and fines of $50,000 for the first offense, and $100,000 for subsequent offenses.

Exemptions. Private clubs and religious organizations are exempt from this law.

Massachusetts Housing Discrimination Law

The *Massachusetts Housing Discrimination Law* is very similar to the federal law, except that it also applies to discrimination against the handicapped. (Mass. Gen. Laws, Ch. 151B.) The reason for a state statute that duplicates the federal law is to give victims of discrimination a state remedy that may be easier to pursue than a federal one.

To summarize this law, it is illegal to refuse to rent to a person on the basis of race, color, national origin, ancestry, religion, creed, sex, sexual orientation, marital status, family composition (the presence or lack of children), veteran status, disability (physical or mental), age, or source of income (i.e., public assistance, etc.). Each of these categories is called a *protected class*.

The most obvious method of discrimination is for the landlord to openly state to the prospective tenant that he or she does not rent to people of the tenant's (protected) class; however, courts have found discrimination to exist with much more subtle conduct. It may be deemed discriminatory if a landlord imposes a more probing application process on a person of a protected class than he or she would impose on other applicants. Also, telling a tenant that he or she may not be comfortable living in your unit because the neighbors are of another class has also been found to be discriminatory.

In addition, taking a security deposit from a tenant of a protected class when your normal practice does not include the taking of security deposits may be deemed discriminatory. Refusing to rent a unit to a blind person because that person has a guide dog is also a violation of the law.

Moreover, refusing to make reasonable accommodations to allow a disabled person to rent your apartment or refusing to rent your unit to a family with children (even if lead paint exists) is conduct that has been found to be discriminatory and punishable.

Penalty. A person who violates the *Massachusetts Housing Discrimination Law* may be required to pay the expenses incurred by the tenant in obtaining alternative housing, storage space, and all associated costs. The tenant may also recover money damages for mental anguish and humiliation. In addition, large civil penalties may be imposed against the landlord. Landlords should be aware that it is not uncommon for representatives from government agencies (commonly called *testers*) to pose as interested tenants and test your compliance with the discrimination laws.

Exemptions. An owner-occupier landlord of a dwelling containing three units or less, who is over sixty-five years of age, and is disabled or suffering from a chronic illness, may lawfully refuse to rent to a prospective tenant with children if the presence of children would constitute a hardship.

In addition, since the Sanitary Code (discussed later in Chapter 4) establishes a minimum amount of square footage space per occupant, a landlord would be justified in refusing to rent to tenants if that ratio would be violated. Presently, the Sanitary Code requires every dwelling unit to contain at least 150 square feet of floor space for the first occupant and 100 square feet of space for each additional occupant.

Lastly, the owner-occupant of a two-family house is exempt from discrimination of all protected classes, except discrimination with regard to tenants receiving rental subsidy or public assistance.

3 LEASES AND RENTAL AGREEMENTS

Once you have found a suitable tenant to rent your unit, the next decision to make is what type of rental arrangement (*tenancy*) will govern your relationship. There are two basic types of tenancies to choose between:

1.   a tenancy-at-will or
2.   a lease.

There are significant differences between the two that should be studied so you can choose the one more suitable to you and your situation.

Tenancy-at-Will

A *tenancy-at-will* is the simplest form of rental arrangement. It arises when the parties (you and your tenant) agree to rent the unit for a certain amount of money and without a certain termination date. The tenancy-at-will continues to be in effect from rental period to rental period—typically month-to-month.

Features   A tenancy-at-will may be terminated by either you or your tenant with or without a reason. Moreover, the rental amount may be changed (usually increased) simply upon a rental period's notice to the tenant. (The procedure for increasing the rent is discussed in Chapter 7.)

Many landlords prefer this type of tenancy for a couple of reasons. It allows them the greatest flexibility in dealing with their tenants. They are always only a full rental period away from being able to increase the rent or terminate the tenancy for any lawful reason that comes up.

> **Example:** A landlord who is contemplating selling the building in the near future may want to have all tenants-at-will, in case the prospective purchaser wants to buy the building vacant.

Many tenants wish to be free to relocate or to purchase their own home.

Written Agreement

Many landlords do not realize that a tenancy-at-will can be in the form of a written agreement and not just oral. Many small and nonprofessional landlords usually enter into oral tenancies-at-will with their residential tenants. However, a tenancy-at-will may be a written agreement with many landlord-favorable terms included to define the relationship. Issues that may be addressed in writing are:

- ✪ who is responsible for shoveling the snow and putting out the trash;

- ✪ the proper care of the unit;

- ✪ responsibility for utilities;

- ✪ the allowance of pets; and,

- ✪ the landlord's right to enter the unit.

Moreover, Massachusetts law requires that the landlord pay for the tenant's heat and hot water unless there is a written agreement to the contrary.

A written tenancy-at-will agreement eliminates doubts about commonly-disputed terms and eliminates the need to rely on case law or statutes, which are often tenant-oriented, in the absence of a written agreement. You may use the **TENANCY-AT-WILL AGREEMENT** found in Appendix E or create your own. (see form 8, p.211.) As with most any agreement, the provisions of a written **TENANCY-AT-WILL AGREEMENT** are somewhat negotiable. However, if you present your tenant with a written agreement to govern the tenancy, it is likely that the tenant will read and sign it without disputing its terms.

> *Landlord Tip:* If you decide on a tenancy-at-will, put your agreement in writing, include terms that are favorable to you and tailor them for each situation. Your attorney will be able to draft such an agreement.

Leases

In contrast to the tenancy-at-will, a *lease* is a formal agreement between the parties that must be in writing. Generally speaking, a lease is for a specific set period, usually for one year. From the landlord's perspective, a lease fixes the term in which a tenant agrees to rent the unit, thereby providing more predictability and stability. A landlord whose tenant has signed a one-year fixed-term lease starting September 1st can now expect to receive rental income for that unit through August of the following year. With a tenant-at-will, there can be no such expectation.

As a corollary to its *fixed* quality, however, the lease provides the landlord with less freedom to terminate the tenancy as compared with the tenancy-at-will. Although a nonpaying tenant may be evicted in the same manner regardless of the type of tenancy, tenants under a lease may not have their tenancies terminated during their lease period unless they violate a specific lease provision.

Standard leases typically provide for only a seven day **NOTICE TO QUIT** period as opposed to the minimum thirty days required with a tenancy-at-will. In addition, the rental amount is usually fixed for the entire period of the lease, unless otherwise provided.

Basic Provisions   The minimum elements that a lease must contain to be valid are:

- ✪   name of *lessor* (landlord) or agent;

- ✪   name of *lessee* (tenant);

- ✪   description of the premises;

- ✪   rental rate;

✪ starting date; and,

✪ a *granting clause* (this is a legal term for a clause that specifically gives, or grants, the lessor the use of the property, such as "Lessor hereby leases to Lessee...").

NOTE: *There have been cases where a lease has been held to be valid where one or more of these terms has been omitted if there was an objective means to determine the missing term. Such exceptions, however, are beyond the scope of this book.*

Prohibited Provisions

Since a lease is a type of contract, the parties are free to negotiate almost any type of provision to be included in the lease. However, the law does forbid certain provisions. The parties cannot enter into an agreement containing the following types of provisions:

✪ the tenant waiving his or her right to eviction by due process of law;

✪ the tenant waiving his or her right to legal recourse against the negligent or intentional acts of the landlord;

✪ making the tenant responsible for all needed repairs;

✪ a penalty for rental payments less than thirty days late; or,

✪ obligating the tenant to make payments to the landlord for increases in real estate taxes unless the lease provision states the following:

• the tenant is obligated to only pay his or her proportionate share depending on his or her unit size;

• the exact percentage of the increase the tenant shall pay; and,

• that if the landlord receives an *abatement*, which is a discount on taxes allowed by the municipality, the tenant will receive his or her proportionate share.

📖 A landlord who inserted a provision in his lease requiring the tenant to pay constable fees for the **NOTICE TO QUIT** if his rent payments were late constituted unfair and deceptive practices under Mass. Gen. Laws, Chapter 93A and the landlord was forced to pay $2,000 in civil penalties and $8,000 in attorney's fees. (*Commonwealth of Massachusetts v. Chatham Development Co. Inc.*, 731 N.E. 2d 89 (2000).)

These types of provisions are deemed unlawful in order to protect the tenant who typically negotiates with less *bargaining power*. These same forbidden provisions also may not be included in a written **TENANCY-AT-WILL AGREEMENT**.

Standard Leases and Terms

Separate standard leases exist for an apartment unit or for the rental of a single family home. A standard **FIXED TERM APARTMENT LEASE** (see form 9, p.213) and a **FIXED TERM SINGLE FAMILY DWELLING LEASE** (see form 10, p.217) are provided in Appendix E. It is common for uninformed landlords to use apartment leases for single-family rentals and vice-versa. Be careful to use the right form as the terms vary for the specific use. In addition, a lease may be for a *fixed term* or *self-extending*.

Standard leases contain provisions relating to:

✪ the names and present addresses of the parties;

✪ the date of execution;

✪ a description of the premises to be rented;

✪ the term of the lease (a *fixed-term* lease ends on a certain date while a *self-extending* lease continues to be in effect unless terminated by either party by a certain date, effective on a certain future date); and,

✪ the amount and due date for the rent.

Most standard leases also contain other clauses to govern the relationship, such as:

✪ the responsibility of heat and other utilities;

✪ the permissible care and the expected cleanliness of the unit;

✪ any restrictions for pets;

✪ late penalties;

✪ subletting and occupation by other guests;

✪ access to common areas;

✪ responsibility for repairs; and,

✪ the landlord's right to enter.

If you decide to use one of these standard leases, make certain that you have read over the entire lease. If you do not want a certain provision included in your agreement, be sure to strike out that undesirable portion and have each party initial the deletion. Alterations and additions may be made in the same manner. In any event, landlords should be clear and precise in the wording of any lease provision as the courts will usually interpret any ambiguity against the landlord.

NOTE: *Leases for more than seven years must be recorded in the Registry of Deeds for the district in which the property lies.*

Once the lease (or tenancy-at-will agreement) is drafted and executed, copies must be given to your tenants within thirty days.

Commercial Leases

Commercial landlords, like their residential counterparts, may choose to have a tenancy-at-will without a written lease governing the relationship. However, commercial landlords often utilize leases to incorporate certain terms in writing that would otherwise not be allowed. It is common for the commercial landlord to require his or her tenant to:

✪ keep the unit and its mechanical systems in the same repair as when the tenancy commenced;

✪ pay a security deposit and waive the right to any interest;

✪ indemnify the landlord against any accidents and injuries sustained on the property;

✪ pay the property taxes; and,

✪ to insure the leased premises.

A **COMMERCIAL LEASE** is included in Appendix E. (see form 11, p.221.)

NOTE: *As commercial leases tend to be for longer periods than residential leases, landlords must remember that leases longer than seven years must be recorded with the applicable Registry of Deeds.*

Suggested Clauses

The following clauses are not required by any law, but are suggested to avoid potential problems during the tenancy:

✪   security and/or damage deposit;

✪   last month's rent;

✪   use clause (limiting use of the property);

✪   maintenance clause (spelling out who is responsible for what maintenance);

✪   limitation on landlord's liability;

✪   limitation on assignment of the lease by tenant;

✪   clause granting attorney's fees for enforcement of the lease;

✪   clause putting duty on tenant for own insurance;

✪   late fee and fee for bounced checks;

✪   limitation on number of persons living in the unit;

✪   requirement that if locks are changed, landlord is given a key (forbidding tenants to change locks may subject the landlord to liability for a break-in);

✪   limitation on pets;

✪   limitation on where cars may be parked (not on the lawn, etc.);

✪   limitation on storage of boats, etc. on the property;

✪   clause regarding tenant's abandoned property;

✪ in a condominium—clause stating that the tenant must comply with all rules and regulations of the condominium; and,

✪ in commercial leases—clauses regarding the fixtures, insurance, signs, renewal, eminent domain, and other factors related to the business use of the premises.

Creative Clauses There are several books on the market and real estate seminars traveling the country that promote creative leases. They have clauses that allow the landlord to charge late rent to a tenant's credit card or to add $50 or $100 late fees, among other things. Some of these clauses will work, but some of them are so strong that judges have held them to be overreaching and illegal. If you plan to use some creative clauses that may be too strong, you should have an attorney review them before you put them into a lease.

Rules and Regulations

Not every tenancy situation that arises can be foreseen by the written lease or tenancy-at-will agreement. To *fine-tune* the details of the tenancy at any time after it has started, a landlord may look to incorporate *rules and regulations* as part of the tenancy. Rules and regulations allow a landlord to better control his or her property and *run a tighter ship*. Some examples of rules and regulations that may be beneficial include the following.

✪ *Tenants may not use the common area washer and dryer before 8:00 A.M. or after 10:00 P.M.*

✪ *Tenants may only park in the designated parking space in the lot.*

✪ *Stereo and television volumes must be lowered after 9:00 P.M.*

✪ *Each tenant is to be responsible for removing his or her trash from his or her unit and disposing of it in the outside dumpster.*

✪ *Tenants may only use the backyard for playing and recreation.*

✪ *Tenants may not have guests for longer than one week without landlord's written permission.*

The rules and regulations must be allowed for in the written lease or tenancy agreement. The following is suggested language to use in the lease or tenancy-at-will agreement to incorporate the already-existing rules and regulations, or rules and regulations that the landlord may adopt in the future.

The rules and regulations cannot change the terms of the tenancy and cannot deprive a tenant of a right that he or she already had. When the rules and regulations change, the new set should be posted in a common area and a copy should be given to each tenant.

> RULES AND REGULATIONS—Tenant agrees to conform to such lawful rules and regulations that are reasonably related to the purpose and provisions of this lease, as shall from time to time be established by the Landlord in the future for the safety, care, cleanliness, or orderly conduct of the leased premises and the building of which they are a part, and for the benefit, safety, comfort, and convenience of all the occupants of the said building.

Landlord Tip: Successful landlords use rules and regulations. Rules and regulations establish with specific certainty what a tenant must or must not do and what the landlord will not allow. Good tenants will appreciate the rules and regulations and the landlords who enforce them.

Options

Both residential and nonresidential leases may contain clauses that grant the tenant an option to extend the lease for another term or several terms. These options often provide for an increase in rent during the renewal periods. Some guidelines on options include the following.

✪ An option to renew a lease is valid and enforceable, even if not all of the terms are outlined.

✪ Some terms may be left open for future negotiation or arbitration, but where no terms are stated, the court can assume that the terms will be the same as the original lease. (Be sure to draft your options carefully!)

✪ Leases that can be renewed indefinitely are not favored by the courts. Where doubt exists as to the terms, they may be limited to one renewal term.

Options to Purchase

A lease may also contain an option for the tenant to purchase the property under certain terms. An option to purchase will usually be enforceable according to its exact terms.

Forms

The landlord should be careful to choose a good lease form. Many forms on the market contain provisions that do not comply with Massachusetts law and can be dangerous to use.

Forms 8, 9, and 10 in this book are leases promulgated by the *Greater Boston Real Estate Board*. Form 11 is a commercial lease developed and used by the author. You may also need to use other forms as explained elsewhere in the text.

Signatures

If you do not have the proper signatures on the lease, you could have problems enforcing it or evicting the tenants.

Landlord

If the property is owned by more than one person, it is best to have all owners sign the lease.

Tenant

It is best in most cases to have all adult occupants sign the lease so that more people will be liable for the rent.

Business Entities

If the landlord or tenant is a business such as a corporation or LLC, be sure that the lease is signed by a properly authorized representative. A provision such as "Tenant represents that he has the appropriate authority on behalf of ABC

Corporation to enter into this lease" can be added. A careful landlord will also require a *corporate resolution* showing that a certain person has authority to sign on behalf of the business.

Initials   Some landlords have places on the lease for the tenant to place their initials. This is usually done next to clauses that are unusual or very strongly pro-landlord. However, even initials might not help if a judge really does not like a clause.

Backing Out of a Lease

Contrary to the beliefs of some tenants, there is no law allowing a *rescission* (cancellation) period for a lease. Once a lease has been signed by both parties, it is legally binding on them. A lease can be backed out of if it was entered into under fraud, impossibility, or for an illegal purpose.

Fraud   If one party fraudulently misrepresents a *material fact* concerning the lease, the lease may be unenforceable. A material fact is one that one of the parties reasonably relied on to be true in agreeing to enter into the lease. (*Golding v. 108 Longwood Avenue*, 325 Mass. 465 (1950).)

Impossibility   The lease may not be enforceable if the lease states that the premises are rented for a certain purpose and it is impossible to use the site for that purpose.

Illegality   If a lease is entered into for an illegal purpose, then it is void and unenforceable by either party.

4 HANDLING DEPOSITS

The taking of deposits may be the single-most misunderstood and problematic area for landlords. The word *deposit* refers to the security deposit and the last month's rent deposit. This is money the tenant pays in advance for the benefit and security of the landlord. The laws are very protective of the tenant to ensure the landlord properly handles it.

Unfortunately, if certain detailed, yet legally-required, steps are not strictly followed, the landlord may be forced to forfeit a deposit and could be liable for significant civil penalties. A landlord who understands and abides by these laws, however, will be both secure in his or her investment and free from the imposition of any penalties.

Under Massachusetts law, at the beginning of the tenancy, a landlord can only request and take a payment for the following:

✪ the first month's rent;

✪ the last month's rent;

✪ a security deposit; and,

✪ the purchase and installation of a new lock and key.

Any other amount requested and received is illegal. The amount of the last month's rent and the security deposit must be calculated at the same rate as the first month's rent.

Example: If a tenant moves into an apartment with a rent of $600 per month on September 10, and pays $400 for the balance of September, the landlord can request a last month's rent and security deposit in the amount of $600 each—the amount equivalent to the initial rental rate.

Security Deposits

The security deposit laws are more involved than those for the last month's rent. If they are closely followed, a security deposit can prove to be very valuable. The law imposes four requirements on a landlord in the initial taking of a security deposit:

1. provide a receipt;

2. provide a statement of present condition;

3. deposit the funds into an interest-bearing account; and,

4. maintain the proper records.

A landlord who has his or her tenant sign a lease waiving any of these requirements forfeits the right to retain any portion of the security deposit.

Receipt Upon taking the appropriate security deposit from your tenant, you are obligated by law to provide a receipt. This receipt must indicate the amount of the deposit, your name (and if taken by your agent, the agent's name with words to the effect that it is received on your behalf), and a description of the leased premises. You (or your agent receiving the security deposit) must sign your name on the receipt. You may use the **RECEIPT FOR SECURITY DEPOSIT AND LAST MONTH'S RENT DEPOSIT** in Appendix E. (see form 6, p.207.)

Landlord Tip: As with any document or writing you give to your tenant, keep a copy of the security deposit receipt for your records.

Statement of Present Condition

Since returning the security deposit to your tenant is partially based upon the condition of the unit when he or she vacates, the landlord must be able to document the condition of the unit at the beginning of the tenancy. Therefore, the law requires landlords to deliver a **STATEMENT OF CONDITION** to the tenant at the commencement of the tenancy or upon receipt of the security deposit—whichever is later. (see form 5, p.205.) The **STATEMENT OF CONDITION** must contain a complete listing of any damage existing on the premises, including any violations of sanitary, building, or housing codes. The statement must be signed by you or your agent, and also must include the following notice in twelve-point, bold-face type at the top of its first page.

This is a statement of the condition of the premises you have leased or rented. You should read it carefully in order to see if it is correct. If it is correct, you must sign it. This will show that you agree that the list is correct and complete. If it is not correct, you must attach a separate signed list of any damage which you believe exists in the premises. This statement must be returned to the lessor (landlord) or his agent within fifteen days after you receive this list or within fifteen days after you move in, whichever is later. If you do not return this list, within the specified time period, a court may later view your failure to return the list as your agreement that the list is complete and correct in any suit that you may bring to recover the security deposit.

If the tenant disagrees with your assessment of the condition and returns your statement with a separate list of damages, you then have an additional fifteen days to return a copy of the tenant's list with your signed agreement as to the additional item or items or a clear statement as to your disagreement.

Landlord Tip: Take photographs or video the entire unit before the tenant moves in to properly document its initial condition.

Interest-Bearing Account

The security deposit, although entrusted to the landlord on a temporary basis, is the tenant's money. The law requires the landlord to place any security deposit taken into a separate, interest-bearing account of a bank located within the Commonwealth of Massachusetts. The account must identify the funds as a security deposit for your tenants, and be kept separate from your own funds and incapable of being reached by your creditors.

The security deposit must also be transferred to any subsequent owner upon the sale of the property. For this reason, if you have rental units in more than one building, you should have separate security deposit accounts for the tenants in each building.

Upon the deposit of the security deposit funds in the appropriate banking institution, you must provide the tenant with a receipt indicating the name and location of the depository bank and the amount and account number of the deposit. The receipt must be delivered to the tenant within thirty days of collection of the deposit. You may use the **STATEMENT DOCUMENTING DEPOSIT OF SECURITY DEPOSIT** in Appendix E. (see form 7, p.209.) As stated before, keep a copy of the receipt given to the tenant for your records. Failure by the landlord to deposit the funds results in the forfeiture of the entire deposit.

> *Landlord Tip:* Use a computer or reminder system to keep track of each tenant's anniversary date so that the interest may be paid in a timely manner.

If the deposit is held for one year or more, the landlord must pay to the tenant, on the anniversary date of the tenancy, interest at five percent, or at the same rate as paid by the bank if it is less than five percent. The landlord, at this time, must also give the tenant a statement showing the name and location of the bank, the amount of deposit, the account number, and the amount of interest payable to the tenant.

In lieu of actually paying the accrued interest, the landlord may include a letter, with a copy of his or her bank statement, showing the interest and offering the tenant the option of deducting it from the next rental payment. If the tenancy terminates before the anniversary date, the tenant must receive all accrued interest within thirty days of termination.

Any interest earned by the tenant's security deposit (at five percent or the bank rate if less than five percent) belongs exclusively to the tenant and may not be applied by the landlord to any *arrears* owed by the tenant. However, the landlord may retain any interest over and beyond the five percent as compensation for administrative costs.

Maintaining Records　　The Massachusetts security deposit laws also require that you properly maintain detailed records with regard to the security deposits you take. Your records must contain detailed information of any damage done to each of your units for which a security deposit was taken, returned to the tenant, or for which you brought suit against a tenant to recover. In addition, you also are required to keep a record of the occupancy termination date of any tenant you charged with damages.

If you made repairs to remedy the damages, you must keep a record of the nature of the repairs, the dates the repairs were made, and the costs of the repairs. Have receipts to prove the repairs. Your records also must contain copies of each **RECEIPT FOR SECURITY DEPOSIT AND LAST MONTH'S RENT** (form 6) and **STATEMENT OF CONDITION** (form 5) given to each tenant.

Massachusetts law allows your tenant or a prospective tenant to request to inspect these records. Therefore, you must have them available for your tenants during normal business hours. If you wrongfully fail to make these records available to your tenant or prospective tenant, he or she is entitled to the immediate return of the security deposit taken plus any accrued interest.

You are required to maintain these records for up to two years from the date of the termination of the tenancy or occupancy upon which the security was conditioned.

Landlord Tip For efficient and effective record-keeping, set up separate folders for each unit you rent. Within each folder, maintain an individual file for each tenant who has rented the unit. This way, you are able to better follow the history of each individual unit.

To summarize, the four requirements that apply to security deposits are:

1. receipt to the tenant upon taking deposit;

2. **STATEMENT OF PRESENT CONDITION** provided to the tenant;

3. deposit money into a bank account with a second receipt to the tenant; and,

4. maintain records.

Other than these, you need not concern yourself with the security deposit until the tenancy terminates. At that time, you must determine whether you are entitled to keep any or all of the security deposit, and if so, the legal procedures for doing so.

**Returning the
Security Deposit**

A security deposit must be returned to your tenant within thirty days after the termination of a tenancy-at-will or after the end of the tenancy according to a written lease. However, you may deduct funds from the security deposit in the three following situations.

1. For any unpaid rent that has not been lawfully withheld or deducted by the tenant (the withholding of rent is further discussed in Chapter 10).

2. For any unpaid taxes the tenant is obligated to pay according to a tax escalation clause in the lease.

3. For a reasonable amount necessary to repair any damages to the tenant's unit caused by the tenant or a person under his or her control.

A deduction from the security deposit made by you for any other reason is unlawful and subjects you to civil liability.

The first two exceptions to the requirement that security deposits must be returned are straightforward. The third is somewhat more complicated. Before you deduct from or keep the security deposit for repairs, you must provide the tenant with an itemized list of damages. You must sign your name to this list under *the pains and penalties of perjury*, meaning that you swear by the contents of the list.

The list should include the precise nature of the damage and the repairs necessary to correct the damage, along with any written documents in support, such as estimates, bills, or receipts. In addition, you cannot deduct from the security deposit for any item that was listed in the **STATEMENT OF CONDITION** (form 5) unless that damage has been since repaired and the new damage is unrelated. A sample letter that can be used to accompany the **STATEMENT OF CONDITION** can be found on the following page.

VIA CERTIFIED MAIL

June 15, 2004

Philip Tenant
456 New Address
Boston, MA

Re: Retention of Security Deposit
        123 Main Street #2, Boston, MA

Dear Mr. Tenant,

As you are aware, you occupied 123 Main Street #2, Boston, MA as my tenant from June 1, 2003 to May 30, 2004 pursuant to a lease. Moreover, upon commencement of your occupancy, you paid a security deposit of $500.00. As you may also recall, at the time of your taking occupancy, you and I signed a Statement of Condition for the apartment indicating that it was free of any defects. (Please find a copy of this Statement of Condition enclosed for your reference.)

Following your move from the premises, I conducted an inspection of your former unit. Please be advised that there was a cracked window in the master bedroom. I retained a window contractor to replace the window on June 10, 2004 at a cost of $200.00. Please find enclosed a copy of said invoice.

Therefore, please find enclosed the return of your security deposit in the amount of $307.50, which is derived as follows:

Original security deposit amount:	$500.00
Bank interest accrued:	$ 7.50
Less: Damages	
Window repair:	$200.00
Balance of Deposit Due:	$307.50

Enclosed, please find my check in the amount of $307.50 representing the balance of the security deposit due back to you. Thank you for your kind attention to this matter.

I HEREBY STATE THAT THE ABOVE ITEMIZED LIST OF DAMAGES IS TRUE AND ACCURATE UNDER THE PAINS AND PENALTIES OF PERJURY.

Very truly yours,

Mirka Landlord

Commercial Tenancies

The Massachusetts security deposit law is less stringent for commercial tenancies. As a commercial landlord, you still must hold the deposit in an interest-bearing account in a bank located in Massachusetts, safe from the claims of any of your creditors. The commercial tenant also must receive a receipt showing the bank name, location, the amount of deposit, and account number. Also, the law requires that commercial landlords maintain a record of each security deposit as detailed for residential tenancies. However, commercial landlords are exempt from the annual interest payments as required for their residential counterparts. In addition, the law does not require commercial landlords to provide their tenants with the **STATEMENT OF CONDITION** upon the taking of the security deposit.

Last Month's Rent

The other deposit you are allowed to take is for the *last month's rent*. The last month's deposit is a safety net for the landlord to protect against the tenant's vacating the unit without paying for his or her final month. The landlord should not permit the tenant to apply his or her last month's rent deposit unless it is the last month of a lease, or, if a tenancy-at-will, the landlord issues a **NOTICE TO QUIT** or the tenant provides notices that he or she is terminating the tenancy.

As stated before, the deposit for the last month's rent must be calculated at the same rate as the initial rent. The law does not have the same amount of requirements for the last month's rent as it does for the security deposit.

Receipt

Upon receiving a deposit from your tenant for the last month's rent, you are required to provide him or her with a receipt including:

- ✪ the amount of the rent;

- ✪ the date it is received;

- ✪ its intended application as rent for the last month of the tenancy;

- ✪ the name of the person receiving it, and if received by an agent, the name of the landlord;

- ✪ a description of the rented premises;

✪ a statement indicating that the tenant is entitled to interest on the deposit at the rate of five percent per year; and,

✪ a statement that the tenant is obligated to provide the landlord with a forwarding address at the termination of the tenancy indicating where such interest may be sent.

These requirements are also satisfied by the **RECEIPT FOR SECURITY DEPOSIT AND LAST MONTH'S RENT DEPOSIT**. (see form 6, p.207.)

Interest Payable
As with the security deposit, at each anniversary date of the tenancy, the landlord must pay to the tenant the accrued interest on the last month's rent deposit and give the tenant a statement indicating the amount payable. However, unlike security deposits, you do not have to keep the last month's rent deposit in a separate bank account. If the landlord chooses to keep it in a separate, interest-bearing bank account, the landlord only needs to pay whatever interest the bank paid in interest, or five percent, whichever is less. If the deposit is not kept in a separate, interest-bearing account, the landlord needs to pay the tenant five percent interest. Along with the interest statement, the landlord should either pay the tenant the interest due or advise him or her to deduct the amount from the next rent payment.

Failure to pay the tenant the accrued interest upon the termination of the tenancy will subject the landlord to civil liability including damages up to three times the amount of interest due to the tenant.

If the tenant does not stay for one complete year, the landlord is responsible for paying all accrued interest within thirty days of the termination.

> *Landlord Tip:* If you are conscientious enough to follow the proper procedures for taking deposits, then you owe it to yourself to request that your tenant provide both a security deposit and a last month's rent deposit for your protection.

Commercial Tenancies
The provisions of the last month's rent law as detailed, including the payment of interest upon the anniversary, apply to commercial tenancies as well as to residential tenancies.

Deposits upon the Sale or Transfer of Property

Whenever a landlord sells or transfers his or her interest in the rental property, he or she also must transfer all security deposits, last month's rent deposits, and all accrued interest to the buyer. However, under Massachusetts law, the new owner is liable under the deposit laws regardless of whether the deposits were transferred to him or her or not.

Within forty-five days of the sale or transfer (date of closing), the new owner is responsible for notifying the tenant in writing that the deposit was properly credited and that he or she has assumed responsibility for the deposits. The notice must also contain the new owner's name, business address, and business telephone number and the name, business address, and business telephone number of any agent.

Landlord Tip: If you purchase property containing tenants, be sure to negotiate (using an attorney) an indemnification clause in your purchase and sale agreement. Your seller then agrees to *indemnify* (fully reimburse) you if the tenants bring any claims or actions regarding their deposits taken by your seller.

5 RESPONSIBILITY FOR MAINTENANCE

This chapter details your rights and responsibilities as landlord to maintain the property. It also covers the rights and obligations of your tenant. A sound understanding of the parameters within law allows the parties to operate will allow you to confidently manage your property.

> *Landlord Tip:* Set a formal, business-like tone with the tenant from the start. Your rental property is an important investment for you and the tenant must realize that you will treat it as such.

Landlord's Duties and Tenant's Rights

A landlord has many responsibilities and duties by virtue of renting his or her unit to a tenant. Some of these responsibilities are stated clearly in writing in the lease or tenancy agreement.

Other responsibilities are not so obvious, as they are required by statutes and regulations deeply hidden in law books. Unfortunately, responsibilities of this type are just as important as those printed in your lease and usually are the type that tenants know more about than landlords.

A landlord's failure to uphold either of these types of responsibilities may allow the tenant the right to withhold rent, assert valid defenses and counterclaims to an eviction action, sue the landlord civilly, and even pressure the authorities to charge the landlord criminally.

If your relationship with your tenant is governed by a lease or written tenancy agreement, its provisions may dictate the nature of some of your responsibilities. For example, standard leases require that the landlord:

- ✪ provide reasonably hot and cold water and reasonable heat;

- ✪ make necessary repairs at the landlord's expense; and,

- ✪ insure the building against risk of loss due to fire.

However, the great majority of a landlord's legal duties are not disclosed in a standard lease. Instead, they are imposed by laws, regulations, and court decisions, all of which are virtually inaccessible to the common landlord. Nevertheless, as the saying goes, *ignorance of the law is no excuse*.

Sanitary Code   By far, the single largest source of law imposing obligations on landlords is the Sanitary Code (the Code), which is a set of *regulations* (specialized laws promulgated by an administrative body) adopted by the Commonwealth's Department of Public Health. The Code is found in the Massachusetts Code of Regulations (Mass. Code Regs.). As with all laws, the Code is always subject to change. It is important to review the text of the Code that is included in Appendix B.

The Code's purpose is to:
> *protect the health, safety, and well-being of the occupants of housing and of the general public, to facilitate the use of legal remedies available to occupants of substandard housing, to assist boards of health in their enforcement of this code and to provide a method of notifying interested parties of violations of conditions which require immediate attention.*

The local board of health in each city and town has the responsibility for enforcing the provisions of the Code.

The Code applies to residential property and establishes minimum standards of fitness for humans to live in. The landlord, and sometimes the tenant, is responsible for complying with the Code. Its provisions dictate the minimum requirements in housing for areas such as:

✪ kitchens;

✪ bathrooms;

✪ electrical;

✪ plumbing;

✪ door and window locks;

✪ smoke detectors;

✪ insects and other pests; and,

✪ garbage and rubbish collection.

Depending on the specific code section, a violation of a provision is deemed either relatively minor in nature or is a *condition deemed to endanger or impair health or safety*. As you may guess, a violation of a provision of the latter type makes the landlord vulnerable to a host of penalties, including the justified withholding of rent by the tenant (discussed further in Chapter 10), civil suits, civil fines, and criminal penalties.

> *Landlord Tip:* Refrain from hiring an outside contractor or repair person who was suggested to you by your tenant. Get your own.

When a question arises during the course of the tenancy regarding maintenance responsibility, you should first consult the latest version of the Sanitary Code for your answer. You should see to it that you and your units are in compliance with these provisions so as to avoid significant problems.

> *Landlord Tip:* Keep all receipts, estimates, and invoices for repairs made to the unit.

A landlord who strives to comply with the Sanitary Code protects him- or herself against what is probably the tenant's biggest weapon. As stated earlier in Chapter 1, the best way to prove that the unit complied with the Sanitary Code at the commencement of the tenant's occupation is to obtain a certificate of compliance from your local board of health prior to the tenant moving into the dwelling. The same is true with the certificate of occupancy from your local building inspector and fire inspector.

Additional Regulations

If a tenant complains about a certain condition and requests that it be repaired, you should consult the Sanitary Code. Chances are the Code will state the minimum requirements for that condition, as well as whose responsibility it is to rectify any substandard situation. Other regulations that, to a lesser degree, control a landlord's duty to provide safe and sanitary housing include:

✪   the Massachusetts State Plumbing Code;

✪   the Massachusetts State Fuel Gas Code;

✪   the Massachusetts State Electrical Code; and,

✪   the Massachusetts State Building Code.

Besides the right to live in a unit that complies with these minimum standards of fitness, a tenant has many other rights granted by law. These additional rights, such as the right to repair and deduct and the right to quiet enjoyment, are discussed in Chapter 10 of this book.

Commercial Tenancies

One of the largest differences between residential and commercial tenancies is the applicability of the Sanitary Code. As discussed earlier in this chapter, a residential landlord must be in compliance with the very specific requirements contained in the Code. The violation of an important provision will be deemed to affect the health or safety of the tenant and subjects the landlord to civil liability, as well as the possibility of criminal punishment.

The Code, however, does not apply in commercial tenancies. The law presumes that the commercial tenant has more bargaining power and needs less protection than its residential counterpart. In addition, the law seeks to protect the habitability and safety of a person's home. The commercial tenant instead must look to the lease itself.

Notwithstanding the exemption from the Code's requirements, the commercial landlord must still comply with the Building Code and other applicable construction codes, as well as with the local zoning ordinances.

Landlord's Rights and Tenant's Responsibilities

While the Sanitary Code and many other statutes often make it seem that landlords have all of the obligations and tenants have all of the rights, landlords do have certain rights and tenants actually do have some duties. To some extent, the nature of the landlord's rights and the tenant's obligations depends on what type of tenancy or agreement governs the parties.

As discussed in Chapter 3, for example, a landlord cannot have a tenant sign a lease that waives his or her right to legal recourse against the landlord. In the absence of specific provisions in an agreement or in the absence of a lease or written tenancy agreement, the law grants a set of rights to the landlord and imposes a set of duties on the tenant.

Tenant's Responsibilities

Tenants have obligations that arise from the terms of the rental agreement and the law.

For example, a standard lease will require the tenant:

✪ to pay a certain rental amount on a set date;

✪ to pay utility bills separately;

✪ to refrain from altering the unit;

✪ to maintain the unit in a clean condition;

✪ to refrain from any illegal or noisy use; and,

✪ to conform to any rules and regulations of the landlord.

The laws of Massachusetts also impose obligations on the tenant, although they are not proportionate to those imposed on the landlord. These legally-imposed obligations exist regardless of the type of tenancy.

As with the landlord's obligations, the Sanitary Code is the primary source for the obligations given to the tenant. The following are the more important provisions in the Code for which the tenant (*occupant*) is responsible or jointly responsible with the landlord. (These sections come from the Code of Massachusetts Code of Regulations, Title 105.)

Section 410.352: Occupant's Installation and Maintenance Responsibilities.

(A) The occupant shall install in accordance with accepted plumbing, gasfitting and electrical wiring standards, and shall maintain free from leaks, obstructions or other defects all occupant-installed and optional equipment, including but not limited to, refrigerators, dishwashers, clothes washing machines and dryers, and garbage grinders.

(B) Every occupant of a dwelling unit shall keep all toilets, wash basins, sinks, showers, bathtubs, stoves, refrigerators and dishwashers in a clean and sanitary condition and exercise reasonable care in the proper use and operation thereof.

Section 410.451: Egress Obstructions.

The occupant shall be responsible for maintaining free from obstruction all means of exit leading from his unit and not common to the exit of any other unit.

Section 410.505: Occupant's Responsibility Respecting Structural Elements.

The occupant shall exercise reasonable care in the use of the floors, walls, doors, windows, ceiling, roof, staircases, porches, chimneys, and other structural elements of the dwelling.

Section 410.555: Extermination of Insects, Rodents and Skunks.

(A) The occupant of a dwelling containing one dwelling unit shall maintain the unit free from all rodents, skunks, cockroaches and insect infestation, and shall be responsible for exterminating them, provided, however, that the owner shall maintain any screen, fence or other structural element necessary to keep rodents and skunks from entering the dwelling.

Section 410.600: Storage of Garbage and Rubbish.

The owner of any dwelling that contains three or more dwelling units, the owner of any rooming house, and the occupant of any other dwelling place shall provide as many receptacles for the storage of garbage and rubbish as are sufficient to contain the accumulation before final collection or ultimate disposal, and shall locate them so as to be convenient to the tenant and so that no objectionable odors enter any dwelling.

Section 410.601: Collection of Garbage and Rubbish.

The owner of any dwelling that contains three or more dwelling units, the owner of any rooming house, and the occupant of any other dwelling place shall be responsible for the final collection or ultimate disposal or incineration of garbage and rubbish by means of....

Section 410.602: Maintenance of Areas Free from Garbage and Rubbish.

(A) *Dwelling Units.* The occupant of any dwelling unit shall be responsible for maintaining in a clean and sanitary condition and free of garbage, rubbish, other filth or causes that part of the dwelling which he exclusively occupies or controls.

(B) *Dwellings Containing Less than Three Dwelling Units.* In a dwelling that contains less than three dwelling units, the occupant shall be responsible for maintaining in a clean and sanitary condition, free of garbage, rubbish, other filth or cases of sickness the stairs or stairways leading to his dwelling unit and the landing adjacent to his dwelling unit if the stairs, stairways, or landing are not used by another occupant.

Section 410.620: Curtailment Prohibited.

No owner or occupant shall cause any service, facility, equipment, or other utility which is required to be made available by 105 CMR 410.000 to be removed from or shut off from any occupied dwelling except for such temporary period as may be necessary during actual repairs or alterations and where reasonable notice of curtailment of service is given to the occupant, or during temporary emergencies when curtailment of service is approved by the board of health.

Remedies for Tenant's Violations

If you believe that your tenant is in violation of any of the above provisions for which he or she is responsible, you should first send him or her a letter. In the letter, clearly describe the problem or the condition that exists and refer to the appropriate section of the sanitary code in which the tenant is in violation. Allow the tenant adequate time to correct the condition and inform him or her that a future violation will be sufficient cause for the termination of the tenancy.

If you want to buttress your support for the tenant being in violation of the sanitary code, you should contact your local board of health and request that it conduct an inspection. If, after the inspection is completed, the tenant fails to comply, you may wish to pressure the board of health to force compliance either with penalties or criminal process.

Standard leases require tenants to comply with all applicable state and local laws and regulations, including the Sanitary Code. If the tenant fails to comply, you may complete the necessary repairs yourself and seek reimbursement from the tenant. You may also choose to evict the tenant for this breach of the lease.

Alternatively, you may file an *injunction* in the appropriate court, asking that the tenant be ordered to comply. You should be sure to demonstrate to the court, through photographs and the board of health's report, the conditions for which the tenant is responsible. Representation by a competent attorney is recommended for any court procedure.

In order to identify your rights and obligations and the rights and obligations of your tenant, you should first look to your lease or written tenancy agreement. If you do not have one or if it is silent or not specific as to a certain term, your answer probably lies in an outside source of law. Most likely, if your question pertains to the maintenance or sanitary condition of the unit and the responsibilities of each party, the Sanitary Code contains your answer.

6 LANDLORD LIABILITIES

The law concerning who is responsible for injuries and crime on rental property has changed considerably over the last couple decades. For hundreds of years landlords were not held liable. Now, landlords are often liable, even for conditions that are not their fault.

Injuries on the Premises

Property insurance for rental property is significantly more expensive than it is for owner-occupied single family homes. The primary cause for this is negligence laws that allow tenants who are injured on the property to make a claim on the owner's insurance. An owner who injures him- or herself in the same manner but in his or her own private home would have no such recourse. A landlord, therefore, needs to know the circumstances in which he or she will be vulnerable if a tenant claims injury.

Areas under Landlord's Control
The landlord has a duty to inspect and repair common areas in a rental building with more than one unit. This does not apply to a single family home. In a duplex, a landlord may state in the lease that the tenants assume the duty to take care of the common areas.

Areas Not under the Landlord's Control

The general rule is that a landlord is not liable for injuries on parts of the premises that are not under his or her control, except in the following circumstances:

- ✪ where there is a danger known to the landlord;

- ✪ where the condition of the premises is in violation of a law with which the landlord is responsible to comply;

- ✪ where there is a pre-existing defect in construction;

- ✪ where the landlord undertakes the repair of the premises or is required by the lease to do the repairs;

- ✪ where the landlord did a negligent act; or,

- ✪ where the premises was a nuisance at the time of making the lease or would become one upon tenant's expected use of the premises.

Cases Holding a Landlord Not Liable

The following are cases that held that a landlord would not be liable for injuries.

NOTE: *The decisions in some of the earlier cases may have been modified by the decisions in later cases.*

- 📖 When an employee of a commercial tenant sued the owner of a building for injuries sustained when a lobby door swung and hit her while she stood in the lobby, the landlord agency was not liable as 1) it did not contract to make the repairs; and therefore, did not make them negligently; and 2) the injury was not in a common area over which the landlord had control. (*Tuchinsky v. Beacon Property Management*, 45 Mass. App. Ct. 469 (1998).)

- 📖 Where a tenant was injured from a fall from a window of her third floor apartment, the landlord was not liable as his failure to install window guards did not violate the warranty of habitability. (*Lynch v. James*, 44 Mass. App. Ct. 448 (1998).)

- 📖 Where a child tenant was injured when another child threw a stick at him in the play area of the residential complex, the landlord agency was not liable as it had no duty to erect a fence around or supervise the playground area, nor was there reason for the landlord to foresee that parents and guardians would not provide adequate supervision. (*Roderick v. Brandy Hill Co.*, 36 Mass. App. Ct. 948 (1994).)

Cases Holding a Landlord Liable
The following cases are examples of when a landlord was held liable for injuries to a tenant or a guest.

📖 Where a child tenant ingested lead-based paint on the rental premises, the landlord was liable because he failed to remove the lead paint as required by statute. The owner may be liable without proof either that the owner knew there were materials containing dangerous levels of lead paint on the premises or that the owner was negligent in not removing offending materials. (*Bencosme v. Kokoras*, 400 Mass. 40 (1987).)

📖 When a tenant was injured after the railing of his third floor porch gave way, the landlord was liable because this was considered to be a *common passageway* and the landlord is required to keep it in such condition that others will not be injured. (*Crowell v. McCaffrey*, 377 Mass. 443 (1979).)

📖 A superior court judge has cleared the way for a guest of a tenant to use the powerful Mass. Gen. Laws, Chapter 93A consumer protection statute as an additional means of recovery against the landlord. Mass. Gen. Laws, Chapter 93A allows a plaintiff, if he or she is ultimately successful, to recover up to triple the amount of his or her actual damages. Prior to this decision, only tenants could avail themselves of this statutory remedy against their landlord. It remains to be seen whether this ruling will hold up on appeal. (*Malonson v. Arsenault*, Lawyers Weekly No. 12-008-04 (February 2004).)

Snow and Ice
One major area of claims by tenants against landlords is for injuries that allegedly occur on snow or ice. Typically, the tenant alleges that he or she fell on snow or ice somewhere on the landlord's property. The tenant's likelihood of success is based significantly on whether the snow and ice accumulated naturally or unnaturally.

A natural accumulation of snow or ice occurs when precipitation merely falls from the sky and either accumulates as snow or freezes as ice. An unnatural accumulation occurs when some human or man-made structure interferes with the natural accumulation or freezing process. An example of unnatural accumulation of ice occurs when water comes from eaves or a downspout and then freezes. A tenant who falls and is injured due to an unnatural accumulation of snow or ice will likely be successful in a claim against the landlord.

One additional fact that could determine the success of the tenant's claim concerns the location of the snow or ice. While a landlord has a duty to warn against known defects in the common areas, the Sanitary Code requires specification for *areas of egress* (exits from the property) when it comes to snow and ice. Mass. Code Reg., Ch. 105, Sec. 410.452 states:

> *The owner shall maintain all means of egress at all times in a safe, operable condition. All exterior stairways, fire escapes, egress balconies and bridges shall be kept free of snow and ice.*

A tenant who falls in one of these areas, or falls as a result of an unnatural accumulation of snow or ice, has a better likelihood of success.

Protection from Liability for Injuries

The basis for liability of landlords for injuries is the failure of the landlord to perform some duty imposed by law or by the lease. A landlord cannot avoid the duties imposed by law, but he or she can avoid putting extra duties in the lease. Any promise you make to a tenant, such as to install window guards or handrails, can be the basis of your liability if you fail to provide them or install them improperly.

Regarding protection from snow or ice, a landlord should assign the duty to remove snow and ice from certain exit areas to the tenant. This should be done in writing within the lease or written tenancy agreement. In addition, the landlord could enter into a separate service contract with the tenant to clear the snow and ice to emphasize the tenant's obligation. The landlord could agree to pay the tenant a fee during the winter months in exchange for the tenant taking on this obligation. Additionally, a landlord must position downspouts so they empty out in areas where tenants or others do not walk. After remedying the downspout locations, a landlord should take photographs of them to show that they do not empty out into areas where people will walk.

A landlord should always carry adequate insurance to cover possible accidents on rental property. If you find the cost is more than you would expect, this expense should be shared by the tenants in the form of higher rent payments.

Crimes against Tenants

The liability of landlords has also been greatly expanded in the area of crimes against tenants. The former theory of law was that a person cannot be held liable for deliberate acts of third parties. This had been the theory for hundreds of years. It has recently been abandoned in favor of a theory that a landlord must protect his or her tenants from crimes.

Basis for Liability   The newer theory is that where the landlord can foresee the possibility of criminal attack, he or she must take precautions to prevent it. But some have said that this means any time an attack is possible, the landlord must protect the tenant. This would include nearly every tenancy, especially in urban areas. New Jersey has gone so far as to hold landlords strictly liable for every crime committed on their premises. This liability for crime, unlike the warranty of habitability, applies to both residential and commercial tenancies. It has not yet been extended to single family homes.

> Where a landlord disconnected his tenant's burglar alarm and the tenant was later burglarized, the landlord was held liable because it was a foreseeable consequence of the landlord's conduct. (*Gidwani v. Wasserman*, 373 Mass. 162 (1977).)

> Where a police officer was murdered during a narcotics raid on a unit of an apartment building, the landlord was not liable as it was not foreseeable that the raid would result in murder, as there was no evidence of firearms in the unit. (*Griffiths v. Campbell*, 425 Mass. 31 (1997).)

> Where an employee of a commercial tenant was raped on the grounds, the landlord was not liable for negligence because the attack was not foreseeable and the landlord did not owe a duty to the employee. (*Whittaker v. Saraceno*, 635 N.E.2d. 1185 (1994).)

Protection from Liability for Crimes

The law is not clear in Massachusetts as to just how far courts will go in holding landlords liable for crimes against tenants. A clause in a lease that makes a tenant responsible for locks and security may provide some protection to landlords in some situations, especially in single-family homes and duplexes.

But in some inner-city apartment complexes where crime is common, landlords may be required to provide armed guards or face liability. Again, insurance is a must and this additional cost will have to be covered by rent increases.

7 CHANGING THE TERMS OF THE TENANCY

It is common for either the tenant or the landlord, sometime during the lease term, to want to change a term of the lease or tenancy agreement or simply alter the current arrangement. For example, the tenant may want to sublease the apartment for the three summer months he or she will be away. Conversely, the landlord may want to raise the rent of a tenant-at-will. If the terms of the lease or tenancy agreement do not allow for such a change, the parties must mutually agree. This chapter discusses these typical changes, what the landlord's rights are relevant to each change, and what the landlord must do to lawfully effectuate the change.

Assignment or Sublease by Tenant

As a general rule, unless it is prohibited in a lease, a landlord cannot stop a tenant from assigning his or her lease to someone else or from subletting all or a portion of the premises.

Assignment
An *assignment* is where a tenant assigns all of his or her interest in a lease to another party. The other party takes over the tenant's position. The original tenant is the *assignor* and the new tenant is the *assignee*. The assignee then deals directly with the landlord.

If a lease contains a covenant to pay rent and the landlord does not release the original tenant upon the assignment, the landlord may sue the original tenant if the new tenant does not pay. (*Dwyer v. Lavigne,* 319 Mass. 26 (1946).)

Sublease   A *sublease* is where the tenant enters into a new rental agreement with a third party. The original tenant is called the *sublessor* and the new tenant is the *sublessee.* Generally, the sublessee does not deal directly with the landlord, but deals only with the sublessor.

Waiver   If a landlord knowingly accepts rent from an assignee or a sublessee of a lease, the landlord waives the right to object to the assignment or sublease. However, if the landlord was unaware of the assignment or sublease, it does not constitute a waiver.

Approval   Some leases provide that a lease may only be assigned with the approval of the landlord. Absent language in the lease to the contrary, a landlord may, even unreasonably, withhold consent to allow a tenant to assign, sublet, or permit other individuals to occupy the rental premises. (*Slavin v. Rent Control Board of Brookline,* 406 Mass. 458 (1990); *21 Merchants Row Corp. v. Merchants Row, Inc.,* 412 Mass. 204 (1992).)

Sale of Property by Landlord

A landlord has the right to sell property covered by a lease, but the new owner must uphold the terms of the existing lease. The new owner cannot cancel the old leases or raise the rent while the leases are still in effect (unless the leases have provisions allowing the landlord to do so). The new owner must make any repairs to the property that the old owner would have been required to do under the terms of the lease. In most cases, a landlord is relieved of his or her obligations under a lease upon sale of the property.

When selling property, a landlord must specify in the sales contract that the sale is *subject to* existing leases (the new owner must still abide by the lease). Otherwise, the buyer may sue for failure to deliver the premises free and clear of tenants. At closing, the leases should be assigned to the buyer. (See Chapter 4 for more information on the landlord's obligations regarding the tenant's deposits upon the sale of the property.)

Foreclosures A foreclosure sale is a sale by the holder of mortgage (mortgagee) of the property to a third party as a result of the original owner (mortgagor) defaulting on loan payment obligation or some other mortgage provision. A bank is usually the holder of the mortgage. When property is purchased at a *foreclosure sale*, the leases of the tenants are terminated if they were signed after the date of the mortgage and if the tenants were joined as parties to the suit.

Raising the Rent

The landlord's ability to raise the rent is conditioned on the type of tenancy. Under most leases, the rent is fixed for the term of the lease and the landlord cannot raise it until that term expires and the parties enter into a new lease. Some leases, especially long-term leases, provide for periodic adjustments of the rent.

With a tenancy-at-will, however, the landlord has more flexibility in increasing the rent. The parties who enter into a tenancy-at-will do so after they reach a mutual understanding as to the terms of the tenancy, among the most important of which is the rental amount. Therefore, any increase (and technically, any decrease as well) in the rental amount may not be changed by the landlord without the consent of the tenant.

As a result, it is improper to call the tenant or send a letter stating that the rent will be increased to a certain amount as of a certain date. Rather, in order to properly change this basic term, the tenancy needs to be terminated with a **NOTICE TO QUIT**, including an offer to the tenant to form a new tenancy at the desired higher rental amount.

The *notice to terminate* the tenancy, as discussed further in Chapter 9, must be given an amount of time in advance that is equivalent to at least a full rental period. In most cases, this is at least one full month.

Example: If you have a tenancy where your tenant pays you monthly on the first of each month and you want to increase your tenant's rent beginning on January 1st, you will need to serve him or her with a **NOTICE TO QUIT/RENTAL INCREASE NOTICE** before the end of November, so that the tenant has a full rental period's notice—the month of December.

The **NOTICE TO QUIT/RENTAL INCREASE NOTICE** can be used for this purpose. (see form 14, p.229.) If the tenant fails to vacate before the date of termination, the law recognizes that he or she has agreed to commence a new tenancy at the increased rental amount and now is responsible for paying that amount.

If the tenant continues to occupy the premises but pays only the old rental amount once the old tenancy has terminated, you may choose to act upon the **NOTICE TO QUIT** (as the tenancy has been terminated) and bring eviction proceedings. Before accepting the old rental amount, you should be sure to reserve the right to accept the money (albeit in the wrong amount) without waiving your right to pursue the eviction. (see form 15.) Before you raise the tenant's rent, be sure that the tenant will not be able to assert a claim for retaliation. (see Chapter 10 for more information.)

Commercial Tenancies

The commercial landlord may raise the rent in accordance with the same provisions as outlined for residential tenancies. As commercial leases are often over the course of many years, landlords want to protect themselves against inflation over this period. Many standard commercial leases contain a consumer price escalation provision that determines the amount, if any, by which the rent will increase for each subsequent year. The customary standard used is the *Consumer Price Index* (CPI), which is published monthly by the U.S. Department of Labor. CPI information may be obtained from your local newspaper, by calling the U.S. Department of Labor Statistics Bureau CPI Information Hotline at 617-565-2325, or on the department's website at **www.bls.gov**.

Example: Suppose a ten-year lease begins in September of 2002 at a rent of $1,000 per month and the CPI index is 177.7 in that month. The terms of the lease specify that the annual rental rate is to be determined each successive September based on the CPI number for that month.

Now suppose that in September of 2003, the CPI is 184.0. The new rental rate will be the product of $1,000 x (184.0/177.7); or $1,035.45 per month. Paragraph 3(b) of the **COMMERCIAL LEASE** is such a rent escalation clause based on the CPI. (see form 11, p.221.)

Modifying the Lease

If you agree to modify the terms of your lease with a tenant you should put it in writing. If you do not and you allow a tenant to do things forbidden in the lease you may be found to have waived your rights. You may use the **AMENDMENT TO LEASE/RENTAL AGREEMENT** for this purpose. (see form 12, p.225.)

8 PROBLEMS DURING THE TENANCY

It is safe to expect problems to occur at some point during most tenancies. A landlord who is aware of the likely problems, what his or her rights are in each case, and how to properly address each problem will be able to resolve any issue at the earliest possible stage.

Landlord's Access to the Premises

Massachusetts law allows the landlord to enter the tenant's unit in limited situations. A landlord may enter:

- ✪ to inspect the premises;

- ✪ to make repairs in the premises;

- ✪ to show the unit to a prospective tenant, purchaser, mortgagee, or its agent;

- ✪ pursuant to a court order;

✪　　if the premises appears to have been abandoned by the tenant; or,

✪　　to inspect the premises within the last thirty days of the tenancy, or after either party has given notice to the other of intention to terminate the tenancy, for damages that would be cause for deduction from the security deposit.

Although not required by law, it would be wise and courteous for the landlord to give the tenant twenty-four hours written notice of his or her intent to enter. A provision in a lease or tenancy agreement giving the landlord authority to enter for any other situation will be deemed void by a court.

Commercial Tenancies　　Massachusetts law does not impose restrictions on the commercial landlord's ability to enter the leased unit. Often with written leases, the parties negotiate their own parameters governing the landlord's entry.

> *Landlord Tip:* To document your entry into the tenant's unit, you should send the tenant a written letter giving notice of your anticipated entry and the specific reason. As always, keep a copy of this letter for your records. Also, if you believe your entry will be disputed by the tenant, it will be beneficial to bring along an independent party to serve as a witness, such as a police officer.

Violations by the Tenant

There are many things tenants can do to violate the lease terms. Some of the more common violations are discussed in the following sections.

Rent Due Date　　Unless otherwise stated in a lease, rent is due at the beginning of each rent payment period. The tenant's failure to pay the rent on or before the due date is a violation of the tenancy.

Vacating Early　　If the tenant breaches the lease by vacating the property before the expiration of the lease, the landlord has three options:

1. terminate the lease and accept surrender of the property *for the landlord's own account* (relieving the tenant of further liability);

2. take possession of the premises *for the account of the tenant*, and hold the tenant liable for the difference in rent due under the lease and the rent eventually received; or,

3. let the unit sit vacant and sue the tenant for the full rent as it comes due.

The law in this area is very complicated. The main decisions by the Massachusetts Appellate Court are confusing and contradictory. They have caused confusion in the appellate courts and many landlords have lost in their attempts to collect damages from tenants.

Problems. The problem in most of the cases where landlords have lost their suits against tenants is that they have tried to terminate the lease and sue for the rent, combining option 1 with option 2 above. When this is done, the courts have usually found that the landlord accepted a *surrender of the premises* and lost all rights to sue for damages. Surrender of the premises is a term that refers to the landlord assenting to the tenant's vacating the premises prior to the termination date of the lease and agreeing to not hold the tenant responsible for any rental loss incurred. In other words, the landlord is deemed to let the tenant out of the lease.

📖 Where the landlord accepts the keys from the vacating tenant and then re-rents the unit to another tenant, a court has held that the landlord accepted the surrender by the first tenant, thereby relieving the first tenant of liability. (*Taylan Realty Co. v. Student Book Exchange, Inc.,* 354 Mass. 777 (1968).)

Possible Solutions. The usual problem in the court cases is a misinterpretation of the landlord's intent. To avoid this, the landlord should analyze the options and make his or her intent clear, either in the form of a certified letter to the tenant or in the allegations of the complaint.

✪ Where the landlord has many vacant units, he or she can elect option 3 and just sue the tenant for the rent due without trying to rent the unit.

✪ If the landlord expects to rent the unit out at a lower rate, the landlord should make clear that he or she is taking possession for the account of the tenant and will hold the tenant liable for the difference.

Bad Checks   The procedure for collecting on bad checks is contained in Massachusetts General Laws (Mass. Gen. Laws), Chapter (Ch.) 93, Section 40A. It provides for criminal penalties and a penalty of $100 to $500, in addition to the amount of the check. The procedure is to send a notice by certified mail and then file suit on the check. A **DEMAND FOR PAYMENT OF DISHONORED CHECK** can be used for this notice. (see form 21, p.243.) However, if a tenant cannot immediately make good on a check, the landlord would be better advised to immediately start the eviction process, rather than sue on the bad check.

Damage to the Premises

If the tenant does intentional damage to the premises, the landlord can terminate the tenancy and can also get an injunction against the tenant. (see Chapter 9.) If there is not enough security deposit to pay for the damage, the landlord can sue the tenant either in small claims court or regular court.

Violations by the Landlord

Tenants are protected from *reprisals* by landlords. A tenant may assert the defense of *reprisal* if the landlord attempts to increase the rent, terminates the tenancy, or commences a summary process action within six months of one of the following activities by the tenant:

✪   complaining of code violations or other law violations to the landlord;

✪   reporting the violations to the local board of health;

✪   organizing or joining a tenant's union or organization; or,

✪   suing the landlord to enforce rights as tenant.

If the landlord begins eviction proceedings within six months of one of the above actions by the tenant, the court will presume that the eviction was commenced solely in retaliation by the landlord. The court may dismiss the eviction action. If the eviction action is for nonpayment of rent, however, the law switches the burden to the tenant to prove that the landlord had some other unlawful motive for the eviction besides nonpayment. This burden is difficult to overcome.

Interrupting Utilities

Under Massachusetts General Laws, Chapter 186, Section 14, a landlord who terminates or interrupts utilities, such as water, heat, light, electricity, gas, elevator, garbage collection, or refrigeration can be held liable for three month's rent for each violation or the actual amount of damages—whichever is greater—plus the tenant's court costs and attorney fees.

This can be frustrating to a landlord whose tenant is intentionally wasting utilities to hurt the landlord. The correct response in such a situation would be to get an emergency restraining order. As this is a complicated process, you should consult a lawyer.

Destruction of the Premises

If the premises is damaged by fire, hurricane, or other casualty, such an event does not automatically terminate the lease. If there is no applicable provision in the lease, the destruction of the premises does not terminate the tenancy and relieve the tenant of his or her obligations to pay rent if the tenant rented the entire building. However, if the tenant merely rented a unit or apartment in the destroyed building, the lease will be terminated.

Where a lease provided for the termination of the lease if any part of the premises were destroyed, the court decided that the landlord may terminate the lease due to the partial destruction of the premises, even if it causes a hardship to the tenant. (*D. A. Schulte, Inc. v. American Realty Corp.*, 256 Mass. 258 (1926).)

9 TERMINATING A TENANCY

As the saying goes, *All good things must come to an end.* This chapter discusses the termination of the tenancy (whether it occurs due to the lease expiring or due to the will of either party). At this point of your relationship with your tenant, the governing law is highly technical and the pace is very fast.

Although this book sets out the procedure and the steps involved, summary process (or eviction) is not to be taken lightly. It is not recommended that anyone handle it without legal representation.

Landlord Tip: Retain a capable attorney at the earliest stage possible to represent you in an eviction matter.

Landlord's Termination of Residential Tenancy

The procedure for terminating the tenancy between you and your tenant will vary depending on the type of tenancy and the reason for the termination. Fixed-term leases terminate by *operation of law*. The stated expiration date contained within the lease terminates the lease without the landlord or tenant having to do any affirmative act. Tenancies-at-will, on the other hand, must be terminated by either party through written notice to the other party. Additionally, the landlord may terminate the tenancy for nonpayment of rent regardless of the type of tenancy. Moreover, tenancies of either type may be terminated *for cause* (for a violation of a term or of a rule or regulation).

No-Fault Termination (with a Lease)

A fixed-term lease, by definition, contains a specified date on which the tenancy ends (except for any lease renewal or extension provisions). Under a fixed-term lease, no termination notice needs to be given by either party. There are a few options available when a lease approaches its expiration date.

- ✪ If you are satisfied with your tenant, you may want to negotiate a new lease, with or without one or more different terms.

- ✪ If you are satisfied but wish to convert the tenancy from a fixed term under a lease to a more flexible tenancy-at-will, you may do nothing and continue to collect the same rent amount or some new rent amount as mutually agreed.

- ✪ If you are dissatisfied with the tenant and do not arrange to extend the tenancy in any manner, you simply wait for the end of the term and for the tenant to vacate. If the tenant fails to vacate on or before the expiration date, the tenant is deemed by law to be a *tenant at sufferance* (also called a *holdover tenant*) and has no legal right to continue to occupy the premises. You will then need to follow the procedures for eviction.

Since a holdover tenant is more than a trespasser, as he or she entered the unit under a lawful tenancy agreement, you must still pursue a court summary process action to lawfully remove the tenant from the premises. Although notice need not be given to a tenant at sufferance, it may prove beneficial and possibly cost-effective to serve him or her with such a notice to encourage him or her to vacate the premises without court action.

Experienced landlords and attorneys will commonly serve such a tenant with a **48 HOUR NOTICE TO QUIT**. (see form 16, p.233.) Also, be sure not to accept any money from the tenant designated as rent. In order to preserve your rights to evict the tenant at sufferance, you may only accept money designated as *rent arrears* or *use and occupation*.

If a landlord fails to *reserve his or her rights* in writing to the tenant, the tenant may successfully argue in court that, by accepting the money, the landlord waived his or her right to pursue any eviction and instead chose to let the tenancy continue and accept rent. A *reservation of rights* clause should be included in any notice served upon the tenant. (The reservation of rights clause is more deeply examined on page 74.)

> *Landlord Tip:* Although not legally required, providing a holdover tenant with a **48 HOUR NOTICE TO QUIT** or other short-term notice may succeed in causing the tenant to vacate; thereby eliminating the time and expense of pursuing a summary process action.

No-Fault Termination (with a Tenancy-at-will)

As a landlord in a tenancy-at-will relationship, you enjoy the benefit of not needing a cause to terminate. You may terminate the tenancy at your *will*.

Example: You may choose to no longer be a landlord, you may wish to have your daughter move in upon her return from college, or you may be selling the building containing the unit and the terms of the purchase and sale agreement require it to be vacant.

> *Landlord Tip:* Do not let on to your tenant that you are considering eviction proceedings prior to serving the **NOTICE TO QUIT**. Any extra notice given to the tenant may be detrimental to you. A tenant, upon learning orally that you are intending on terminating that tenancy, unscrupulously may use the opportunity to take various actions to set up a possible defense or counterclaim to an eviction action.

Although you may terminate the tenancy without cause, you still must comply with legal procedures, including providing proper notice. In Massachusetts, for the typical tenancy-at-will where the rent is due monthly, the landlord must provide thirty days notice of termination or a full rental period, whichever is longer.

Example: If you serve the tenant with a **30 DAY NO FAULT NOTICE TO QUIT** on May 30th, and rent is due from your tenant the first day of each month, the tenancy will terminate no earlier than July 1st. If, instead, you serve your tenant with a **30 DAY NO FAULT NOTICE TO QUIT** on June 2nd, the tenancy terminates in thirty days or a full rental period, whichever is longer. Since June's rental period started on the 1st, the tenancy will terminate after the next full rental period (July), or on August 1st. (see form 17, p.235.)

Although not recommended, service received on the 1st day of a certain month may terminate a tenancy on the 1st day of the next month; however, if there are less than thirty-one days in the month in between (*i.e.*, February), the notice will be invalid as the notice period must be equal to a full rental period or thirty days, whichever is longer.

If your rental agreement requires rent to be paid in periods more frequent than monthly, say weekly or bi-monthly for example, at least thirty days notice is required.

With a **30 Day No Fault Notice to Quit** (form 17) without cause, the landlord does not need to provide a reason for the termination. However, if the landlord does state a reason, he or she will be required to prove it at the time of any court hearing or trial. The benefits of including reasons in the **30 Day No Fault Notice to Quit** include preventing the tenant from asserting the *withholding of rent* as a defense and preventing the tenant from receiving a *stay of execution* from the court. A stay of execution is a court order that allows the tenant to remain in the property beyond the time that the judgment and execution call for him or her to vacate. Stays of execution are further discussed in Chapter 10.

The **30 Day No Fault Notice to Quit** must state clearly that you are exercising the right to terminate the tenancy. Common language is—*Quit and deliver up the premises*. The notice also must clearly state when the termination is effective. Typical language indicating the date of termination is—*effective at the end of the last day of (month)*.

> *Landlord Tip:* Refrain from listening to and buying your tenant's excuses for not paying rent. Your mortgage holder will not listen to yours.

Termination Due to Nonpayment of Rent

The situation that landlords probably loathe most is when their tenants fail to pay any or all of the rent due. After all, landlords—especially small, non-professional landlords—greatly depend on this money to pay their monthly mortgage or other budgeted expenses. The law recognizes the seriousness of a nonpaying tenant and provides the landlord with a faster termination process. This procedure applies to tenants-at-will as well as tenants under lease. It requires the **14 Day Notice to Quit**. (see form 18, p.237 for the tenants-at-will and form 19, p.239 for lease tenants.)

Landlord Tip: With tenants who have not been with you long (under six months or so) and whose credit is unproven, do not hesitate to serve them with a **14 DAY NOTICE TO QUIT** the first time they are five to ten days late with the rent. (see form 18, p.237 for tenants-at-will and form 19 p.239 for lease tenants.) If they then pay, there is no harm done and you have established your formal tone. If they do not pay, you may begin eviction proceedings immediately and minimize your losses.

A landlord is allowed to give notice to a nonpaying tenant that the tenancy will terminate in fourteen days after receipt of the notice. Unlike no-fault terminations, the law does not require the notice to be effective on a certain rental date, nor does it require it to be equivalent to a full rental period. The termination is effective fourteen days after receipt. Also, the landlord is not required to first demand that the outstanding rent be paid before serving the **NOTICE TO QUIT.**

A landlord must look to the terms of the lease or the **TENANCY-AT-WILL AGREEMENT** to determine when the rent is due. (see form 8, p.211.) Normally, the rent is due the first day of each month. Therefore, a tenant may be served with a **14 DAY NOTICE TO QUIT** as early as the second day of the month, or the day after the rent is due and unpaid. (see form 18, p.237.)

In practice, landlords wait about ten days as the check may be in the mail. The time and expense of serving a **NOTICE TO QUIT** on a tenant prior to the ten days elapsing probably makes it impractical. Landlords under a lease, as well as landlords under a tenancy-at-will, may terminate the tenancy with a **14 DAY NOTICE TO QUIT**. The difference, however, lies in the required contents of the written notice and in the tenant's ability to pay-up and *cure,* or restore, the tenancy.

Contents of the 14 DAY NOTICE TO QUIT *and the tenant's right to cure.* Massachusetts law has specific requirements for how the **14 DAY NOTICE TO QUIT** should read, especially for tenants-at-will. In addition, the law allows your tenant a period of time in which to *cure* the tenancy by timely paying the amount of outstanding rent due. The tenant's ability to cure and the time period in which it must occur depends on the type of tenancy.

The form of the **14 DAY NOTICE TO QUIT** itself is simple. It need not recite the amount owed; however, in practice, it usually does. The notice must state that the tenant is to vacate the unit on a certain date at least fourteen days after the receipt of notice. Typically, the notice will state—*quit and deliver up the premises now occupied by you at the expiration of fourteen days from receipt of this notice.*

It is recommended that the notice specify and describe the premises from which the tenant must vacate. A form for a **14 DAY NOTICE TO QUIT** for nonpayment of rent to a tenant-at-will is included in Appendix E. (see form 19, p.239.)

Reservation of Rights. After you serve a **14 DAY NOTICE TO QUIT** for nonpayment to your tenant, be aware if he or she offers, and you accept, some or all of the money due. The law will presume that you have rescinded your decision to terminate the tenancy, and by accepting the money, you have agreed to enter into a new tenancy. Therefore, you should include a *reservation of rights* clause in the **14 DAY NOTICE TO QUIT**.

This clause allows you to accept money from the tenant without waiving your right to terminate the tenancy and pursue a *summary process action* if necessary. This is done by labeling the money payment as "rent arrears and/or use and occupation only." In other words, in order for you to both keep the money paid by the tenant after a **NOTICE TO QUIT** and terminate the tenancy, you must accept the money, not as *current rent*, but instead as either money paid for *outstanding rent owed* or for *the use of the premises without any tenancy agreement* (use and occupancy). The following reservation of rights clause is used in notices to quit for nonpayment.

> Please note: Any monies tendered by the tenant and accepted by the landlord or his agent after receipt of this notice are accepted for use and occupation and/or for rent arrears only and not as rent and without in any way waiving any and all rights under this notice or under any subsequent summary process proceeding. The landlord hereby reserves the right to accept monies re-establishing any new tenancy.

Even though this clause is included in your **NOTICE TO QUIT**, it is also very important to follow up your subsequent receipt of any monies from your tenant with a separate, written letter restating this reservation of rights. You may use the **RESERVATION OF RIGHTS LETTER** for this purpose. (see form 15, p.231.)

Curing the violation. The *tenant-at-will* has an absolute right to *cure* (re-establish) the tenancy if he or she has not been served with a previous **NOTICE TO QUIT** for nonpayment within the last *twelve* months *and* he or she pays the *full* amount of rent owed within ten days after receipt of the **14 DAY NOTICE TO**

QUIT. Therefore, if your tenant is a tenant-at-will; has not been served with a prior **NOTICE TO QUIT** for nonpayment within the last twelve months; and pays the full amount owed within ten (10) days of having received your **NOTICE TO QUIT** for nonpayment, you will not be able to go forward with the eviction and the tenant remains.

This money must be paid in full to the person the tenant customarily pays the rent or as otherwise directed within the letter (e.g., to the landlord's attorney). The landlord or his attorney must apprise the tenant of this right in the **14 DAY NOTICE TO QUIT** with the following language.

> If you have not received a **NOTICE TO QUIT** for nonpayment of rent within the last twelve months, you have a right to prevent termination of your tenancy by paying or tendering the full amount of rent due to your landlord, your landlord's attorney, or the person to whom you customarily pay your rent within ten days after your receipt of this notice.

If the **NOTICE TO QUIT** fails to include the above notification, the tenant who otherwise qualifies will be allowed to cure the tenancy up until the time his or her answer is due in the summary process action—a minimum of an additional two weeks.

The tenant under a lease may similarly cure his or her tenancy that was terminated by the landlord with a **14 DAY NOTICE TO QUIT**. (see form 19, p.239.) Massachusetts law, however, allows the tenant under a lease to cure the tenancy by paying the landlord the full amount of rent due plus interest and the court filing costs before the date on which the answer in the eviction action is due. While a tenant under a lease benefits by having more time to cure a default than a tenant-at-will, the law requires that the tenant also pay interest and the court costs. Massachusetts law does not require the landlord to include a *right to cure* notice in the **14 DAY NOTICE TO QUIT** to a tenant under a lease. (see form 1, p.195.)

Termination of Tenancy for Cause

The final category for which tenancies may be terminated is *termination for cause*. As previously stated, a tenancy-at-will may be terminated without reason, but if a reason is included in the **NOTICE TO QUIT**, the landlord must prove facts to support this reason. As previously stated, if the landlord is successful in proving this *cause*, the law rewards him or her for the extra effort by prohibiting the tenant from asserting a *rent-withholding* defense and from obtaining a stay of execution. (see Chapter 10.) Tenancies under a lease, however, may be terminated only for cause, including nonpayment.

> *Landlord Tip:* It is much easier to evict a tenant for cause when you can show a violation of a written term of a tenancy or of a rule or regulation. Therefore, always incorporate rules and regulations into your written lease or tenancy agreement.

To determine if cause exists, start by examining the terms of the lease. A standard lease contains provisions that, if violated by the tenant, can result in the lease's termination. Standard provisions mandate:

- ✪ prohibition of unlawful, noisy, or otherwise offensive use of the premises;

- ✪ compliance with any landlord-imposed rule or regulation;

- ✪ prohibition of pets on the premises without landlord approval;

- ✪ prohibition of assignment or subletting of the premises; and,

- ✪ compliance with payment of any additional real estate taxes.

The landlord may terminate the lease upon a violation of one of these or other similar provisions. A lease that contains these provisions will also contain a clause that governs the termination of the lease upon a violation. The **NOTICE TO QUIT** will be served according to the terms of this termination clause.

Although Massachusetts law requires a fourteen day notice for a violation due to nonpayment, standard leases usually provide for only seven days notice for any other breach. You may use the **7 DAY NOTICE TO QUIT** for a tenant under a lease. (see form 20, p.241.)

Prior to serving the tenant with a **NOTICE TO QUIT** cause, you should furnish him or her with a written *letter of admonishment*. This letter need not be of any specific form, but it should:

- ✪ set out the wrongful act(s) or conduct of the tenant;

✪ cite to the provision in the lease, tenancy-at-will agreement, or rules and regulations in which it is in violation; and,

✪ give a firm warning that any future violation of that provision (or any other provision) will be cause for termination of the tenancy.

This warning letter will serve to give the tenant the benefit of the doubt in any *less-than-serious* situations and will allow you to later show the court that there has been a history with this tenant and that he or she continues to be in violation. This will help show the judge that you were not predetermined to evict the tenant and that, as a result of exercising patience and discretion earlier, your case for eviction for cause has merit.

In addition to specific grounds for termination contained within the lease itself, you may immediately terminate the tenancy of a tenant who is using the premises for any of the following:

✪ prostitution;

✪ lewdness;

✪ illegal gaming;

✪ illegal keeping and sale of alcoholic beverages;

✪ illegal keeping, sale, or manufacture of controlled substances; or,

✪ illegal keeping of weapon, explosive, or incendiary device.

As the law for this type of eviction is complicated, the landlord is advised to seek the assistance of a capable attorney when seeking to immediately evict a tenant under this law. (Mass. Gen. Laws, Ch. 139, Sec. 19.)

When tenancies-at-will are in writing and when they include written rules and regulations, it is easy to understand the tenant's obligations. A landlord, therefore, may point to one or more of these various violated terms in support for terminating the tenant's tenancy-at-will for cause.

Service of the Notice to Quit

To be effective, the **NOTICE TO QUIT** must be served upon the tenant and receipt must be proven. There is no required method for serving the tenant with the notice. However, a notice that cannot be proven to have been received by a tenant may jeopardize your eviction.

> *Landlord Tip:* Have a *constable* serve your **NOTICE TO QUIT**. Although there is a fee for this service, the constable's signed statement on your notice is evidence that the tenant was served and all but eliminates the tenant's excuse of never receiving it. The constable will sign his or her *return* on your copy of the notice itself, indicating who, where, when, and how service was made.

Landlord's Termination of Commercial Tenancy

A commercial tenancy-at-will must be terminated with a **14 DAY NOTICE TO QUIT** for nonpayment as explained in the section concerning residential tenancies. (see form 18, p.237.) A tenancy under lease, however, may be terminated according to the terms specified in the lease. Therefore, Massachusetts law allows the landlord to negotiate a shorter notice period into his or her **COMMERCIAL LEASE**. (see form 11, p.221.)

Termination for Nonpayment

Standard **COMMERCIAL LEASES** require the landlord to send written notice of nonpayment to the tenant. If the tenant does not pay and cure the default within ten days of receipt of the written notice, the landlord would then serve a *notice of termination* on the tenant and immediately start the court eviction procedure.

If the lease does not contain a termination due to nonpayment provision, the landlord must use a **14 DAY NOTICE TO QUIT**. In this case, the tenant is allowed to cure his or her tenancy by paying the entire rent due plus interest and costs of the action by the day on which the answer is due in the subsequent summary process action.

Termination for Cause

Commercial tenancies terminated for cause are typically a result of a breach of a provision in the written lease. The commercial lease normally contains a default provision that governs such occurrences. If the tenant fails to cure the default as described in the landlord's written notice within the prescribed amount of time, the landlord may terminate the lease.

It should be noted that although many commercial leases are worded to suggest that the landlord may physically remove the tenant from the premises upon a default (*enter into and upon the premises and expel the said tenant*), the landlord should not understand this to mean *self-help* without due process of the law. Self-help refers to the landlord physically removing the tenant without going to court. Instead, the landlord usually must send a written termination notice to the tenant. As you are now aware, if the tenant still continues to occupy despite receiving notices, the landlord must then start the court eviction procedures.

Special Rules for Public Housing

All subsidized housing programs require that their tenants sign leases with the landlord. Some subsidy programs require that the parties use the programs' special lease or its addendum. Other programs simply require that the housing authority approve the landlord's lease. The leases contain restrictions on the landlord's right to evict the tenant. Although the reasons vary depending on which subsidy program the tenant is using, the landlord is typically only able to evict a tenant for:

✪ serious violations of the lease;

✪ nonpayment of rent;

✪ tenant misconduct; and,

✪ landlord's business reasons (*i.e.*, desire to use the apartment for family use or to charge a higher rent than what the subsidy program pays).

NOTE: *If you want to evict the tenant for a business reason, the lease will likely require that this only be done at the end of the first year of the lease. The landlord must also give ninety days written notice in advance. If the housing authority believes that this is not your good faith reason, your eviction may be denied.*

When terminating the tenancy, the landlord must send the tenant a **NOTICE TO QUIT** as detailed at the beginning of this chapter. The landlord must also provide the local housing authority a copy of this notice. The lease may also require further language in the **NOTICE TO QUIT**. Be sure to carefully consult your lease for any additional language as an eviction based on a faulty termination notice may be dismissed against you.

Federally subsidized housing is governed by the Code of Federal Regulations (C.F.R.) as well as Massachusetts law. If you have any questions regarding your rights or required procedures, you should review the following federal regulations.

✪   Evictions from certain subsidized and HUD-owned projects (24 C.F.R. Part 247).

✪   Lease and Grievance Procedure (24 C.F.R. Part 966).

Death of a Tenant

If a lease contains a clause binding the *heirs, successors, and assigns* of the lessee, then the lease continues after the death of the tenant unless cancelled by the agreement of the landlord and the heirs. Without any such explicit language, the lease terminates upon the death of a tenant.

Options to Cancel

Generally, when a lease allows only one party to cancel it at will, the lease is not considered binding and the courts will allow either party to cancel it at will. A lease will probably be held valid if the option to cancel is contingent upon the occurrence of some event.

10 | EVICTING A TENANT

Unfortunately, the service of the **NOTICE TO QUIT** merely terminates the tenancy. It does not require the tenant to move out. A court summary process action (eviction) is necessary to remove tenants still present in your unit after the tenancy has been terminated. The ultimate hearing in the summary process action occurs at least two to three weeks after the termination date stated in the **NOTICE TO QUIT**.

Many tenants know that they have at least this additional time before they will be required to move. Many also bank on being able to convince the judge to allow them additional time after the hearing before they must vacate. Your knowledge of the summary process procedure will allow you to minimize your losses by scheduling the court hearing at the earliest possible time and ensure that the tenant is not able to defeat the eviction on any technical procedural grounds.

Self-Help by Landlord

The only way a landlord may recover possession of a dwelling unit is if the tenant voluntarily surrenders it to the landlord, abandons it, or if the landlord gets a court order giving the landlord possession. As explained later in this chapter, *self-help methods*, such as shutting off electricity or changing locks, can result in thousands of dollars in fines. In some cases, the tenants' lawyers have abused the system and allowed nonpaying tenants to remain in possession for months, but most of the time the system allows delinquent tenants to be removed quickly.

Residential landlords are specifically forbidden to use self-help methods to evict tenants even if the lease allows it. As explained under the subsection on "Violations by the Landlord" on page 66, if a landlord directly or indirectly terminates utilities such as water, electricity, gas, elevators, lights, garbage collection, or refrigeration or if the landlord locks up the unit or takes off the doors, windows, roofs, walls, etc., the landlord is liable for damages of at least three months rent plus court costs and attorney's fees.

> A case where the landlord changed the locks to a room rented by the tenant for additional storage after the tenant complained of his apartment rent being increased, and a case where the landlord changed the locks to the tenant's apartment after the tenant gave verbal notice that he was leaving, but before he had vacated, are two examples of where Massachusetts courts have found against the landlord as a result of trying to engage in *self-help*. In each case, the court awarded the tenant judgment in the amount of three times the rent plus reasonable attorney's fees. *Ianello v. Court Management Corporation*, 400 Mass 321 (1987) and *Dew v. Laufauci*, 2001 Mass App. Div. 95, respectively.

Surrender or Abandonment

To surrender a dwelling, tenants must tell the landlord that they are leaving or leave the keys. If the tenants leave the keys and remove all of their possessions, then the landlord would be safe to assume abandonment. However, if the tenant leaves behind property that appears to have some value, the landlord should not assume that the tenant has abandoned it unless there is some other evidence, such as the tenant having the electricity shut off or having mail forwarded.

Settling with the Tenant

Although in many evictions the tenants do not answer the complaint and the landlord wins quickly, some tenants can create nightmares for landlords. Clever tenants can delay the case for months and vindictive tenants can destroy the property with little worry of ever paying for it. Therefore, in some cases, lawyers advise their clients to offer the tenant a cash settlement to leave.

Example: A tenant may be offered $200 to be out of the premises and leave it clean within a week.

Of course it hurts to give money to a tenant who already owes you money, but it could be cheaper than the court costs, vacancy time, and damages to the premises. You will have to make your own decision based upon your tenant.

Using an Attorney

The tenant may, in some cases, just be waiting for the eviction notice before leaving the premises. In such a case, the landlord may regain the premises no matter what kind of papers he or she files. But in other cases, tenants with no money and no defenses have retained free lawyers who find technical defects in the case. This can cause a delay in the eviction and could cause the landlord to be ordered to pay the tenant's attorney fees. A simple error in a landlord's court papers can cost him or her the case.

A landlord facing an eviction should consider the costs and benefits of using an attorney compared to doing it without an attorney. One possibility is to file the case without an attorney and hope the tenant moves. If the tenant stays and fights the eviction, an attorney can be hired to finish the case. Some landlords, who prefer to do their own evictions, start by paying a lawyer for a half-hour or hour of time to review the facts of the case and point out potential problems.

Whenever a tenant has an attorney, the landlord should also have one.

📕 A winning tenant was awarded $8,675.00 in attorney's fees that was figured at $150 an hour and then doubled.

 📖 The fact that a tenant obtained free counsel from a legal aid program in connection with the summary process matter brought by landlord did not bar award of attorney's fees to the program. (*Darmetko v. Boston Housing Authority*, 378 Mass. 758 (1979).)

If the lease says that the tenant must pay the landlord's attorney's fees if the landlord sues the tenant, the law implies that the tenant has the same right if he or she wins. (Mass. Gen. Laws, Ch. 186 Sec. 20.) Therefore, it is important to have an attorney if the tenant has one. Otherwise, the tenant's attorney might find some technical flaws in your case and end up winning.

Who Can Sue

An owner can represent him- or herself or herself in court and does not need an attorney. As a general rule, no one can represent another person in court except a licensed attorney, and only an attorney can represent a corporation. Not even a corporate officer can represent a corporation. It is a criminal offense for a non-lawyer to represent another party in court. In some cases, where a real estate agent or other agent of a landlord signed leases in his or her own name as rental agent, the agent could go to court without the owner of the property. This is because the agent is the party to the contract.

Summary Process Action

Summary process is the legal term used to refer to the eviction process in the courts. The word *summary* refers to the fast pace in which the entire process moves. Although a landlord of a nonpaying or problem tenant will never agree that the process is fast, summary process, which usually takes two to three weeks to receive a court hearing, is very fast when compared with regular civil lawsuits that can take up to two years to get to trial. The fast pace means that there are usually only a few days in between each step of the process. Therefore, the landlord must keep on top of the procedure.

NOTE: *Be sure to see the Eviction Flow Chart on page 178.*

Summons and Complaint

The initial step in summary process is service of the *Summary Process Summons and Complaint* upon the tenant. The Summary Process Summons and Complaint is a single court document that informs the tenant of the date, time, and place of the court hearing, as well as the reason for the lawsuit. It also includes the amount of money, if any, the landlord is seeking. This Summary Process Summons and Complaint may only be served after the tenancy has been terminated in accordance with the **NOTICE TO QUIT**. A sample Summary Process Summons and Complaint is provided in Appendix D.

A summary process action may be brought in the appropriate district court including the Boston Municipal Court, the Superior Court, and the Housing Court. The majority of evictions are filed either in the district court, including the Boston Municipal Court, or the Housing Court. Because of jurisdictional requirements, if you are filing an eviction action in either Middlesex County or Norfolk County and are seeking $25,000 or more in damages from the tenant, the action needs to be brought in the *Superior Court* of that county. If you do not, the tenant may dismiss the action and force you to do it all over again, even if you prevailed in the district court. As you must use the Summary Process Summons and Complaint form of the particular court in which you file your action, you first must decide in which court you may bring your action.

District Court. A *district court* is a court that has jurisdiction over a certain district consisting of one or more cities and towns. Unlike other civil lawsuits, summary process jurisdiction is not dictated by the residence of the parties involved, but rather by the location of the property at issue.

Example: If the property to which your eviction action pertains is located in one of the following communities: Reading, North Reading, Woburn, Winchester, Burlington, Wilmington, or Stoneham; you must file your summary process action in the Woburn District Court. The Chelsea District Court would likewise have jurisdiction over evictions for properties located in Chelsea and Revere. The Boston Municipal Court has jurisdiction over properties located within the downtown area of the City of Boston.

Housing Court. There is a Housing Court that handles summary process in five divisions throughout Massachusetts. If your rental property at issue is located within one of these Housing Court districts, you may also bring your eviction there. The five divisions are:

✪   Boston Division;

✪   Hampden County Division;

✪   Worcester County Division (for all of Worcester County, plus Bellingham, Ashby, and Townsend);

✪   Northeastern Division (for Essex County, Lowell, Billerica, Chelmsford, Dracut, Dunstable, Groton, Pepperell, Shirley, Tewksbury, Tyngsborough, and Westford); and,

✪   Southeastern Division (for Bristol and Plymouth counties).

Choice of court. As you may have noticed, if your property is located in one of several certain cities and towns, you have a choice as to the court in which you file your summary process matter.

Example: If your unit is in South Boston, you may bring the summary process action either in the South Boston District Court or in the Boston Division of the Housing Court. If you live in Hopedale (Worcester County), you may bring your action in the Milford District Court or in the Worcester County Division of the Housing Court. If your unit is on Commonwealth Avenue in Boston, you can bring the eviction in either the Boston Municipal Court (BMC) or in the Boston Division of the Housing Court.

Difference between the courts. Besides location, there are other differences between the district courts (and the BMC) and the Housing Court that will aid you in your selection. First, the filing fee for a summary process matter in any district court or for the BMC is currently $195, whereas in the Housing Court it is only $135.

Second, the Housing Court has a staff of *Housing Specialists* who will be assigned to help mediate and resolve the case. This often can benefit a landlord without an attorney.

Third, an appeal from a district court (except in Middlesex and Norfolk counties) or BMC decision goes to the Superior Court where the whole hearing or trial is repeated (called a *de novo* hearing). An appeal from the Housing Court (and from the Superior Court) is to the Appeals Court for the appeal of an *error of law* or *abuse of discretion* only. Appeals from Middlesex and Norfolk counties are to the appellate division of the court.

If your unit is located in a city or town that allows you to have a choice where to file, you should weigh the above factors in your decision making. A district court and Housing Court directory appears in Appendix C to assist you in finding the correct court for your eviction.

Obtaining the complaint. Once you have selected the appropriate court in which to file the summary process action, you must obtain a Summary Process Summons and Complaint from that court. (A sample Summary Process Summons and Complaint may be found in Appendix D. If you choose to be represented by an attorney, he or she will have this form and will complete it for you.) You may then complete the Summary Process Summons and Complaint so that it may be served upon your tenant.

Completing the Complaint. In the places indicated, you must:

- ✪ fill in the name of your tenant(s);

- ✪ the address of the rented unit;

- ✪ the name of the appropriate court;

- ✪ the dates corresponding to the entry date, answer date, and hearing date;

- ✪ your name and address;

- ✪ the reason for the eviction; and,

- ✪ an itemized amount of back rent due (if any).

The trickiest part of completing the Summary Process Summons and Complaint is filling in the correct dates. As previously stated, the landlord is able to select the date for the court hearing. In most cases, the courts have summary process hearing sessions on each Thursday.

The first step is to figure out when you will be able to have the Summary Process Summons and Complaint served upon your tenant by a constable. Most constables are very flexible and will be able to serve it within only a few days. The entry date (the day that you file the summary process action with the court) must be within seven to thirty days after the tenant has been served. Most courts have Mondays as the entry date for summary process matters.

Example: If your constable serves your tenant with the Summary Process Summons and Complaint on Monday, June 1st, the earliest you can enter the action would be Monday, June 8th. The latest date you could enter the action, given the June 1st date of service, is Monday, June 29 (the last Monday within thirty days). Most likely, you will want to enter the action and schedule a hearing at the earliest opportunity after the tenant has been served.

To summarize, select the dates as follows.

✪ Ascertain the date in which your **NOTICE TO QUIT** terminates the tenancy.

✪ Have your Summary Process Summons and Complaint ready for the constable to serve the day after the tenancy terminates (e.g., the fifteenth day after the tenant receives the **14 DAY NOTICE TO QUIT**).

✪ Schedule the entry date for the first Monday at least seven days away from the date of service (e.g., if the constable served the Summary Process Summons and Complaint on your tenant on Wednesday, August 2nd, you may then select Monday, August 14th as your earliest entry date).

This procedure will ensure that you obtain the earliest possible hearing date. The instructions on the Summary Process Summons and Complaint and the summary process clerk at the court can provide you with additional assistance.

Once you schedule the entry date, the answer date and the hearing date are automatic. The answer date (the day by which your tenant must respond in writing to your complaint and file any counterclaims or discovery) is the following Monday, one week after the entry date. Finally, barring any holiday or special circumstance, the hearing date will usually be on the Thursday of that week, three days after the answer date and ten days after the entry date.

NOTE: *Some housing courts have various days of the week for their hearing day.*

The Summary Process Summons and Complaint also requires you to indicate the reason for eviction. You should indicate that the tenant was duly served with the specific **NOTICE TO QUIT** (or is a tenant at sufferance), and has not (timely) paid or vacated, depending on the facts in your case.

Example: A reason may read: *you were duly served by a constable with a fourteen-day Notice to Quit for nonpayment of rent and have failed to pay or vacate.*

Service. Once you have completed the Summary Process Summons and Complaint, you can now forward it to a constable or a sheriff authorized to serve civil process in the town where your unit is located. If you are unaware of any constables, check your local Yellow Pages or the clerk's office in the town or city hall where your unit is located.

Unlike the service of the **NOTICE TO QUIT**, where the use of the constable is recommended, a constable (or sheriff) is mandatory for service of the Summary Process Summons and Complaint. Once the constable or sheriff has made service upon your tenant, he or she will return the Summary Process Summons and Complaint to you with his or her signed *return* evidencing the date, time, and manner of service. (A typical service by a constable or sheriff costs about $30 depending on the travel distance and other factors). You are then set to file your summary process action in court.

Proper filing. The summary process rules require that in order to properly file a summary process action, you must include the following:

☐   the Summary Process Summons and Complaint;

☐   the notice terminating the tenancy (**NOTICE TO QUIT**), with proof of service;

☐   a certificate of eviction if the unit is controlled by rent control laws;

☐   an affidavit of condominium conversion compliance (where applicable); and,

☐   the entry fee.

As this package of documents must be filed in the court on or before the Monday entry date as indicated on the Summary Process Summons and Complaint, you should file the package in person with the court if you believe the mail will not allow ample time. The package should be mailed to or entered with the summary process clerk in the civil clerk's office in the court. Once you have filed your package, you may check with the clerk for the *docket number* your case has been assigned for future reference. This is the court-assigned file number for the court action.

Tenant's Answer   After the landlord serves and files the Summary Process Summons and Complaint, the tenant will have an opportunity to respond. The tenant, or his or her attorney, will be able to protect his or her interests and challenge the eviction by serving and filing his or her own documents, including an *answer* and any counterclaims and discovery requests.

The tenant may serve and file his or her answer on or before the date when the answer is due as stated in the Summary Process Summons and Complaint. The answer may be thought of as the counterpart to your Summary Process Summons and Complaint. The tenant will either admit or deny various allegations contained within your complaint (e.g., admit that he is a tenant of yours but denies that any rent is owed). The tenant may assert *affirmative defenses* to justify his or her position and to prevent the landlord from obtaining a judgment (e.g., *the Summary Process Summons and Complaint was not completed and filed properly* or *the tenant was lawfully withholding the rent*).

Counterclaim. In the majority of cases, where a tenant or a tenant's attorney files an answer, it is accompanied by a set of counterclaims. Unlike an affirmative defense, which is like the shield a knight uses as defensive protection in battle, a counterclaim is more like the knight's lance and is used by the tenant to seek money damages by alleging that the landlord violated one of the tenant's rights. An example of a typical counterclaim is claiming a violation of the security deposit law entitling the tenant to the return of the deposit and three times the amount of the deposit as a penalty. Affirmative defenses and counterclaims are examined in depth later in this chapter. A sample answer and counterclaim is provided in Appendix D.

You are not required by law to respond to the counterclaims, but a response may very well serve your interests. If your tenant, and more significantly, an attorney on behalf of your tenant, files an answer with counterclaims and request for discovery, you should immediately retain your own attorney, if you have not done so already.

Discovery. The third part of the tenant's response is a *request for discovery*. The tenant is allowed to demand that up to thirty written *interrogatories* (questions) concerning the eviction be answered by you. Also, the tenant may serve you with up to thirty *requests for admissions* in which you will be required to either admit or deny the validity of a written statement regarding the eviction. Finally, the tenant can request that you produce documents relevant to the eviction. The landlord is required to respond to these discovery requests within ten days of receipt.

Besides aiding a tenant with more facts with which to defend against the eviction, a discovery request also has a tactical purpose—it automatically postpones the hearing date for two weeks.

Example: If the original hearing date was scheduled for Thursday, May 4th, the timely filing of discovery requests on or before the answer date will automatically postpone the hearing two weeks to Thursday, May 18th.

The court requires the tenant to inform you of this new date. A sample tenant-discovery request is included in Appendix D. Although you have a right to serve the tenant with discovery requests, this should be reserved for only the most hotly contested cases as it will delay your ability to have a court hearing by two weeks.

NOTE: *If you do not submit discovery requests to the tenant by the answer date, you must request permission from the court through a motion. As this will delay the eviction hearing, the tenant will rarely oppose your request.*

The filing of these documents by your tenant means that he or she is strongly contesting the eviction. Therefore, you should seriously consider retaining your own attorney to ensure that your rights will be asserted and your interests protected.

Transfers. Another tactic commonly used by tenants to delay the eviction procedure is to ask the district or superior court to *transfer* the case to the Housing Court. If your unit is located in a city or town for which a Housing Court and a district court both have jurisdiction (see Appendix C) and you entered the case in the district court, the tenant may transfer the case to the Housing Court. The law allows the tenant to transfer the case to the Housing Court at his or her will, as long as he or she does so no later than the day before the hearing.

The effect of this transfer is to delay the eviction proceedings for a minimum of one to two weeks. The court will provide you with notice of the transfer and the new hearing date in the Housing Court.

Tenant's Possible Defenses

Chapter 4 discussed the landlord's duties with respect to taking the security and the last month's rent deposits. Chapter 5 illustrated the important duties of the landlord with respect to the maintenance of the unit and property. This section of this chapter explains the various defenses and claims that a tenant may assert for breaches of these and other duties of the landlord. As mentioned before, these claims and defenses are typically alleged by the tenant in his or her answer and counterclaims.

Understanding the various defenses and claims a tenant may lawfully make will allow you to better perform your duties, as well as better evaluate the tenant's case and help predict the likelihood of your success in an eviction case.

Procedural Defenses

A tenant may attack a *procedural* component of a case, hoping to have the court dismiss the eviction action—or at least postpone it. A procedural component of a case is the manner in which the case was filed in court and served upon the defendant. The following are common procedural defenses asserted.

The court does not have jurisdiction. Here, the tenant challenges the jurisdiction of the court to hear the summary process case.

Example: If your tenant lives in your unit in Medford, but you mistakenly bring the case in the Malden District Court instead of the Somerville District Court, the tenant will prevail on a *motion to dismiss for lack of jurisdiction*. The court will probably dismiss the case *without prejudice*, which means that you will be able to refile the eviction case in the Somerville District Court. However, you will have wasted valuable time and all expenses incurred to date.

The Summary Process Summons and Complaint were not served correctly. This defense attacks the manner in which the tenant received notice of the eviction action. The tenant may allege that the Summary Process Summons and Complaint was served less than seven or more than thirty days before the matter was entered in court (the entry date). As previously discussed, the law helps to protect the tenant by prohibiting the landlord from giving notice of the eviction hearing too far in advance (more than thirty days) or too close in time (less than seven days). In such a situation, the court will probably dismiss the case *without prejudice* (meaning you must start over).

"Notice to Quit" Related Defenses. The tenant may raise a few defenses relating to the **NOTICE TO QUIT**. The tenant may allege that the notice was never sent or was never received. You can effectively combat these defenses by filing the original **NOTICE TO QUIT**, containing the constable's return, with the court. If you did fail to serve the **NOTICE TO QUIT**, the court will dismiss the action.

Similarly, the tenant may allege that the Summary Process Summons and Complaint was served before the notice period expired.

Example: If you served the tenant with a **14 DAY NOTICE TO QUIT** on August 1st, effective August 15th, but served the Summary Process Summons and Complaint on the tenant on August 12th, the tenant would have a legitimate defense and likely would prevail on a motion to dismiss.

Additionally, the tenant may defend by asserting that the Summary Process Summons and Complaint was served by an unauthorized person. If it was not served by a constable or sheriff authorized to serve process in the applicable town or by a person authorized by the court, the case likewise will be dismissed. You should be sure to confirm with the constable or sheriff that he or she is authorized to serve a Summary Process Summons and Complaint in the town where your unit is located.

Substantive Defenses

A tenant often will defend against an eviction action by asserting a *substantive defense* (or defenses). This is a defense that attacks the heart of the landlord's case.

Withholding of rent. This is probably the most widely-used—and one of the most powerful—defenses available for the residential tenant. The Massachusetts rent withholding law allows both the tenant-at-will and the tenant under a lease to defend against an eviction for nonpayment of rent and an eviction without cause. (Mass. Gen. Laws, Ch. 239, Sec. 8a.) However, this defense is not applicable to an eviction with cause.

In using this defense, the tenant essentially justifies withholding rent based upon the landlord's breach of an important (*material*) provision of the lease or tenancy agreement or a breach of the *warranty of habitability* (discussed later in this chapter). In most cases, tenants refer to sanitary, building, or other structural code violations to support this defense.

Unfortunately for the landlord, the tenant may assert this defense without many strings attached. The tenant is not required to notify the landlord in writing that he or she is withholding some or all of the rent. The tenant need only show that the landlord had notice of the poor conditions before the tenant began to withhold the rent. The tenant may assert this defense even if it was not the tenant who notified the landlord.

NOTE: *The tenant may rely on the local board of health's notice of violations to the landlord as the basis to begin withholding. In addition, the law does not require the tenant to deposit the withheld rent into an escrow account.*

As far as the law is concerned, the tenant may spend every last cent of the *withheld rent payment* and still lawfully claim that he or she is withholding it. Therefore, it is possible, and unfortunately usual, for a landlord to first learn of the tenant's defense of the withholding of rent after the tenant serves his or her answer and counterclaims.

The law, however, does include some limitations on the tenant's ability to assert this defense. As previously mentioned, the landlord's breach must be material and not simply minor in nature. In addition, the tenant will not be able to rely on this defense unless all four of the following conditions exist.

1. The landlord, his or her agent, or the person who normally collects the rent knew of the conditions before the tenant was in arrears with the rent.

2. The landlord cannot show that the conditions complained of were caused by the tenant (the tenant will have to show that any violation entirely within the unit was not his or her fault).

3. The unit is not located in a motel, hotel, or lodging house where the tenant has lived for less than three months.

4. The landlord does not show that the conditions could not be corrected without the premises being vacated.

If the tenant cannot demonstrate all of the four above requirements, his or her withholding of rent defense will fail.

The tenant may not automatically withhold the entire rent when a material breach occurs. The tenant is only entitled to withhold that portion of the rent that compensates him or her for the *loss in value* of the unit due to its poor condition. In considering the amount of loss in value, a court will consider the effect of the condition(s) on the tenant's *use and enjoyment* of the unit.

> **Example:** If the apartment unit had no heat for the first two weeks of January, the effect on the tenant's use and enjoyment of the unit would be much greater than had the unit been without heat for the first two weeks of June.

The key here is not simply for the tenant to show the existence of a code violation, but rather to show that the violation or condition greatly affected his or her use and enjoyment of the unit. The absence of heat for the first two weeks of January would arguably render the value of the apartment unit to be negligible and would allow the tenant to withhold most, if not all, of the rent for the affected period. On the other hand, a defective heating system in the first two weeks of June, although a code violation, would hardly affect the tenant's use and enjoyment of the unit; thereby not allowing much, if any, rent to be withheld.

The great majority of cases fall somewhere in between these examples and each presents its own set of facts for the court to consider. Many courts have found it almost impossible for code violations and other conditions to render a unit completely worthless, especially if the tenant continues to occupy it. Therefore, a tenant who withholds the entire rent is probably mistaken and poorly advised.

In an eviction for nonpayment, the court will allow the tenant to stay (award him or her *possession*) if the amount of rent withheld is less than or equal to the loss in value of the unit due to the defect.

> **Example:** Assume the rent for Unit A is $1,000 per month, but due to a significant code violation the tenant pays only $800 for rent and withholds $200 (after giving notice to the landlord). Next, assume that the landlord brings an eviction action against the tenant for nonpayment of rent.
>
> At the hearing, the judge determines that the code violation rendered the value of the unit to be only $700 for the month. Therefore, since the unit's loss in value due to the defect ($300) is greater than the amount of rent withheld ($200), the court will allow the tenant to stay.

If the landlord does demonstrate that the tenant withheld too much and that back rent is due, the court will allow the tenant to remain in possession if he or she pays the difference within seven days after the date of judgment.

Repair and deduct. A residential tenant may be compensated for code violations and other conditions through a procedure less drastic than the withholding of rent. The "Repair and Deduct" law allows the tenant of a unit containing violations of the *standards of fitness for human habitation*, as determined by the Sanitary Code and other laws, to deduct from his or her rent an amount that corresponds to the expense incurred in the correction of the condition. (Mass. Gen. Laws, Ch. 111, Sec. 127L.)

The "Repair and Deduct" law establishes a procedure so that the tenant cannot capriciously deduct just any expense from the rent. The condition or violation must endanger or materially impair the health, safety, or well-being of the tenant. This condition must be certified by the local board of health or by a court. Also, the owner must have been notified in writing of the existence of the violation, have failed to contract with a third party within five days to repair the condition, and have failed to substantially complete all necessary repairs within fourteen days after the notice.

If these prerequisites are satisfied, the tenant may undertake repairs and may subsequently deduct the cost from the rent due. However, the tenant is restricted from deducting repair expenses in an amount greater than four months rent in any twelve-month period.

Reprisal by landlord. Residential tenants are protected from *reprisals* by landlords. Reprisals refer to unlawful retaliation by the landlord against the tenant. A tenant may successfully defend against a summary process action if he or she can show it is the result of doing any of the following:

❂ trying to obtain damages and/or enforce a federal, state, or local law, regulation, by-law, or ordinance that regulates residential housing;

❂ deducting money from his or her rent as a result of paying the gas or electric bill, where the landlord is contractually responsible for paying said bill, in order to prevent the utility company from shutting off the service;

✪ reporting to the local board of health or housing inspection department a violation or a suspected violation of any health or building code or any other local, state, or federal regulation that regulates residential housing;

✪ complaining of any such local, state, or federal regulation or law violation in writing to the landlord or the landlord's agent;

✪ organizing or joining a tenant's union or association; or,

✪ making or expressing an intention to make a rental payment to an organization of condo unit owners where the landlord is late with the condo fee payments.

If the tenant is able to show that the **NOTICE TO QUIT** upon which the summary process action is based, or that the summary process action itself was commenced within six months of any of the tenant's above-listed actions, the court will *presume* that the action is in reprisal. Once reprisal is presumed, the landlord will need very solid evidence that the summary process was started for a legitimate reason.

If the landlord begins eviction proceedings within six months of one of the above actions by the tenant, a court will presume that the eviction was commenced solely in retaliation by the landlord and the court may dismiss the eviction action. If the eviction action is for nonpayment, however, the law switches the burden to the tenant to prove that the landlord had some other unlawful motive for the eviction besides nonpayment. This burden is difficult to overcome.

Acceptance of rent after **NOTICE TO QUIT**. The landlord who brings an eviction action for the nonpayment of rent must be careful not to waive his or her right to pursue the eviction by accepting rent from the tenant. As discussed in Chapter 9, if a landlord accepts money as *rent* from a tenant after the tenancy terminates, the tenant may convincingly argue in court that the landlord *waived* (cancelled) the **NOTICE TO QUIT** and re-established the tenancy.

To prevent this event, the landlord should include the *reservation of rights* paragraph in the **NOTICE TO QUIT**, as well as send the tenant a **RESERVATION OF RIGHTS LETTER** upon the acceptance of any monies from the tenant. (see form 15, p.231.) The letter should clearly state that the money is being accepted for *use and occupancy* and/or for *rent arrears* only and not as rent. Failure to take these precautionary measures may result in dismissal of the eviction action. If a tenant offers to pay the full amount of rent arrears due but the landlord wants to evict the tenant, regardless of what is repaid, a landlord may refuse this money as long as the applicable cure period (as discussed in Chapter 9) has expired. If a landlord who files a nonpayment of rent eviction accepts all of the rent arrears due, the court will likely dismiss the case, regardless of how the landlord labeled the monies received.

Tenant's Counterclaims

In addition to defenses that seek to immunize the tenant from liability, the tenant may also assert *counterclaims* against the landlord. Successful counterclaims may deprive the landlord of some or all of the recovery sought, including regaining possession. It may also actually result in money damages against the landlord. The following are some common counterclaims.

Breach of the Warranty of Habitability

The landlord is obliged to provide the tenant with housing fit for human habitation. The tenant's obligation to pay rent is dependent on the landlord's providing safe and habitable housing. For the most part, the Sanitary Code (the Code) sets the standard for *habitable* housing. Breach of the *warranty of habitability* occurs when there is a violation that endangers or materially impairs the health, safety, or well-being of the tenant.

The landlord has limited options in defending against a claim of a breach of the warranty of habitability. A landlord may not argue that he or she did not cause the condition or is in the process of remedying it. Liability attaches upon the landlord being given notice of the uninhabitable condition. To successfully defend against this claim, the landlord must show that the condition did not exist as alleged, that he or she did not have any knowledge of the condition, or that the condition was directly caused by the tenant.

In measuring the amount of any damages to be awarded the tenant for the landlord's breach of the warranty of habitability, the court will look at the time the landlord first knew or received notice of the condition, whichever occurs first. The court then compares the *value of the unit as warranted* with the *market value* of the unit given the defective conditions.

The value of the unit as warranted presumes that it complies with the warranty of habitability and contains no violations impairing the health, safety, or well-being of its occupants. This value is often deemed to be the rent amount. Courts often use a discretionary number to calculate the extent of the reduction in value. The court then will take this difference, if any, and multiply it over the period of time for which the landlord had notice of the condition.

Example 1: A court may decide that the unit's lack of hot water, a condition deemed to endanger or impair the health or safety of the tenant according to the Sanitary Code, reduced the value of the unit by twenty percent. This percentage reduction in value is then used to assess the tenant's damages.

Example 2: Assume the tenant pays $600 per month for rent and the court considers this to adequately approximate its value as warranted. Now let us assume that the tenant, on January 1st, makes the landlord aware of the unit's exposed electrical wiring, the infestation of cockroaches, and lack of smoke detectors. Next assume that the defective conditions go unremedied by the landlord for ninety days. Also assume that all of these defective conditions actually exist as alleged by the tenant and were not caused by him or her. Finally, assume that the court, after hearing all the facts, decides that the conditions and code violations reduced the tenant's use and enjoyment of the unit by fifty percent.

Given this scenario, a court will award the tenant $900 ($600 x 50% = $300.00 per month x 3 months = $900).

NOTE: *Rarely will a court find that conditions and violations reduce the use and enjoyment of the unit by a full 100 percent. After all, if the tenant still occupied the unit, some use and enjoyment must have been possible.*

Deposit Violations As discussed in Chapter 4, taking a security deposit or last month's rent deposit from a tenant requires following specific legal procedures. The taking of these deposits is one of the most misunderstood areas for landlords. This is unfortunate since the violation of a deposit procedure enables the tenant to have a civil remedy against the landlord.

Security deposit violations. With regard to the security deposit, the amount of damages in which the tenant is entitled depends on the nature of the violation. The following examples show some of the most common security deposit violations and the corresponding damages allowed the tenant under law.

✪ *Failure to deposit the funds in the proper interest-bearing account.* The tenant is entitled to the immediate return of the deposit plus damages in an amount equal to three times the security deposit plus interest at the rate of five percent from the date when payment became due plus court costs and reasonable attorney fees. (see Chapter 4 for further discussion.)

✪ *Failure to transfer the security deposit to the landlord's successor.* The tenant is entitled to the immediate return of the security deposit plus damages in an amount equal to three times the security deposit plus interest at the rate of five percent from the date when payment became due plus court costs and reasonable attorney fees.

✪ *Use of a provision in a lease that attempts to obtain a waiver by the tenant of his or her security deposit rights.* The tenant is entitled to the immediate return of the security deposit.

✪ *Failure to furnish the tenant with an itemized list of damages within thirty days after the termination of the tenancy.* The tenant is entitled to the immediate return of the security deposit.

✪ *Failure to return the security deposit or balance after deducting any appropriate amounts, together with interest, after thirty days after termination of the tenancy.* The tenant is entitled to:

- the immediate return of the security deposit;

- damages (three times the security deposit plus interest at the rate of five percent from the date when payment became due);

- court costs; and,

- reasonable attorney fees.

If you violate one of these security deposit requirements, the tenant or the tenant's attorney may likely request the immediate return of the security deposit together with interest and a penalty of three times the security deposit and attorney's fees. Massachusetts case law states that if the landlord returns the deposit with any accrued interest when the tenant first demands it (whether demand is first made by letter or in a lawsuit—no other efforts by the tenant or his or her attorney are required), the landlord is not required to pay any attorney's fees or three times the deposit.

Last month's rent violations. A violation of the last month's rent procedures does not entail penalties as severe as those for the security deposit. If the landlord fails to tender a receipt to the tenant, upon payment of the last month's rent, the tenant will be entitled to the immediate return of the deposit. If the landlord fails to pay interest on the last month's rent within thirty days after the termination of the tenancy, the tenant will be entitled to damages in an amount equal to three times the interest to which the tenant is entitled plus court costs and reasonable attorney fees. There is no penalty if the landlord fails to deposit the last month's rent into a bank account.

Wrongful Acts by Landlord and Breach of Quiet Enjoyment

Massachusetts also has laws in place to protect the residential tenant from willful or intentional acts by the landlord that interfere with the tenant's enjoyment of the premises. This law, which is commonly referred to as the *Wrongful Acts by Landlord* statute or *Breach of Quiet Enjoyment* statute, calls for the landlord, upon a violation, to pay the actual amount of damages or the equivalent to three month's rent, whichever is greater, plus court costs and attorney's fees. (Mass. Gen. Laws, Ch. 186, Sec. 14.)

Under this statute, a landlord is prohibited from intentionally failing to furnish utilities to the tenant such as hot water, heat, light, power, gas and telephone service. A landlord may not transfer the responsibility of payment for any utility to the tenant without the tenant's knowledge or consent. Additionally, a landlord may not remove a tenant from the premises without going through the proper court procedure.

Acting on your own, such as by changing the locks on a tenant's unit or physically removing his or her property, will subject you to civil damages equivalent to three months rent, court costs, and attorney fees. In addition, the statute provides for the Commonwealth of Massachusetts to pursue the landlord criminally.

A landlord may not interfere with the *quiet enjoyment* of the tenant's premises. Quiet enjoyment may be thought of as the tenant's right to live peacefully and freely in his or her unit or free from any direct or indirect interference by the landlord. Massachusetts courts, for example, have found the ringing of smoke alarms for more than one day in an apartment building to be a breach of quiet enjoyment. In addition, the failure to provide essential services such as heat, light, or hot water have been found to breach quiet enjoyment.

Following a breach, a tenant may recover the difference in value between what he or she should have received and what he or she, in fact, did receive.

Unfair and Deceptive Practices

Regardless of the type and nature of the eviction, a tenant who files counterclaims against a landlord will invariably allege a violation of the *Consumer Protection Statute*, or, as it is commonly referred, Chapter 93A. Enacted by the Massachusetts legislature to provide an equitable balance between merchants and consumers, Chapter 93A awards a tenant up to three times more than what he or she actually lost plus attorney's fees if the landlord engaged in *unfair or deceptive acts or practices*.

Unfortunately for landlords, what constitutes an unfair or deceptive act or practice is continually evolving. There is no clear cut definition. Fortunately, however, Chapter 93A may only be used by tenants against larger landlords and not against those who are the owner-occupiers of two or three-family houses.

A tenant may allege a violation of Chapter 93A in two ways: 1) in an action brought by the tenant or 2) in a tenant's counterclaims to an eviction action brought by the landlord. The first option requires that the tenant send the landlord a *demand letter* that should describe the act or conduct constituting the alleged unfair or deceptive practice. In addition, the letter must, by its terms, allow the landlord thirty days to make an offer of settlement.

As the law and procedure is too complex for this book, you are advised to consult your own attorney immediately upon your receipt of any letter that purports to be such a demand letter.

The second manner the Chapter 93A action may be alleged, by way of the tenant's counterclaim, is the more common of the two. When alleged in the counterclaim, the tenant need not send a demand letter.

Massachusetts courts have found various acts of landlords to be deemed *deceptive and unfair* and therefore in violation of Chapter 93A.

Example: A landlord was held liable for including a paragraph in the lease stating that, unless the tenant informed him of a problem within two days of his occupancy, the apartment was deemed to be in habitable condition. This paragraph was deemed to be a waiver of the tenant's right to a habitable apartment.

A landlord who fails to comply with the Sanitary Code may likewise be found liable under Chapter 93A. In addition, the violation of any consumer (tenant)-oriented law by a landlord may subject the landlord to Chapter 93A liability.

If a landlord requires tenants to pay their own utility bills although the units in the building are not separately metered, the tenant may pursue a Chapter 93A claim. As Chapter 93A allows the landlord to limit his or her liability exposure by timely responding to the tenant's demand letter, the landlord is strongly encouraged to immediately seek counsel upon the receipt of such a letter.

Where certain acts or conduct on the part of the landlord could constitute more than one counterclaim for the tenant, the law usually will allow recovery only under one and will prohibit the tenant from *piggybacking* his or her claims.

Example: The landlord's failure to provide heat is a breach of the Sanitary Code, violates the warranty of habitability, violates the tenant's right to quiet enjoyment, and, assuming the landlord is *in the business* of renting apartments, is a violation of Chapter 93A.

As it is not the law's intention to bury the landlord with compounded damages for the same act or conduct, the tenant is usually allowed to recover under one theory that yields the largest recovery.

Reprisal In addition to serving as a defense to an eviction, a tenant may also assert reprisal as a counterclaim. (Mass. Gen. Laws, Ch. 186, Sec. 18.) Again, the tenant will need to show that the landlord retaliated after the items listed on page 96. If the tenant is able to show this, he will be able to obtain a judgment of between one and three month's rent, or his actual damages, whichever is greater, plus attorney's fees and costs. In addition, the tenant may be able to show that within six months of any of the tenant's actions on page 96 the landlord served a **NOTICE TO QUIT** (except one for nonpayment of rent), raised the rent, or did something else to significantly alter the terms of the tenancy. The court will then presume that the notice was sent in reprisal. Once reprisal is presumed, the landlord will need very solid evidence that the notice was sent for another legitimate reason.

Commercial Tenant's Defenses and Counterclaims

Defenses A commercial tenant has far fewer defenses against a summary process action and far fewer counterclaims to assert against the landlord. As a result, all else being equal, it is generally easier to evict a commercial tenant than a residential tenant.

The commercial tenant may utilize the same procedural defenses to a summary process action as the residential tenant. He or she may not invoke the majority of the substantive defenses discussed earlier in this chapter, namely, the withholding of rent, repair and deduct, and reprisal. These defenses may only be used by the residential tenant.

The commercial tenant may invoke other general defenses, however. One such common defense is *waiver*. This is where the tenant alleges that the landlord, by accepting rent after the tenant's alleged breach or after notice of termination, waived his or her right to rely on the breach for eviction and essentially *cancelled* the notice of termination sent to the tenant. The landlord may generally preserve his or her ability to keep the rent and pursue a summary process action if a prompt **RESERVATION OF RIGHTS LETTER** is given to the tenant. (see form 15, p.231.)

Counterclaims As with defenses, the commercial tenant has fewer possible counterclaims against a landlord. Unlike the residential tenant, the commercial tenant is not able to utilize the powerful warranty of habitability and the Sanitary Code. Instead, the commercial tenant's counterclaims invariably focus on contractual issues. The commercial tenant typically alleges breach of contract, fraud, misrepresentation, or Chapter 93A. (See pages 102–103 in this chapter for a Chapter 93A discussion.)

Settlement

After serving and filing the *Summary Process Summons and Complaint*, after the tenant files an answer and any counterclaims, and after both parties engage in discovery, the summary process hearing day arrives. In most Massachusetts courts the hearing day is Thursday.

In summary process cases, the following major issues are presented:

✪ whether the landlord is entitled to possession (the right to eject the tenant from the unit);

✪ if answer to the above is yes, the deadline for vacating the unit;

✪ the amount of any rent due; and,

✪ whether the tenant wins any counterclaims and for how much.

Because of these variables, the summary process lends itself to compromise. The landlord may be vulnerable under some counterclaims or the **NOTICE TO QUIT** may be deemed defective by the court. It may be in the landlord's interest to sacrifice some demands in order to secure his or her main objective.

Example 1: Instead of risking not winning possession in court, the landlord may strike a settlement deal with the tenant whereby the parties agree to a reduction in the rent due in exchange for the tenant relinquishing possession.

Example 2: The landlord is evicting a tenant without fault and wants to regain possession at the earliest possible time. Instead of taking a chance before the judge, who will be able to use his or her discretion in allowing the tenant more time to vacate, the landlord and tenant agree to a certain date. Here, the landlord could even offer to assist the tenant with his or her moving expenses if he or she vacates before a certain date.

Even where the landlord's case appears sound, it still may be beneficial for the landlord to compromise.

Example: Let us assume that your tenant is *judgment proof*, meaning he or she has no assets from which to pay a court judgment for back rent owed. In addition, assume that your first priority is to remove this nonpaying tenant as expeditiously and inexpensively as possible. Finally, assume that your instinct suggests this tenant may intentionally defy a court order and continue to remain in possession, forcing you to pay the significant expense of a constable and movers to regain possession.

With this set of facts, it may be wise to enter into an agreement whereby you forego the back rent due (knowing that it would be almost impossible to collect anyway) if the tenant moves out by a certain date.

If you make it appear that you have worked out a mutually-agreeable compromise, rather than having the court impose its order, the tenant may be less defiant and more likely to uphold his or her promise.

> *Landlord Tip:* Eviction actions are often heated and contentious. Resist the urge to let your emotions control your decision-making. Think with your head and not with your heart.

A settlement prior to the hearing must be in writing and is usually called an **AGREEMENT FOR JUDGMENT**. (see form 22, p.245.) The settlement is submitted to the court for approval and, once approved, it becomes a court order with the same power and effect as if it were the court's decision after a hearing.

The form and style of an **AGREEMENT FOR JUDGMENT** vary, but there are certain provisions that you should be sure to include. You want to spell out for the court that the landlord has possession and the date allowing the landlord to remove the tenant from the premises, if needed.

The agreement should also state that the tenant waives any and all claims he or she has or may have had against the landlord. You also should include a provision where the tenant waives the right to appeal or to seek a *stay of execution* (permission from the court to remain in the rental unit for more time than initially agreed (or ordered)). If the agreement calls for the tenant to pay back rent, it should specify how much money is due and when, where, and how payments are to be made.

Finally, the agreement should indicate that the tenant is signing voluntarily and knowingly chooses not to be represented by an attorney (if this is the case). The original **AGREEMENT FOR JUDGMENT** must be filed with the summary process clerk and the parties should keep copies. You may use the **AGREEMENT FOR JUDGMENT** in Appendix E for this purpose. (see form 22, p.245.)

Hearing

If no settlement agreement can be reached with your tenant, then the matter will be decided by the court. It should be noted that some courts, especially the Housing Courts, will attempt to forward your case to a *mediator* within the court. A mediator is a court-appointed independent person whose purpose is to help the parties arrive at a mutually-acceptable agreement. The mediator will listen to both sides and advise the parties of their rights and what the probable result would be if the case were to be decided by a judge.

The mediator's ultimate objective is to encourage the parties to reach a settlement and help them draft an **AGREEMENT FOR JUDGMENT**. If you are unrepresented by an attorney, the mediator will serve to inform you of the relative strengths and weaknesses of your case. Depending on his or her input, you may decide to settle or refuse to compromise and take your eviction case before the judge.

The summary process hearing session typically begins at 9:00 A.M. although in some courts it begins at 2:00 P.M. Upon arriving, ask a court officer or a clerk in the civil clerk's office for the correct courtroom. When the session starts, the summary process clerk will *call the list* of the cases scheduled. Answer *plaintiff* after your name is called. If your tenant has shown up at court, he or she will answer *defendant* and the matter usually will be held for a *second call*, upon the completion of the entire list. This means that the case will be heard after the court finishes confirming the attendance of the parties on all the remaining cases scheduled for that day.

Default   If your tenant fails to appear, you will win by *default* and the court will enter a *default judgment*. Before you leave the court after a default, check with the clerk to see if you need to file a **AFFIDAVIT RE: NONPAYMENT OF RENT; NONMILITARY AFFIDAVIT AND COMPETENCY**. (see form 23, p.247.) This is an affidavit signed by you stating the amount in which the tenant is indebted to you and that, to your knowledge, the tenant is not a member of the armed services of the United States or its allies, and therefore, this is not the reason for his or her absence in court. Be sure to request that the *execution* is issued. (The execution is explained starting on p. 112.) A couple of days later, you will receive a copy of the judgment in the mail. This judgment is just as valid and effective as if you won after a full hearing before the judge.

Court Hearing   If your tenant does appear, your case will be called again and the clerk will ask both of you to approach the judge's bench. Because the hearing is recorded on audiotape, the judge will have you introduce yourself *for the record*. The judge will then take a moment to review the documents the parties have previously filed—the **NOTICE TO QUIT**, the Summary Process Summons and Complaint, and the answer and discovery responses and counterclaims, if any. After looking at these papers, the judge may ask you to state your case or may begin by asking the defendant if he or she has any defenses.

The proceeding varies from court to court and judge to judge and may proceed informally with the parties standing in front of the judge with a loose application of the rules of evidence. Or, it may be more formal with the parties taking the witness stand and being subject to *cross-examination* (questioning by the opposing party). You should only address the judge and avoid addressing the tenant directly. The judge is properly addressed as *Your Honor*. When one or both of the parties is represented by an attorney, the process is almost always a formal trial with the witness stand, direct and cross-examination, and the rules of evidence.

Assuming you are not represented and the judge asks you to *state your case*, be sure to cover the following elements:

- ✪ you are the owner of the leased premises and the defendant is your tenant at that location;

- ✪ whether a lease governs the tenancy;

- ✪ the type of **NOTICE TO QUIT** served upon the tenant and how it was served;

- ✪ for a nonpayment eviction, the amount owed and the corresponding dates;

- ✪ for an eviction for cause, the reason or reasons for the **NOTICE TO QUIT** and any supporting documentation or witnesses; and,

- ✪ your desired relief, be it possession and/or back rent.

The judge will then look to the tenant and inquire as to any defenses he or she may have. Although the tenant is required to file an answer by the Monday prior to the hearing date, the judge will often overlook this deadline and allow the tenant to present any defenses for the first time at the hearing. (It should be noted, however, that a tenant who does not file an answer is barred from bringing up any counterclaims at the hearing/trial.) You should be prepared to address any potential defense the tenant may mention. Many times with a simple nonpayment eviction, the tenant has no defenses and merely informs the court of his or her poor financial condition as the reason for nonpayment.

The judge will probably allow you to pose direct questions to your tenant for him or her to answer and vice-versa. You should prepare a few questions in advance. Choose those that you believe will likely elicit favorable testimony for your side.

If the judge seems to be decidedly in your favor, stop talking. Any further communication after you have the judge in your corner will only serve to test the judge's patience and jeopardize your case.

If, instead, the judge is wavering in his or her decision, politely yet firmly remind the judge of your version of the facts. The judge may render the decision *from the bench* or may state that it will be taken *under advisement* and mail you the decision. In either case, you will receive a judgment in the mail informing you of the court's decision.

Appeals

A few days after the court hearing, you will receive a judgment and possibly the court's written decision. Most summary process judgments are in two parts— one awards or denies possession for the landlord, and the other awards any money damages for back rent due. A sample of a summary process judgment is shown including Appendix D.

Absent an appeal, the successful party will be entitled to an *execution* from the court ten days after the entry of judgment. The execution, as discussed on pages 112–114, is the official court document that will allow you to regain possession of your unit, as well as secure your right to any money damages as stated in the judgment.

A party has ten days from the date of the judgment to file an appeal. As noted before, an appeal from the district court is to the superior court for a retrial, whereas an appeal from the Housing Court or superior court is to the Massachusetts Appeals Court on a question of law. An appeal from a district court in either Middlesex or Norfolk counties is to the appellate division of the district court. It is recommended that you have an attorney represent you on an appeal to the superior court, especially on an appeal to the Massachusetts Appeals Court or the appellate division of the district court.

A notice of appeal must be filed with the court that entered judgment within this ten day period. The notice will prevent (*stay*) any execution from issuing. In addition, the party who is appealing (the *appellant*) is required to file a bond with the court.

If it is the tenant who is appealing, the court may require, as part of the bond, all rent already owed, the rent to accrue during the pendency of the appeal, and any damage or loss of the landlord, including costs of the action. This is to help ensure that the landlord does not suffer any loss of rent due to the appeal.

The party (usually the tenant) may make a motion to waive the appeal bond if he or she is *indigent* (financially incapable of paying). In order for the court to waive the appeal bond, the tenant must show that, in addition to being indigent, he or she has *nonfrivolous* defenses. Nonfrivolous defenses are defenses that are based on sound legal principles and not asserted merely to delay.

Post-Judgment Motions

After the entry of judgment, but prior to the expiration of the ten days, there are a couple of motions that tenants can—and often do—file. A motion is an official request, usually in writing, made by a party asking the court for some specific relief.

Motion to Remove Default   If the tenant failed to appear for the court summary process hearing and was subsequently defaulted, he or she may file a motion with the court and attempt to have the court remove the default judgment. The person who files the motion (the *moving party*) must give the opposing party a copy of the motion, with a notice of any court hearing for the motion.

When a tenant files a *Motion to Remove Default*, the court will require him or her to show two things.

1.   There must have been a significant and legitimate reason (*good cause*) for absence.

2.   The court will require him or her to demonstrate that he or she has a nonfrivolous defense to the action.

Although the court has much discretion, the court will likely deny the motion if he or she fails to satisfy one of these two requirements. The landlord should inform the court of any facts known to him or her that undermine the tenant's *excuse* for his or her absence or that expose the tenant's defense as being without merit.

Motion for Stay of Execution

After the court hearing or the filing of an **AGREEMENT FOR JUDGMENT** (form 22) by the parties and after judgment has been entered, tenants frequently file a *Motion to Stay the Execution*. A tenant usually cites difficulties in securing alternative housing as reason for requesting a postponement of the execution. If the tenancy was terminated for fault or nonpayment, the law does not allow the court to stay the execution. You should politely remind the court of this. However, if the tenancy terminated without fault of the tenant or by operation of law (*e.g.*, the lease expired), the court may consider the tenant's motion.

The court may grant the tenant a stay of up to six months, provided the tenant pays the court the amount of rent that would be due for the period of the stay and for any additional amount as the court may deem reasonable. If the tenant is sixty years of age or older or has a physical or mental handicap, the court may grant a stay of up to twelve months. At the court hearing on the tenant's motion for a stay of execution, the tenant must demonstrate that although he or she has used reasonable efforts to secure similar and suitable premises, he or she is unable to do so. It is the landlord's job to show any facts that contradict the tenant's contention of reasonable efforts.

> *Landlord Tip:* To defend against the tenant's motion for stay of execution, come to the hearing with a newspaper's *apartment for rent* classifieds, letters from real estate brokers showing the availability of similar premises in the same or surrounding towns, and any other evidence to undermine the tenant's assertion of reasonable efforts and good faith attempts to find other housing. Also, if true, inform the judge that no other landlord has contacted you regarding a reference for this tenant.

Execution

The *execution* is the official document issued by the court granting the landlord the right to regain possession of the unit and forcibly remove the tenant, if necessary. If the landlord was also awarded judgment for back rent, the court may issue a separate *money judgment execution* or may issue one execution for both possession and the money.

The landlord is entitled to the summary process execution either:

- ✪ at the expiration of ten days from the entry of judgment, according to the specified date in the parties' **AGREEMENT FOR JUDGMENT** (form 22);

- ✪ upon the expiration of any final stay of execution granted by the court; or,

- ✪ upon the successful outcome of the landlord in any appeal.

Once the landlord obtains the execution for possession from the court, he or she should make arrangements for it to be served and *levied on* (acted upon) by an appropriate constable or deputy sheriff. As previously discussed, the constable must be authorized to act in the town in which your unit is located.

Time Limits   The execution for possession is valid only for three calendar months after its date of issue. Massachusetts law requires that a constable or deputy sheriff give the tenant at least forty-eight hours written notice prior to physically removing the tenant and his or her possessions (called *levying on the execution*). The written notice must contain:

- ✪ the constable or deputy sheriff's name, business address, telephone number, and signature;

- ✪ the name of the court; and,

- ✪ docket number of the case.

The notice must state that at a specified date and time, at least forty-eight hours in the future, the constable or deputy sheriff will levy on the execution and will physically remove the tenant and his or her personal possessions from the premises.

Many judges do not count weekends in calculating the forty-eight hours.

Example: If the constable serves the *Forty-Eight Hour Notice* on Friday at nine o'clock in the morning, the earliest day the execution could be levied upon would be the following Tuesday at nine o'clock in the morning.

The law also prohibits the constable or sheriff from levying on the execution:

✪   on a Saturday, Sunday, or legal holiday;

✪   before nine o'clock in the morning; or,

✪   after five o'clock in the evening.

> *Landlord Tip:* You may want to have the constable or deputy sheriff give your tenant more than forty-eight hours notice so that the tenant will have enough time to move him- or herself and save you from paying the expensive moving and storage costs. A good constable or deputy sheriff also may be able to personally speak with your tenant and convince him or her into moving him- or herself before the movers remove his or her property.

Fees   Your constable (or attorney) will help you retain and schedule a bonded and insured moving company to move the tenant out of the property. A moving company will charge an average of about $1,250 for a four room unit, with each additional room costing $200 to $300 extra. This amount typically includes moving, packing, and three months of storage. An additional $200 to $300 can be expected for the constable's fee.

This money is required to be prepaid by the landlord. The tenant's property will be stored by the moving company for a period of up to six months. If the tenant fails to claim it, the moving company will be able to sell the property at a public sale to recoup its costs.

Payment of Rent or Judgment

If the judgment and execution are based upon nonpayment of rent, the tenant will be able to prevent the constable from levying on the execution if he or she pays the full amount of the judgment plus any amount for use and occupancy that accrued since the date of the judgment. The law, however, allows the landlord to refuse full payment, thereby allowing him or her to proceed with the levy for possession.

The landlord is free, however, to accept some portion of the judgment amount and still remove the tenant as long as he or she does not accept the full amount due. In addition, the landlord's refusal to accept full satisfaction does not prevent him or her from later pursuing the enforcement of the judgment's outstanding balance in another legal proceeding.

Repossession

Upon your regaining possession of the unit, you should have all of the locks changed. In addition, photographs or video should be taken to capture any damage left by the tenant and receipts for remedial repairs should be saved. Within ten days of an execution being satisfied (i.e., within ten days of the landlord regaining possession of the property), the execution must be returned to the court indicating that it has been satisfied.

Money Judgment

A landlord who also has an execution on a money judgment may look to seize the personal property of the tenant to satisfy his or her judgment. Once seized, the constable or deputy sheriff will be able to sell the property through a public auction. Unfortunately, however, much of a residential tenant's personal property, including clothing, household furniture less than $3,000 in value, and tools less than $500 in value, are exempt from any execution.

Any unsatisfied execution on a money judgment should be referred to a knowledgeable attorney for collection. An execution for a money judgment, unlike the execution for possession, is valid in Massachusetts for twenty years. If a tenant pays a money judgment or it is satisfied through seizure of property, the execution must be returned to the court with the notation that it has been satisfied.

Tenant's Bankruptcy

If a tenant files bankruptcy, federal law imposes an *automatic stay* on all actions against the tenant. This provision is automatic from the moment the bankruptcy petition is filed. (11 U.S.C. Sec. 362.) If you take any action in court, seize the tenant's property, or use the security deposit for unpaid rent, you can be held in contempt of federal court. It is not necessary that you receive formal notice of the bankruptcy. Verbal notice is sufficient. If you do not believe the tenant, you should call the bankruptcy court to confirm the filing.

The automatic stay lasts until the debtor is discharged, until the bankruptcy case is dismissed, until the property is abandoned or voluntarily surrendered, or until the federal bankruptcy judge *lifts* the stay.

The landlord may ask for the right to continue with the eviction by filing a *Motion for Relief from Stay* and paying the appropriate filing fee. Within thirty days, a hearing is held. It may be held by telephone. The motion is governed by Bankruptcy Rule 9014 and the requirements of how the tenant must be served are contained in Rule 7004. However, for such a hearing the services of an attorney are usually necessary.

The bankruptcy stay only applies to amounts owed to the landlord at the time of filing the bankruptcy. Therefore, the landlord can sue the tenant for eviction and rent owed for any time period *after* the filing of the bankruptcy petition, unless the bankruptcy trustee assumes the lease. The landlord can proceed during the bankruptcy without asking for relief from the automatic stay under three conditions.

1.   The landlord can only sue for rent due after the filing.

2.   The landlord cannot sue until the trustee rejects the lease (if the trustee does not accept the lease within sixty days of the *Order for Relief,* then Section 365(d)(1) provides that it is deemed rejected).

3.   The landlord must sue under the terms of the lease and may not treat the trustee's rejection as a breach.

In a Chapter 13 reorganization bankruptcy, the landlord should be paid the rent as it comes due.

If the tenant filed bankruptcy after a judgment of eviction has been entered, there should be no problem lifting the automatic stay since the tenant has no interest in the property.

If your tenant files bankruptcy and you decide it is worth hiring a lawyer, you should locate an attorney who is experienced in bankruptcy work. Prior to the meeting with the attorney, you should gather as much information as you can obtain from the tenant or the tenant's file at the bankruptcy court clerk's office (*e.g.*, type of bankruptcy filed, assets, liabilities, case number, etc.).

II | SELF-SERVICE STORAGE SPACE

Self-storage facilities have sprouted up all over Massachusetts in the last ten years or so as a result of our insatiable need for more storage space. Massachusetts General Law, Chapter 105A, applies to real property designed and used for renting individual storage space to tenants.

Rental Agreement

The landlord of a self-service storage facility (called the *operator*) may only lease space to a tenant (called the *occupant*) by entering into a written rental agreement. The rental agreement must contain a statement, in bold type, advising the occupant that:

- ✪ the property stored in the leased space is not insured by the operator for loss or damage;

- ✪ a lien exists on the personal property stored in the leased space for the benefit of the operator; and,

✪ the personal property stored in the leased space may be sold to satisfy the lien if the occupant is in default of the rental agreement.

Operator's Lien

The self-storage facility operator has a *lien* on all personal property stored within each leased space for rent, labor, insurance, or other charges and expenses.

If the occupant defaults, the operator may enforce the lien by selling the property stored in the leased space at a public or private sale. The following items describe how a sale must be done and the result of any sale.

✪ Five days after the occupant is in default, the occupant (and any other person claiming to have an interest in the goods) must be notified of the default. The operator sends a notice by regular mail to the person's last known address.

✪ Fourteen days after the occupant's default, the occupant (and all other persons known to claim an interest in the goods) must be notified by certified mail, return receipt requested, to the last known address of the occupant and all other persons known to claim an interest in the goods, or by hand delivery.

✪ The five-day and fourteen-day notifications must include:

• a statement that the contents of the occupant's leased space are subject to the operator's lien;

• a general description of the contents, if known, by the operator;

• a statement of the operator's claim, indicating the charges due on the date of the notice, the amount of any additional charges that shall become due before the date of sale, and the date such additional charges shall become due;

• a demand for payment of the charges due within a specified time, (must be more than fourteen days after receipt of notification);

- a statement that unless the claim is paid within the time stated, the contents of the occupant's space will be advertised for sale and sold at auction at a specified time and place; and,

- the name, street address, and telephone number of the operator, or designated agent, whom the occupant may contact to respond to the notice.

✪ After the expiration of the time given in the notification, an advertisement of the sale must be published once a week for two consecutive weeks in a newspaper. The newspaper must be one of general circulation in the city or town where the sale is to be held. The advertisement must include:

- a description of the property;

- the name of the person on whose account the property is being held; and,

- the time and place of the sale.

The sale must take place at least fifteen days after the first publication. If there is no newspaper of general circulation in the city or town where the sale is to be held, the advertisement must be posted at least ten days before the sale in at least six conspicuous places in the neighborhood of the proposed sale.

✪ If before any sale, any person claiming a right in the property pays the amount necessary to satisfy the lien and the reasonable expenses incurred in storing the property and preparing for the sale, the property must not be sold, but must be released to the payor.

✪ The sale must be at the self-service storage facility where the personal property is stored or at the nearest suitable place.

✪ The sale must conform to the terms of the notification.

✪ A purchaser of goods sold to enforce an operator's lien gets the property and the original owner cannot get it back without buying it. This is so even if the operator does not comply with the requirements of the law.

NOTE: *The operator may buy at the sale.*

✪ The operator may satisfy the lien from the proceeds of the sale, but must hold the balance to give to the occupant or to any person to whom the operator would have been bound to release the property. (The operator may recover his or her costs but cannot make a profit on the sale.)

✪ The operator shall be liable for damages caused by failure to comply with these itemized requirements for sale. If it is determined that the operator willfully violated these requirements, the tenant would be able to sue the operator for conversion.

Withholding Access

After rent is five days overdue, the operator may deny the occupant access to the storage facility for the purpose of storing or removing any property. However, the occupant is entitled to access for the sole purpose of viewing the contents.

12 MOBILE HOME PARKS

Mobile parks in Massachusetts present a different tenancy relationship and therefore have several unique laws and regulations. (Mass. Gen. Laws, Ch. 140, Secs. 32A-32S.) Unlike other tenants of residential dwellings, mobile park tenants own the dwelling (mobile home) in which they actually live, but instead pay rent for the space in the mobile home park on which the home sits.

Licensing and Registration

In order for a prospective owner of a mobile park (a track of land for three or more mobile, or manufactured, homes) to rent land, he or she must first be properly licensed by the Board of Health from the city or town where the park is located. In addition to the park license fee, the owner will have to pay an additional license fee of $6 to $12 for each mobile home (depending on the particular city or town). The owner can recover this charge from each mobile home owner if made part of the tenancy agreement. Each month the mobile park owner is also responsible for providing the city or town with a list of the names and addresses of each owner or occupant of the mobile homes and the fee amounts collected.

The mobile park owner must also:

- ✪ keep a register of the names and addresses of each mobile home owner or any tenant or subtenant;

- ✪ the date of their entering; and,

- ✪ the date of their leaving the mobile home park.

This register needs to be retained by the mobile park owner for at least one year after the mobile home owner leaves. It must be made available for the inspection of the city or town's authorities.

Requirements and Restrictions

The following are some of the unique requirements and restrictions applicable to mobile home parks.

- ✪ The mobile park owner may use leases, rules, and regulations to govern the park, but no rule can be *unreasonable, unfair, or unconscionable.*

- ✪ If any rule or rent increase does not apply uniformly to all mobile home owners of a similar class, then it is presumed that the rule or rent increase is unfair.

- ✪ A mobile park owner cannot impose any conditions on whom a mobile home owner can do business with regarding the mobile home (*e.g.,* the mobile home dealer, the seller of fuel, or the seller of furnishings).

- ✪ A mobile park owner shall not refuse to allow the transfer of a mobile home located in the park on the ground that such mobile park owner has not sold as many mobile homes as there are sites.

- ✪ A mobile park owner may not charge a fee or collect a commission for the sale of a mobile home located within the park, but may, however, upon the proposed sale of such a home, contract with the mobile home owner to sell the home for a fee not to exceed ten percent of the sale price of such home.

✪ Before new or revised rules governing the mobile home park can become effective, the mobile park owner must first send the proposed rules via certified mail, return receipt requested, to the attorney general and the director of housing and community development. This must be done at least sixty days prior to the date the new rules or changes become effective. In addition, copies of the new rules or changes must be provided to all mobile home owners at least thirty days prior to the effective date.

✪ Any rule or condition of occupancy that is unfair or deceptive is unenforceable.

✪ A mobile park owner who intends to close the park must comply with several requirements, including the following.

- The mobile park owner needs to give each mobile home owner fifteen days written notice, by certified or registered mail, that the park owner will be appearing before a governmental body to request to change the use or discontinue the park.

- Upon the approval by the city or town board of the change of use or discontinuance of the park, the park owner shall give each mobile home owner at least two years written notice, by certified or registered mail. Included in the notice must be the nature of the change of use or discontinuance and the reasons.

- Once notice is given, the park owner must give this notice to any prospective new mobile home owner.

- During the two-year notice period, the mobile park owner must survey all mobile parks within a 100 mile radius to determine if any sites are available during the two-year period. The park owner must prominently post all relevant information obtained. The park owner must perform a second survey no less than 120 days prior to the end of the notice period.

- The park owner must pay the mobile home owner's actual relocation costs or the appraised value of the mobile home.

Terms and Condition of Occupancy

The mobile park owner must disclose in writing all terms and conditions of occupancy to any prospective mobile home owner prior to occupancy, including, but not limited to:

- ✪ the amount of rent;

- ✪ an itemized list of charges or fees;

- ✪ names and addresses of all mobile home owners; and,

- ✪ the rules and regulations.

Said writing shall contain an offer to lease the mobile home lot for a term of five years or, where a valid notice of discontinuance is in effect at the time of such offer, the balance of the period remaining before the effective date of the discontinuance. The writing shall also be signed by the mobile park owner.

The terms and conditions document must also include the following notice printed verbatim in a clear and conspicuous manner:

IMPORTANT NOTICE REQUIRED BY LAW

The rules set forth below govern the terms of your lease or occupancy with this manufactured housing community. If these rules are changed in any way, the addition, deletion or amendment must be delivered to you, along with a copy of the certified mail receipts indicating that such change has been submitted to the attorney general and the director of housing and community development and either a copy of the approvals thereof by the attorney general and said director or a certificate signed by the owner stating that neither the attorney general nor said director has taken any action with respect thereto within the period set forth in paragraph (5) of section thirty-two L of chapter one hundred and forty. This notification must be furnished to you at least thirty days before the change goes into effect. The law requires all of these rules and regulations to be fair and reasonable or said rules and regulations cannot be enforced.

You may continue to stay in the community as long as you pay rent and abide by the rules and regulations. You may only be evicted for nonpayment of rent, violation of law or for substantial violation of the rules and regulations of the community. In addition, no eviction proceedings may be commenced against you until you have received notice by certified mail of the reason for the eviction proceeding and you have been given fifteen days from the date of the notice in which to pay the overdue rent or to cease and desist from any substantial violation of the rules and regulations of the community; provided, however, that only one notice of substantial violation of the rules and regulations of the community is required to be sent to you during any six month period. If a second or additional violation occurs, except for nonpayment of rent, within six months from the date of the first notice, then eviction proceedings may be commenced against you immediately.

You may not be evicted for reporting any violations of law or health and building codes to boards of health, the attorney general, or any other appropriate government agency. Receipt of notice of termination of tenancy by you, except for nonpayment of rent, within six months after your making such a report shall create a rebuttable presumption that such notice is a reprisal and may be pleaded by you in defense to any eviction proceeding brought within one year.

Any group of more than fifty percent of the tenants residing in the manufactured housing community has certain rights under section thirty-two R of chapter one hundred and forty, to purchase the community in the event the owner intends to accept an offer to sell or lease the community in the future. If you wish to receive further information about the financial terms of such a possible purchase, you may so notify the owner at any time by signing the attached Request for Information and returning it to the owner in person or by certified mail. Such request for information shall not obligate you to participate in any purchase of the community. For a proposed sale or lease by the owner which will result in a change of use or a discontinuance of the community you will receive information at least two years before the change becomes effective. Otherwise, Requests for Information or similar notices from more than fifty percent of the tenants residing in the community must be on file with the owner before the owner is required to give you information concerning the financial terms of a sale or lease.

This law is enforceable by the consumer protection division of the attorney general's office.

REQUEST FOR INFORMATION

The undersigned, a tenant in the manufactured housing community known as _____ _____ and located at _____, Massachusetts, desires to receive information concerning any proposed sale or lease of the community as required under Section 32R of Chapter 140 of the General Laws. I understand that this request shall not obligate me to participate in any purchase or lease of the community, but is only a request for information. This notice is being delivered to the owner or owner's manager either in person or by certified mail on _____ (date).

_____

(Tenant - Name)

Sale of the Tenant's Mobile Home

As mobile park owners are often in the business of selling mobile homes in the park, a natural conflict arises when mobile park tenants seek to sell their homes. As a result, laws have been imposed to ensure that the mobile park owner fairly treats the tenant who is looking to sell his or her mobile home. The park owner needs to comply with the following restrictions.

✪ As long as the tenant's prospective buyer meets the current, enforceable rules of the park and provides reasonable evidence of his or her financial ability to pay the rent, the park owner must allow him or her and his or her household to reside in the park.

✪ The park owner may not interfere with the tenant's right to sell his or her home in the park. The park owner may not require that the home be removed after it is sold. If the park owner wishes to upgrade the tenant's lot by placing a new home on it and selling it, he or she will need to bid on the tenant's home when it becomes available for sale.

✪ The park owner may not require the tenant to use the park owner or any other particular broker for any sale. The tenant can sell his or her home directly or use any broker of his or her choosing. If the tenant does select the park owner to sell the home, the park owner may not charge more than 10% of the sale price in commission. In addition, there must be a separate written agreement.

✪ The park owner may not require that a tenant's prospective buyers first stop at the management office to inquire about the availability of other homes. He or she also may not make any false, deceptive, or misleading statements to the potential buyers about the tenant.

✪ The mobile park owner may not require that he or she, or the prospective buyer, inspect the mobile home prior to its sale. The park owner, however, is entitled to inspect the tenant's lot prior to leasing it to a new tenant.

✪ The mobile park owner may not restrict the tenant's ability to place a commercially-reasonable "For Sale" sign on the mobile home.

✪ The mobile park owner may not charge an exit fee when a tenant leaves the park.

(For more specifics on these restrictions, refer to 940 C.M.R. 10.07 contained in Appendix A.)

Termination of the Tenancy

The tenancy of a mobile home owner may only be terminated for one or more of the following reasons:

✪ nonpayment of rent;

✪ substantial violation of any enforceable rule of the mobile home park;

✪ violation of any laws or ordinances that protect the safety or health of the other mobile park residents;

✪ the mobile park owner's closing of the park; and,

✪ in the case of a tenancy-at-will, to create a new tenancy at an increased rent (similar to raising the rent in a normal tenancy as explained in Chapter 7).

In order to properly terminate the tenancy, the mobile home park owner must give the mobile home owner at least thirty days written notice by certified or registered mail. The notice must state one or more of the acceptable reasons for termination. In addition, if the termination is for nonpayment, the notice must state that the mobile home owner has fifteen days from the date of the mailing of the notice to pay the overdue rent or *cure* (fix) the applicable violation.

In addition to the above requirements, the mobile park owner is still not allowed to pursue eviction of the mobile home owner, unless:

✪ the mobile home owner has not paid the overdue rent or cured the applicable violation within twenty days from the date the written notice was received and

✪ if terminated other than for nonpayment, the notice is served within thirty days from the date of the applicable violation. (However, no further notice is required if the same substantial violation occurs within six months from the date the notice was delivered.)

Summary Process and Appeal

If the mobile home owner continues to occupy the premises subsequent to the expiration of a valid **NOTICE TO QUIT**, the mobile park owner now must pursue summary process. (see Chapter 10.) The mobile home owner may therefore raise those relevant defenses and counterclaims that a regular residential tenant would have, including, but not limited to:

✪ Sanitary Code violations;

✪ breach of quiet enjoyment;

✪ retaliatory eviction; and,

✪ unfair and deceptive practices.

The appeal of a mobile home eviction case follows the same procedures as does the normal landlord/tenant appeal. (see page 109.) Therefore, a mobile home owner can also request that the court grant him or her or her a stay of execution.

GLOSSARY

A

answer. The legal document written by the tenant in response to the landlord's complaint or by the landlord in response to the tenant's counterclaim. The answer typically admits or denies each of the relevant allegations of the opposing party and contains affirmative defenses.

assignment (of lease). The taking over of a tenant's rights and obligations in a lease by a successor tenant, such that, if done with the landlord's approval, the original tenant is free from the terms of the lease and from liability.

automatic stay. A statutory-mandated order effective upon the filing of a bankruptcy position making unlawful any further action by a creditor or other party against the bankruptcy filer.

B

bargaining power. The relative ability of one to negotiate given his or her position, knowledge, and resources.

C

certificate of compliance. A document issued by the local city or town, usually by the board of health, certifying that the residential building complies with the Sanitary Code and any other local ordinances regulating habitable housing.

certificate of occupancy. A document issued by the local city or town, usually by the building inspector's office, certifying that the building meets certain local and state codes, including the zoning laws and the state building and fire codes, and is allowed to be occupied as a specific type of dwelling (*i.e.*, a two-family home).

complaint (or summary process summons and complaint). The legal document for a specific court that the landlord completes to initiate the eviction process in the court against the tenant. The complaint states, among other things, the reason for the eviction, the amounts allegedly owed, and the court date.

consumer price index (CPI). A number generated by the United States Government Department of Labor to indicate the cost of living and the change therein over time. The CPI often is used in multiple-year leases so that the rental amount adjusts for inflation.

counterclaim. Refers to the claim brought by a tenant against the landlord in response to his or her commencement of an eviction.

cure. A term used to refer to the tenant's ability to reinstate his or her tenancy. This is usually done by paying the entire amount of rent that is due within ten days of receiving a notice to quit for nonpayment for a tenancy at will if he or she had not received a prior notice to quit within the last twelve (12) months (or, for a tenant under lease, by paying all back rent plus interest and costs before the answer is due in a summary process action).

D

default. The status of a case when the tenant does not appear in court on the day of the summary process hearing. With this status, the landlord will be entitled to the requested relief, absent any motion to remove the default by the tenant.

defense. A legal claim asserted by a party that if proven successfully, will prevent the other party from the relief requested.

de novo. "Of new"; refers to the process by which the losing party in certain district courts can appeal to the superior court for a second trial, all over again.

discovery. Refers to the part of the summary process procedure, occurring after service of the complaint and before the court hearing, wherein the parties are able to learn of the other party's case by having written questions (interrogatories) answered by requesting that the other side produce requested documents (request for the production of documents), and by having the other party admit or deny certain written statements (request for admissions).

E

encapsulation. The process of covering over surfaces containing lead with a thick glue-like substance to eliminate any risk of poisoning.

execution for money damages. A court document obtained after the landlord prevails in court and after any appeal period has expired that entitles the landlord to a stated amount of money.

execution for possession. A court document obtained after the landlord prevails in court and after any appeal period has expired that entitles the landlord to have the tenant physically removed from the premises by the use of constable or sheriff.

H

holdover tenant. A tenant that continues to reside in the unit after the tenancy has been terminated, either by operation of law or by a notice to quit. Also referred to as tenant at sufferance.

L

lease. A tenancy relationship between landlord and tenant whereby there is a defined termination date. A lease must be in writing.

lien. The right given by statute, or otherwise, to a creditor or potential creditor, such as the self-storage landlord, to be entitled to that portion of the debtor's (or potential debtor such as the self-storage tenant) property in the event that the debtor fails to pay.

M

motion. A formal request, typically in writing, by a party asking that the court take some sort of action or grant some requested relief.

N

notice to quit. A legal notice that the landlord serves on his or her tenant to terminate a tenancy at will or to terminate a lease short of its expiration date because of some violation of the lease terms.

O

operation of law. Used to describe the manner in which a lease terminates (by its own stated termination date) as opposed to tenancies that are terminated by a notice to quit issued by the landlord.

P

possession. Term used to describe who legally is entitled to be in physical control of the premises. Possession for the tenant means that the tenant can remain as a tenant, whereas possession for the landlord means that the landlord can lawfully remove the tenant from the premises.

protected class. Any of several ways used to classify individuals and with which the state and/or federal government prohibits a landlord to base housing decisions (e.g., race, national origin, and religion).

Q

quiet enjoyment. Refers to the tenant's implied and unwritten right to live in the premises free of willful or intentional acts directly caused or allowed by the landlord.

R

reprisal. A prohibited act whereby the landlord acts to negatively change the terms of the tenancy (*e.g.*, raise the rent or terminate the tenancy) in response to certain protected activities of the tenant (*e.g.*, complaining of defects to the board of health). Also known as retaliation.

reservation of rights. A type of clause, typically inserted in a notice to quit, whereby the landlord is able to collect monies tendered by the tenant after the tenancy has terminated (and labeling them "rent arrears" or "use and occupancy fees") while also preserving his or her right to pursue summary process.

return of service. Documentation of the date, time, and manner of service of a notice to quit or summary process summons and complaint that a constable or sheriff attaches to the document to prove service upon the tenant.

S

self-help. Refers to prohibited conduct on the part of landlords in attempt to evict tenants without going through court summary process (*e.g.*, changing locks or shutting off utilities).

Sanitary Code. A set of regulations promulgated by the Commonwealth of Massachusetts Department of Public Health that sets out the minimum requirements for habitable housing. A violation of the regulations could cause the landlord to be liable civilly or criminally.

stay of execution. Usually requested by a tenant in a motion, the stay of execution requests that the court order the landlord to delay the removal of the tenant from the premises for some stated reason.

sublease. The granting by the original tenant of some portion (but not all) of his or her rights and interest in the lease. The original tenant is still obligated under the terms of the lease to the landlord.

summary process. The term used to describe the eviction process in the courts.

T

tenancy-at-will. A tenancy relationship between landlord and tenant whereby the relationship continues from period to period (e.g., week-to-week or month-to-month) without a defined termination date. The terms of the tenancy-at-will can be either oral or in writing. If in writing, it is referred to as a tenancy-at-will agreement, as opposed to a lease.

tenant at sufferance. *See holdover tenant.*

W

warranty of habitability. Refers to the implied, unwritten promise contained in every residential tenancy wherein the landlord warrants (promises) that the premises are habitable and that there are no violations of any regulations governing safe and habitable housing.

Appendix A:
Selected Massachusetts
Statutes and Regulations

Included in this appendix are the Massachusetts landlord/tenant statutes that will be most useful to small landlords. There are other statutes that may apply to landlords. You may access all the Massachusetts statutes at some public libraries, most law libraries, and on the Internet at:

www.state.ma.us/legis

This appendix includes the following sections from the Massachusetts General Laws, as well as Section 10.07 of title 940 of the Code of Massachusetts Regulations.

Chapter 140.

Section 32A. Necessity of license; motel defined.

Section 32B. Grant, suspension or revocation of license; expiration; renewal; application fees; inspection; reinstatement.

Section 32C. Examination of licensed camps and cabins; unsanitary conditions.

Section 32D. Rules and regulations; posting.

Section 32E. Operating business without license.

Section 32F. Definition; license requirement; copy sent to city or town clerk; exceptions.

Section 32G. Monthly fees; collection; deposit; lists; payment to treasurers; exemption from taxes; penalties; revocation of license.

Section 32H. Unequipped communities; plans; cost estimates; conditional licenses; suspension or revocation.

Section 32I. Register; retention; inspection; penalty.

Section 32J. Summary process to recover possession; termination of tenancy or lease.

Section 32K. Appeals; reinstatement; reissuance.

Chapter 186.   Estates for Years and at Will

Chapter 239.   Summary Process for Possession of Land

Code of Massachusetts Regulations
Title 940: Office of the Attorney General
Chapter 10.00. Manufactured Housing Community Regulations

Chapter 140: Section 32A. Necessity of license; motel defined.

No person shall conduct, control, manage or operate, directly or indirectly, any recreational camp, overnight camp or cabin, motel or manufactured housing community unless he is the holder of a license granted under the following section. The term "motel", as used in section twenty-seven, in this section, and in sections thirty-two B to thirty-two E, inclusive, shall be construed to mean any building or group of buildings which provide sleeping accommodations for transient motorists and which is not licensed as an inn.

Section 32B. Grant, suspension or revocation of license; expiration; renewal; application fees; inspection; reinstatement.

The board of health of any city or town, in each instance after a hearing, reasonable notice of which shall have been published once in a newspaper published in such city or town, may grant, and may suspend or revoke, licenses for recreational camps, overnight camps or cabins, motels or manufactured housing communities located within such city or town, which license, unless previously suspended or revoked, shall expire on December thirty-first in the year of issue, but may be renewed annually upon application without such notice and hearing. Such application shall include a true and complete copy of the rules and regulations then in effect for an existing manufactured housing community or, if the application is for an original license, the rules and regulations for the proposed manufactured housing community, together with a certificate from the owner or operator of the community certifying, under the penalties of perjury, that the owner or operator has complied with paragraph (5) of section thirty-two L, that the attorney general and the director of housing and community development have been in receipt of such rules and regulations and any amendments or additions thereto for at least sixty days, and that neither the attorney general nor the director of housing and community development has disapproved any portion of such rules and regulations. Unless otherwise established in a town by town meeting action and in a city by city council action, and in a town with no town meeting by town council action, by adoption of appropriate by-laws and ordinances to set such fees, the fee for each original or renewal license shall be ten dollars, but in no event shall any such fee be greater than fifty dollars. Such board of health shall at once notify the department of environmental protection of the granting or renewal of such a license, and said department shall have jurisdiction to inspect the premises so licensed to determine that the sources of water supply and the works for the disposition of the sewage of such premises are sanitary. If upon inspection of such premises said department finds the sources of water supply to be polluted or the works for the disposition of the sewage to be insanitary, or both of such conditions, said

department shall forthwith notify such board of health and such licensee to that effect by registered mail and said board shall forthwith prohibit the use of any water supply found by said department to be polluted. Unless such licensee shall, within thirty days following the giving of such notice, correct the conditions at such premises to the satisfaction of both said department and such board the license so granted shall be suspended or revoked by such board. Any license so suspended may be reinstated by such board when the conditions at such premises, as to sources of water supply and works for the disposition of sewage, are satisfactory to said department and such board. The board of health of a city or town may adopt, and from time to time alter or amend, rules and regulations to enforce this section in such city or town.

Section 32C. Examination of licensed camps and cabins; unsanitary conditions.

Every board of health shall, from time to time, examine all camps, motels, manufactured housing communities and cabins licensed by it under authority of section thirty-two B, and if, upon such examination, such camp, motel, manufactured housing community or cabin is found to be in an unsanitary condition, said board of health may, after notice and a hearing, suspend or revoke such license.

Section 32D. Rules and regulations; posting.

Whoever conducts, controls, manages or operates any camp, motel, manufactured housing community or cabin licensed under section thirty-two B shall post, in a conspicuous place near the entrance to every such camp, motel, manufactured housing community or cabin or in a conspicuous place at the office of the manager on the site, a copy of the rules and regulations adopted thereunder, as most recently altered or amended.

Section 32E. Operating business without license.

Whoever conducts, controls, manages or operates any camp, motel or cabin subject to section thirty-two A to thirty-two C, inclusive, which is not licensed under section thirty-two B, shall be punished by a fine of not less than ten nor more than one hundred dollars.

Whoever conducts, controls, manages or operates any manufactured housing community subject to sections thirty-two A to thirty-two C, inclusive, which is not licensed under section thirty-two A to thirty-two B or which is not managed or operated in compliance with sections thirty-two A to thirty-two S, inclusive, shall be punished by a fine of one hundred dollars for each day in which such violation occurs or continues.

Section 32F. Definition; license requirement; copy sent to city or town clerk; exceptions.

Any lot or tract of land upon which three or more manufactured homes occupied for dwelling purposes are located, including any buildings, structures, fixtures and equipment used in connection with manufactured homes shall be defined as a manufactured housing community. No lot or tract of land may be used for a manufactured housing community unless the owner or occupant thereof is the holder of a license granted under section thirty-two B. The board of health of a city or town shall, forthwith upon granting an original or renewal license under said section thirty-two B for a manufactured housing community, send a copy of such license to the city or town clerk.

A lot or tract of land provided by a state or county fair, agricultural and horticultural society, grange or 4-H club for the use of manufactured homes to accommodate personnel who are to participate in any fair or exhibition conducted by such organization, which fair or exhibition does not continue for a period of exceeding ten consecutive days, or a lot or tract of land provided by a college or university for the use of manufactured homes to accommodate students lacking dormitory facilities shall not be deemed a manufactured housing community.

Section 32G. Monthly fees; collection; deposit; lists; payment to treasurers; exemption from taxes; penalties; revocation of license.

In addition to the license fee provided for under section thirty-two B, each manufactured housing community owner or operator licensed under said section shall, except as hereinafter provided, pay an additional license fee of six dollars per month or a major fraction thereof, on account of each manufactured home, occupying space within such manufactured housing community; provided, however, that in a city by vote of the city council and in a town by vote of the board of selectmen, the amount of such additional license fee may be increased to an amount not exceeding twelve dollars per month. Such additional license fee shall, except as hereinafter provided, be collected by such manufactured housing community operator from the owner or occupant of each manufactured home occupying space in such manufactured housing community at the end of each month or any major fraction thereof, and shall be deposited with the collector of taxes in the city or town in which such manufactured housing community is located not later than the tenth day of the month next following. The manufactured housing community operator shall, not later than the fifth day of each month, file with the licensing authority a list containing the amounts collected together with the name and address of each owner of a manufactured home occupying space during the preceding month or the tenant or subtenant of such space and designating the manufactured homes and the home owners or tenants of the space or such subtenants thereof on account of which no additional license fee is to be collected or deposited under the provisions of the last paragraph of this section. The licensing authority shall forthwith commit the list to the collector of taxes in the city or town in which the manufactured housing community is located for collection. Such collector, shall in the collection of such accounts, have all the remedies provided by sections thirty-five, thirty-six

and ninety-three of chapter sixty for the collection of taxes on personal property. The collector of taxes shall, once in each week or more often, pay over to the city or town treasurer all money received by him during the preceding week or lesser period on account of such license fees. Each manufactured home subject to the license fee provided for in this section shall be exempt from any property tax as provided in clause Thirty-sixth of section five of chapter fifty-nine.

The collector of taxes shall report to the licensing authority any failure to deposit with him any license fee so collected, and any failure by a manufactured housing community operator to collect any license fee provided for under this section or to deposit with the collector of taxes any license fee so collected shall be deemed cause for the revocation of any license granted under section thirty-two B. In addition, any willful failure to deposit with the collector of taxes a licensee fee which has been so collected shall be punished by a fine of not less than ten nor more than one hundred dollars for each fee so collected and not deposited.

No additional license fee imposed by this section shall be collected by the operator of a manufactured housing community, nor shall any such fee be required to be deposited with the collector of taxes in the city or town in which such community is located, on account of a manufactured home which is deemed, by section 514 of the Soldiers' and Sailors' Civil Relief Act of 1940, as amended, not to be located or present in or to have a situs in such city or town for the purposes of taxation in respect to personal property.

Section 32H. Unequipped communities; plans; cost estimates; conditional licenses; suspension or revocation.

An applicant for a license under section thirty-two B for a manufactured housing community which has not been equipped with the buildings, structures, fixtures and facilities necessary to conduct a manufactured housing community shall file with the board a plan showing the buildings, structures, fixtures and facilities and the proposed set-up which he plans to have upon said premises if and when the license may issue, together with an itemized estimate of the cost of the same and, thereupon, the board, with the approval of the state department of environmental quality engineering, shall grant a manufactured housing community license upon the condition that such license shall issue upon the completion of the premises according to the plans and estimate submitted, providing that the proposed manufactured housing community will be in compliance with all applicable laws, ordinances, rules and regulations. Such conditional license may be suspended or revoked in accordance with the provisions of said section thirty-two B.

Section 32I. Register; retention; inspection; penalty.

Every holder of a license for a manufactured housing community shall keep or cause to be kept, in permanent form, a register in which shall be recorded the true name or name in ordinary use, address and registration of each owner of a manufactured home or motor vehicle renting space in such community and each tenant of such space or subtenant of which the tenant may have notified the operator, the date of entering and the date of leaving such manufactured home or motor vehicle. Such register shall be retained by the holder of the license for a period of at least one year after the date of the last entry, and shall be open to the inspection of the licensing authorities, their agents and the police. Whoever willfully and knowingly violates any provision of this section shall be punished by a fine of not less than five dollars nor more than one hundred dollars.

Section 32J. Summary process to recover possession; termination of tenancy or lease.

If the manufactured home owner or person holding under him holds possession of a manufactured home site in a manufactured housing community without right, after the determination of a tenancy or other estate at will or lease as provided in this section, the licensee entitled to the manufactured home site may recover possession thereof by summary process.

Any tenancy or other estate at will or lease in a manufactured housing community, however created, and including any existing contract for occupancy of a manufactured home site in a manufactured housing community, may be terminated by the licensee entitled to the manufactured home site or his agent only for one or more of the following reasons:

(1) nonpayment of rent;

(2) substantial violation of any enforceable rule of the manufactured housing community;

(3) violation of any laws or ordinances which protect the health or safety of other manufactured housing community residents;

(4) a discontinuance in good faith by the licensee, of the use of part or all of the land owned by the licensee as a manufactured housing community subject to any existing contractual rights or agreements between the licensee and the tenants located in the manufactured housing community. No such discontinuance shall be valid for any manufactured home sold the licensee and for which a manufactured home site was made available at the time of said sale, by the licensee, for a period of five years from the date of said sale;

(5) in the case of an existing tenancy at will, to create a new tenancy at will at an increased rent in accordance with the provisions of section twelve of chapter one hundred and eighty-six.

No action shall be maintained under this section unless:

(1) the manufactured housing community licensee has given at least thirty days' written notice, delivered by certified or registered mail, stating the reasons for termination and notifying the manufactured housing community resident that he has fifteen days from the date of the mailing of the notice in which to pay the overdue rent, or cure the substantial violation of the community rules or of the law or ordinance, in order to avoid eviction;

(2) the manufactured home resident has not paid the overdue rent or cured said violations within twenty days from the day on which such written notice was received; and,

(3) such action, other than for nonpayment of rent, is brought within thirty days from the date of the last alleged violation; provided, however, that an action may be maintained under this section without further notice or opportunity to cure, if the same substantial violation of rules, other than nonpayment of rent, occurs within six months from the date on which such notice was delivered. For the purposes of this section, upon the death of a manufactured housing community tenant, such tenancy shall continue in the estate of such tenant for a period of one year from the date of death or one year from the appointment of an executor or administrator, whichever first occurs.

A resident who has been evicted from a manufactured housing community shall have one hundred and twenty days after such eviction in which to sell the resident's manufactured home, subject to the terms of this paragraph. Such resident shall be responsible for the rental amount accruing during the period prior to such sale and shall maintain the manufactured home and lot during such period, on the terms and conditions of the lease or other rental agreement in effect prior to the occurrences of the default or termination of the term of occupancy which resulted in the eviction. If such manufactured home remains on the lot during such period, the owner of the manufactured housing community shall have a lien on the home to the extent such rental amount is not paid or such maintenance is not performed and to the extent of any additional past sums owed to the owner as set forth on any final eviction order issued by a court of competent jurisdiction. Such lien may be perfected by filing in the offices of the town clerk and secretary of state a uniform commercial code statement, prepared by the owner and signed by the former resident at the request of the owner following the issuance of such eviction order. If the former resident fails to sign such statement within ten days after receipt of such statement from the owner, such resident shall not be entitled to the benefits of this paragraph for so long as such failure continues, provided that nothing in the foregoing is intended to prevent the former resident from preparing and filing such a statement. During such one hundred and twenty day period, no person shall reside in such home and the former resident shall use good faith efforts to sell the home.

Section 32K. Appeals; reinstatement; reissuance.

Any person aggrieved by any act, rule, order or decision of the licensing board may appeal to the superior court. After suspension or revocation, the license may be reinstated or reissued if the conditions leading to such suspension or revocation have been remedied and the community is being maintained and operated in full compliance with the law.

Section 32L. Requirements and restrictions applicable to manufactured housing communities.

The following requirements and restrictions shall apply to all manufactured housing communities:

(1) A manufactured housing community licensee may promulgate rules governing the rental or occupancy of a manufactured home site but no such rule shall be unreasonable, unfair or unconscionable.

(2) Any rule or change in rent which does not apply uniformly to all manufactured home residents of a similar class shall create a rebuttable presumption that such rule or change in rent is unfair.

(3) A manufactured housing community owner, directly or indirectly engaged in the business of selling manufactured homes, shall not impose any conditions of rental or occupancy which restrict a resident or prospective resident in his choice of a manufactured home dealer unless the lot on which the home is to be placed is being leased or rented for the first time. A manufactured housing community owner shall not impose any conditions of rental or occupancy which restrict the resident in his choice of a seller of fuel, furnishings, goods, services or accessories connected with the rental or occupancy of a manufactured home lot, provided, however, that such seller is in compliance with applicable law and rules and regulations of the community approved by the attorney general and the director of housing and community development or otherwise then in effect pursuant to paragraph (5) of section thirty-two L of chapter one hundred and forty, including rules imposing reasonable insurance requirements. A manufactured housing community licensee may impose reasonable conditions relating to central fuel and gas meter systems in the community, provided, however, that the charges for such fuel shall not exceed the average prevailing price in the locality.

(3A) No manufactured housing community owner shall refuse to allow the transfer of a manufactured home located in said community on the ground that such manufactured housing community owner has not sold as many manufactured homes as there are sites.

(4) A manufactured housing community licensee shall not impose by any rule or condition of occupancy, any fee, charge or commission for the sale of a manufactured home located in a manufactured housing community. The licensee may, however, upon the proposed sale of such a home, contract with the manufactured home owner to sell the home for a fee not to exceed ten percent of the sale price of such home.

(5) If any manufactured housing community owner promulgates, adds, deletes or amends any rule governing the rental or occupancy of a manufactured home site in a manufactured housing community, a new copy of all such rules shall be sent by certified mail, return receipt requested, for approval to the attorney general and the director of housing and community development at least sixty days prior to the effective date of such promulgation, addition, deletion or amendment. A copy of such rules shall be furnished to each manufactured housing community resident in such community along with a copy of the certified mail receipts signed by a representative of the attorney general and a representative of the director of housing and community development. Such copies shall be furnished by the manufactured housing community licensee to said residents at least thirty days prior to the effective date of such promulgations, addition, deletion or amendment. Nothing in this section shall be deemed to be an approval of such rules by the attorney general or said director. If neither the attorney general nor said director takes any action prior to the proposed effective date of such rules or amendment or addition thereto, such rules may be enforced by the manufactured housing community licensee until such time as the attorney general or said director subsequently disapproves such rules or portions thereof which disapproval shall apply only prospectively, provided that nothing in this sentence shall preclude a private party from challenging such rules or portions thereof in a court of competent jurisdiction prior to or after such disapproval.

(6) Any rule or condition of occupancy which is unfair or deceptive or which does not conform to the requirements of this section shall be unenforceable.

(7) Failure to comply with the provisions of sections thirty-two A to thirty-two S, inclusive, shall constitute an unfair or deceptive practice under the provisions of paragraph (a) of section two of chapter ninety-three A. Enforcement of compliance and actions for damages shall be in accordance with the applicable provisions of section four to ten, inclusive, of said chapter ninety-three A.

(7A) Any manufactured housing community licensee having given notice, pursuant to this section, of a pending change of use or discontinuance shall survey within the period of notice given to tenants, all of the manufactured housing communities within a one hundred mile radius which are known to the licensee or which reasonably can be ascertained by him, to determine if any manufactured home sites are available or will become available during the notice period. The licensee shall prominently post at the community all of the information received regarding such available sites. Such survey shall be done at least once each year during the two year notice period. The second survey shall be completed and posted not less than one hundred and twenty days prior to the end of the notice period. The manufactured housing community owner shall pay to any tenant who is entitled to receive notice pursuant to paragraph (8) at the tenant's election, either (a) his actual relocation costs or (b) the appraised value of the tenant's manufactured home. Relocation costs shall include the costs of disconnecting and moving the home to the new community selected by the resident within the one hundred mile radius, reconnecting the home with all hook-ups so that it is substantially in the same condition as before the move, with any required and comparable appurtenances, and the reasonable costs of suitable lodging until the move and installation are completed. The appraised value of the manufactured home shall be the fair market value of the home and any existing appurtenances but excluding the value of the underlying land, determined by an independent appraiser agreed to by the community owner and the tenant. If the parties are unable to agree on an independent appraiser within thirty days, either may have recourse to the director of housing and community development or the director's designee, who shall appoint such appraiser within thirty days. The parties shall share the cost of the appraisal equally. In making such determination, the appraiser shall assess fair market value based on the price which a willing and able buyer intending to reside in the home would pay for the home and any existing appurtenances, but excluding the value of the underlying land and shall assume that the home is and will continue to be located on a lot which is leased in a duly licensed manufactured housing community, with all hook-ups and existing appurtenances in place for use and occupancy by the resident. In addition, if the home is then actually located on a lot rented to the home owner by the same person or a predecessor or affiliate of such person or predecessor who sold the home in question within the past ten years to the home owner or a predecessor of such owner, then the appraisal also shall take into account the value to the tenant, if any, which is attributable to a below-market contract rental for the balance of the ten years from the date of sale at the rate at which the lot is leased before delivery of the relocation notice, as increased in accordance with the lease and after its expiration by an annual factor not to exceed the increase in the consumer price index set forth in this paragraph for the twelve-month period immediately preceding delivery of the relocation notice. Otherwise no value shall be attributed to actual existing below-market or above-market rental rates. This paragraph shall not be construed to authorize an early termination of an otherwise enforceable lease with a fixed term or to restrict a tenant's rights at law or in equity with respect thereto. Payment of the appraised value or of the estimated relocation costs, as the case may be, shall be made to the tenant no later than the tenant's departure from the manufactured housing community with adjustments made for the total actual relocation costs upon completion of relocation. Any manufactured housing community owner shall provide a rental agreement to each tenant who is entitled to receive notice pursuant to this section. Such agreement shall begin on the date of the issuance of the notice of discontinuance. The provisions of such rental agreement shall not alter in any manner the tenancy arrangement existing between the community owner and tenant prior to issuance of the notice of discontinuance, except with respect to the amount of annual rent, which

may be increased by an amount not to exceed the increase in the Consumer Price Index for Urban Consumers, published by the United States Department of Labor, Bureau of Labor Statistics, for the calendar year immediately preceding the date upon which such rental agreement is commenced plus the proportionate amount of any documented increase in real estate taxes or other municipal fee or charge; provided, however, that the total amount of such increase shall not exceed ten percent of the annual rent charged in the immediately preceding year; provided, however, that if there is a rent control ordinance in existence such increase shall be subject to the provisions of said ordinance and in no event shall any owner whose notice of discontinuance or change of use is not given in good faith be entitled to any increase in rent otherwise permitted hereunder; and, provided further, that once a tenant has received a notice of discontinuance, his rent shall not be increased unless a year has passed from the date of the last increase imposed upon such tenant.

(8) A manufactured housing community owner shall give at least fifteen days written notice, delivered by certified or registered mail, to each manufactured housing community tenant, that the owner will be appearing before a governmental board, commission or body to request a permit for a good faith change of use or discontinuance of the manufactured housing community. No change of use or discontinuance shall be approved or otherwise be effective unless the owner has demonstrated that such change of use or discontinuance is in good faith and the burden of proving such good faith shall be on the owner. Upon a change of use or discontinuance approved by a governmental board, commission, or body, or with respect to a change or discontinuance that requires no local governmental permit or permits, the manufactured housing community owner shall give to each manufactured housing community tenant at least two years written notice, delivered by certified or registered mail, prior to the manufactured housing community owner's determination that a change of use or discontinuance will occur. The owner shall disclose and describe in the notice the nature of the change of use or discontinuance and the reasons therefor.

(9) The manufactured housing community owner shall give each prospective tenant written notice prior to the inception of tenancy that the owner is requesting a change of use or discontinuance before local governmental bodies, or that a change of use or discontinuance has been granted, or that a change of use or discontinuance which requires no governmental approval will occur, noting the effective date of change.

Section 32M. Sale or proposed sale of manufactured home located in licensed community.

Upon the sale or proposed sale of a manufactured home located on a lot in a manufactured housing community and which is not owned by the manufactured housing community licensee, the prospective purchaser and members of his household may not be refused entrance if they meet the current rules of the community.

Failure to comply with the provisions of this section shall constitute an unfair or deceptive trade practice under the provisions of section two (a) of chapter ninety-three A.

Section 32N. Reprisals for report of violations.

Any manufactured housing community licensee or his agent who threatens to or takes reprisals against any manufactured housing community resident or group of residents for reporting a violation or suspected violation of section thirty-two L or section thirty-two M or any applicable building or health code to the board of health of a city or town in which the manufactured housing community is located, the department of public health, the department of the attorney general or any other appropriate government agency, shall be liable for damages which shall not be less than one month's rent or more than five months' rent, or the actual damages sustained by the manufactured housing community resident or group of residents, whichever is greater, and the costs of the court action brought for said damages including reasonable attorney's fees. The receipt of any notice of termination of tenancy by such manufactured housing community resident or group of residents, except for nonpayment of rent, within six months after making such a report of a violation or a suspected violation, shall create a rebuttable presumption that such notice is a reprisal against the manufactured housing community resident or group of residents for making such report and said presumption may be pleaded in defense to any eviction proceeding against such manufactured housing community resident or group of residents brought within a year after such report.

Section 32O. Actions to enforce sections 32L or 32M; mailing copies of orders.

In any action to enforce the provisions of section thirty-two L or section thirty-two M, the clerk of the court shall mail copies of any judgment, decree, permanent injunction or order of the court upon the entry thereof to the attorney general and to the board of health of the city or town in which the manufactured housing community of the licensee is located.

Section 32P. Terms and conditions of occupancy; disclosure in writing; required notice.

All terms and conditions of occupancy must be fully disclosed in writing by the manufactured housing community owner to any prospective manufactured housing community resident at a reasonable time prior to the rental or occupancy of a manufactured home lot. Said disclosure shall include, but shall not be limited to, the amount of rent, an itemized list of any charges or fees, the names and addresses of all the owners of the manufactured housing community, and the rules and regulations governing the use of the manufactured home lot and community. Said

writing shall contain a bona fide, good faith offer to each new tenant and to each person renewing or extending any existing arrangement or agreement for occupancy of premises in a manufactured housing community for a rental agreement with a term of five years or, where a valid notice of discontinuance is in effect at the time of such offer the balance of the period remaining before the effective date of the discontinuance, at fair market rental rates subject to any applicable rent control restrictions, as an alternative to any other proposed term lengths. Such writing shall be signed by the manufactured housing community owner and contain the following notice printed verbatim in a clear and conspicuous manner:

IMPORTANT NOTICE REQUIRED BY LAW

The rules set forth below govern the terms of your lease or occupancy with this manufactured housing community. If these rules are changed in any way, the addition, deletion or amendment must be delivered to you, along with a copy of the certified mail receipts indicating that such change has been submitted to the attorney general and the director of housing and community development and either a copy of the approvals thereof by the attorney general and said director or a certificate signed by the owner stating that neither the attorney general nor said director has taken any action with respect thereto within the period set forth in paragraph (5) of section thirty-two L of chapter one hundred and forty. This notification must be furnished to you at least thirty days before the change goes into effect. The law requires all of these rules and regulations to be fair and reasonable or said rules and regulations cannot be enforced. You may continue to stay in the community as long as you pay rent and abide by the rules and regulations. You may only be evicted for nonpayment of rent, violation of law or for substantial violation of the rules and regulations of the community. In addition, no eviction proceedings may be commenced against you until you have received notice by certified mail of the reason for the eviction proceeding and you have been given fifteen days from the date of the notice in which to pay the overdue rent or to cease and desist from any substantial violation of the rules and regulations of the community; provided, however, that only one notice of substantial violation of the rules and regulations of the community is required to be sent to you during any six month period. If a second or additional violation occurs, except for nonpayment of rent, within six months from the date of the first notice, then eviction proceedings may be commenced against you immediately.

You may not be evicted for reporting any violations of law or health and building codes to boards of health, the attorney general, or any other appropriate government agency. Receipt of notice of termination of tenancy by you, except for nonpayment of rent, within six months after your making such a report shall create a rebuttable presumption that such notice is a reprisal and may be pleaded by you in defense to any eviction proceeding brought within one year. Any group of more than fifty percent of the tenants residing in the manufactured housing community has certain rights under section thirty-two R of chapter one hundred and forty, to purchase the community in the event the owner intends to accept an offer to sell or lease the community in the future. If you wish to receive further information about the financial terms of such a possible purchase, you may so notify the owner at any time by signing the attached Request for Information and returning it to the owner in person or by certified mail. Such request for information shall not obligate you to participate in any purchase of the community. For a proposed sale or lease by the owner which will result in a change of use or a discontinuance of the community you will receive information at least two years before the change becomes effective. Otherwise, Requests for Information or similar notices from more than fifty percent of the tenants residing in the community must be on file with the owner before the owner is required to give you information concerning the financial terms of a sale or lease.

This law is enforceable by the consumer protection division of the attorney general's office.

REQUEST FOR INFORMATION

The undersigned, a tenant in the manufactured housing community known as _____ and located at _____, Massachusetts desires to receive information concerning any proposed sale or lease of the community as required under Section 32R of Chapter 140 of the General Laws. I understand that this request shall not obligate me to participate in any purchase or lease of the community, but is only a request for information. This notice is being delivered to the owner or owner's manager either in person or by certified mail on (date) .

(Tenant - Name)

Section 32Q. Manufactured home defined.

As used in sections thirty-two A to thirty-two P, inclusive, the words "manufactured home" shall mean a structure, built in conformance to the National Manufactured Home Construction and Safety Standards which is transportable in one or more sections, which in the traveling mode, is eight body feet or more in width or forty body feet or more in length, or, when erected on site, is three hundred twenty or more square feet, and which is built on a permanent chassis and designed to be used as a dwelling unit with or without a permanent foundation when connected to the required utilities, and includes the plumbing, heating, air conditioning, and electrical systems contained therein.

Section 32R. Sale or lease of manufactured housing community; home owners' association; notice; right of first refusal.

(a) A manufactured housing community owner shall give notice to each resident of the manufactured housing community of any intention to sell or lease all or part of the land on which the community is located for any purpose. Such notice shall be mailed by certified mail, with a simultaneous copy to the attorney general, the director of housing and community development, and the local board of health, within fourteen days after the date on which any advertisement, listing, or public notice is first made that the community is for sale or lease and, in any event, at least forty-five days before the sale or lease occurs; provided, that such notice shall also include notice of tenants rights under this section.

(b) Before a manufactured housing community may be sold or leased for any purpose that would result in a change of use or discontinuance, the owner shall notify each resident of the community, with a simultaneous copy to the attorney general, the director of housing and community development, and the local board of health, by certified mail of any bona fide offer for such a sale or lease that the owner intends to accept. Before any other sale or lease other than leases of single lots to individual residents, the owner shall give each resident such a notice of the offer only if more than fifty percent of the tenants residing in such community or an incorporated home owners' association or group of tenants representing more than fifty percent of the tenants residing in such community notifies the manufactured housing community owner or operator, in writing, that such persons desire to receive information relating to the proposed sale or lease. Any notice of the offer required to be given under this subsection shall include the price, calculated as a single lump sum amount which reflects the present value of any installment payments offered and of any promissory notes offered in lieu of cash payment or, in the case of an offer to rent, the capitalized value of the annual rent and the terms and conditions of the offer.

(c) A group or association of residents representing at least fifty-one percent of the manufactured home owners residing in the community which are entitled to notice under paragraph (b) shall have the right to purchase, in the case of a third party bona fide offer to purchase that the owner intends to accept, or to lease in the case of a third party bona fide offer to lease that the owner intends to accept, the said community for purposes of continuing such use thereof, provided it (1) submits to the owner reasonable evidence that the residents of at least fifty-one percent of the occupied homes in the community have approved the purchase of the community by such group or association, (2) submits to the owner a proposed purchase and sale agreement or lease agreement on substantially equivalent terms and conditions within forty-five days of receipt of notice of the offer made under subsection (b) of this section, (3) obtains a binding commitment for any necessary financing or guarantees within an additional ninety days after execution of the purchase and sale agreement or lease, and (4) closes on such purchase or lease within an additional ninety days after the end of the ninety-day period under clause (3).

No owner shall unreasonably refuse to enter into, or unreasonably delay the execution or closing on a purchase and sale or lease agreement with residents who have made a bona fide offer to meet the price and substantially equivalent terms and conditions of an offer for which notice is required to be given pursuant to paragraph (b). Failure of the residents to submit such a purchase and sale agreement or lease within the first forty-five day period, to obtain a binding commitment for financing within the additional ninety day period or to close on the purchase or lease within the second ninety-day period, shall serve to terminate the rights of such residents to purchase or lease the manufactured housing community. The time periods herein provided may be extended by agreement. Nothing herein shall be construed to require an owner to provide financing to such residents except to the extent such financing would be provided to the third party offeror in the case of a sale or lease for a use which would result in a change of use or discontinuance or to prohibit an owner from requiring such residents who are offering to lease a community to provide a security deposit, not to exceed the lesser of one-year's rent or the amount which would have been required to be provided by the third party offeror, to be kept in escrow for such purposes during the term of the lease. A group or association of residents which has the right to purchase hereunder, at its election, may assign its purchase right hereunder to the city, town, housing authority, or agency of the commonwealth for the purpose of continuing the use of the manufactured housing community.

(d) The right of first refusal created herein shall inure to the residents for the time periods hereinbefore provided, beginning on the date of notice to the residents under paragraph (b). The effective period for such right of first refusal shall obtain separately for each substantially different bona fide offer to purchase or lease the community, and for each offer substantially equivalent to an offer made more than three months prior to the later offer; provided however, that in the case of a substantially equivalent offer made by a prospective buyer who has previously made an offer for which notice to residents was required by said paragraph (b), the right of first refusal shall obtain only if such subsequent offer is made more than six months after the earlier offer. The right of first refusal shall not apply with respect to any offer received by the owner for which a notice is not required pursuant to said paragraph (b). No right of first refusal shall apply to a government taking by eminent domain or negotiated purchase, a forced sale pursuant to a foreclosure by an unrelated third party, transfer by gift, devise or operation of law, or a sale to a person who would be an heir at law if there were to be a death intestate of a manufactured housing community owner.

(e) In any instance where the residents of the manufactured housing community are not the successful purchaser or lessee of such manufactured housing community, the seller or lessor of such community shall provide evidence of compliance with this section by filing an affidavit of compliance with the attorney general, the director of housing and community development, the local board of health, and the official records of the county where the property is located within seven days of the sale or lease of the community. Any lease of five years or less shall specifically require that such lessee shall not discontinue or change the use of the manufactured housing community during the term of such lease.

(f) In any instance of a sale or lease for which a notice from the owner of the manufactured housing community is not required to be, and is not, given under paragraph (b) and within one year of such sale or lease the new owner or lessee delivers a notice of change of use or discontinuance under paragraph (8) of section thirty-two L, such notice shall provide each tenant in the manufactured housing community with at least four years prior notice of the effective date of the proposed change of use or discontinuance.

Section 32S. Rules and regulations.

The attorney general from time to time shall promulgate such rules and regulations as he deems necessary for the interpretation, implementation, administration and enforcement of sections thirty-two A to thirty-two S, inclusive. Such authority shall be in addition to, and not in derogation of, the attorney general's authority to promulgate rules and regulations under section two of chapter ninety-three A with respect to manufactured housing communities.

Chapter 186. Estates for years and at will.
Chapter 186: Section 1. Long term interests; treatment as freeholder.

If land is demised for the term of one hundred years or more, the term shall, so long as fifty years thereof remain unexpired, be regarded as an estate in fee simple as to everything concerning the descent and devise thereof, upon the decease of the owner, the right of dower as defined in section one of chapter one hundred and eighty-nine therein, the sale thereof by executors, administrators, guardians, conservators or trustees, the levy of execution thereon, and the redemption thereof if mortgaged or taken on execution; and whoever holds as lessee or assignee under such a lease shall, so long as fifty years of the term remain unexpired, be regarded as a freeholder for all purposes.

Section 2. Assignment of dower.

If dower as defined in section one of chapter one hundred and eighty-nine is assigned out of such land, the husband or widow and his or her assigns shall pay to the owner of the unexpired residue of the term one third of the rent reserved in the lease under which the wife or husband held the term.

Section 3. Tenancy at sufferance; liability for rent.

Tenants at sufferance in possession of land or tenements shall be liable to pay rent therefor for such time as they may occupy or detain the same.

Section 4. Liability of tenant for rent for proportion of land in possession.

A person in possession of land out of which rent is due shall be liable for the amount or proportion of rent due from the land in his possession although it is only a part of that originally demised.

Section 5. Action to recover rent; evidence.

Such rent may be recovered in contract, and the deed of demise or other written instrument, if any, showing the provisions of the lease, may be used in evidence by either party to prove the amount of rent due from the defendant.

Section 6. Survival of action.

Such action may be brought by or against executors and administrators for any arrears of rent accrued in the lifetime of the deceased parties, respectively, in the same manner as for debts due from or to the same parties in their lifetime on a personal contract.

Section 7. Remedies of landlords.

The six preceding sections shall not deprive landlords of any other legal remedy for the recovery of rents, whether secured by lease or by law.

Section 8. Recovery of rent accruing before determination of lease.

If land is held by lease of a person having an estate therein determinable on a life or on a contingency, and such estate determines before the end of a period for which rent is payable, or if an estate created by a written lease or an estate at will is determined before the end of such period by surrender, either express or by operation of law, by notice to quit for non-payment of rent, or by the death of any party, the landlord or his executor or administrator may recover in contract, a proportional part of such rent according to the portion of the last period for which such rent was accruing which had expired at such determination.

Section 9. Recovery of rent paid in advance.

If, upon the determination of a tenancy, in any manner mentioned in the preceding section, before the end of a period for which rent is payable, the rent therefor has been paid before such determination, a proportionate part thereof, according to the portion of such period then unexpired, may be recovered back in contract.

Section 10. Rent as a necessary.

Debts for the rent of a dwelling house occupied by the debtor or his family shall be considered as claims for necessaries.

Section 11. Determination of lease for nonpayment of rent.

Upon the neglect or refusal to pay the rent due under a written lease, fourteen days' notice to quit, given in writing by the landlord to the tenant, shall be sufficient to determine the lease, unless the tenant, on or before the day the answer is due, in an action by the landlord to recover possession of the premises, pays or tenders to the landlord or to his attorney all rent then due, with interest and costs of suit. If the neglect or refusal to pay the rent due was

caused by a failure or delay of the federal government, the commonwealth or any municipality, or any departments, agencies or authorities thereof, in the mailing or delivery of any subsistence or rental payment, check or voucher other than a salary payment to either the tenant or the landlord, the court in any such action shall continue the hearing not less than seven days in order to furnish notice of such action to the appropriate agency and shall, if all rent due with interest and costs of suit has been tendered to the landlord within such time, treat the tenancy as not having been terminated.

Section 11A. Termination of lease for nonpayment of rent.

Upon the neglect or refusal by the tenant to pay the rent due under a written lease of premises for other than dwelling purposes, the landlord shall be entitled to terminate the lease either (i) in accordance with the provisions of the lease or (ii) in the absence of such lease provisions, by at least fourteen days notice to quit, given in writing to the tenant. If a landlord terminates the lease by at least fourteen days notice pursuant to clause (ii) of the preceding sentence, the tenant shall be entitled to cure on or before the day the answer is due in any action by the landlord to recover possession of the premises, by paying or tendering to the landlord or to his attorney all rent then due, with interest and costs of such action. The rights to cure provided herein, shall apply only to termination pursuant to clause (ii) and shall not apply to termination in accordance with the provisions of the lease.

Section 12. Notice to determine estate at will.

Estates at will may be determined by either party by three months' notice in writing for that purpose given to the other party; and, if the rent reserved is payable at periods of less than three months, the time of such notice shall be sufficient if it is equal to the interval between the days of payment or thirty days, whichever is longer. Such written notice may include an offer to establish a new tenancy for the same premises on terms different from that of the tenancy being terminated and the validity of such written notice shall not be affected by the inclusion of such offer. In case of neglect or refusal to pay the rent due from a tenant at will, fourteen days' notice to quit, given in writing by the landlord to the tenant, shall be sufficient to determine the tenancy; provided, that the tenancy of a tenant who has not received a similar notice from the landlord within the twelve months next preceding the receipt of such notice shall not be determined if the tenant, within ten days after the receipt thereof, pays or tenders to the landlord, the landlord's attorney, or the person to whom the tenant customarily pays rent, the full amount of any rent due. Every notice to determine an estate at will for nonpayment of rent shall contain the following notification to the tenant: "If you have not received a notice to quit for nonpayment of rent within the last twelve months, you have a right to prevent termination of your tenancy by paying or tendering to your landlord, your landlord's attorney or the person to whom you customarily pay your rent the full amount of rent due within ten days after your receipt of this notice." If any notice to determine an estate at will for nonpayment of rent shall fail to contain such notification, the time within which the tenant receiving the notice would be entitled to pay or tender rent pursuant to this section shall be extended to the day the answer is due in any action by the landlord to recover possession of the premises. Failure to include such notice shall not otherwise affect the validity of the said notice. If the neglect or refusal to pay the rent due was caused by a failure or delay of the federal government, the commonwealth or any municipality, or any departments, agencies or authorities thereof, in the mailing or delivery of any subsistence or rental payment, check or voucher other than a salary payment to either the tenant or the landlord, the court in any action for possession shall continue the hearing not less than seven days in order to furnish notice of such action to the appropriate agency and shall, if all rent due with interest and costs of suit has been tendered to the landlord within such time, treat the tenancy as not having been terminated.

Section 13. Recovery of possession after termination of tenancy at will.

Whenever a tenancy at will of premises occupied for dwelling purposes, other than a room or rooms in a hotel, is terminated, without fault of the tenant, either by operation of law or by act of the landlord, except as provided in section twelve, no action to recover possession of the premises shall be brought, nor shall the tenant be dispossessed, until after the expiration of a period, equal to the interval between the days on which the rent reserved is payable or thirty days, whichever is longer, from the time when the tenant receives notice in writing of such termination; but such tenant shall be liable to pay rent for such time during the said period as he occupies or retains the premises, at the same rate as theretofore payable by him while a tenant at will; provided, that in the case of a rooming house, an action to recover possession of premises occupied for dwelling purposes may be brought seven days after written notice if the rent is payable on either a weekly or daily basis. A tenancy at will of property occupied for dwelling purposes shall not be terminated by operation of law by the conveyance, transfer or leasing of the premises by the owner or landlord thereof.

Section 14. Wrongful acts of landlord; premises used for dwelling or residential purposes; utilities, services, quiet enjoyment; penalties; remedies; waiver.

Any lessor or landlord of any building or part thereof occupied for dwelling purposes, other than a room or rooms in a hotel, but including a manufactured home or land therefor, who is required by law or by the express or implied terms of any contract or lease or tenancy at will to furnish water, hot water, heat, light, power, gas, elevator service, telephone service, janitor service or refrigeration service to any occupant of such building or part thereof, who willfully or intentionally fails to furnish such water, hot water, heat, light, power, gas, elevator service, telephone service, janitor service or refrigeration service at any time when the same is necessary to the proper or customary use of such building or part thereof, or any lessor or landlord who directly or indirectly interferes with the furnishing by another of such utilities or services, or who transfers the responsibility for payment for any utility services to the occupant without his knowledge or consent, or any lessor or landlord who directly or indirectly interferes with the quiet enjoyment of any residential premises by the occupant, or who attempts to regain possession of such premises by force without benefit of judicial process, shall be punished by a fine of not less than twenty-five dollars nor more than three hundred dollars, or by imprisonment for not more than six months. Any person who commits any act in violation of this section shall also be liable for actual and consequential damages or three month's rent, whichever is greater, and the costs of the action, including a reasonable attorney's fee, all of which may be applied in setoff to or in recoupment against any claim for rent owed or owing. The superior and district courts shall have jurisdiction in equity to restrain violations of this section. The provisions of section eighteen of chapter one hundred and eighty-six and section two A of chapter two hundred and thirty-nine shall apply to any act taken as a reprisal against any person for reporting or proceeding against violations of this section. Any waiver of this provision in any lease or other rental agreement, except with respect to any restriction on the provision of a service specified in this section imposed by the United States or any agency thereof or the commonwealth or any agency or political subdivision thereof and not resulting from the acts or omissions of the landlord or lessor, and except for interruptions of any specified service during the time required to perform necessary repairs to apparatus necessary for the delivery of said service or interruptions resulting from natural causes beyond the control of the lessor or landlord, shall be void and unenforceable.

Section 15. Non-liability of landlord; provisions in lease or rental agreement.

Any provision of a lease or other rental agreement relating to real property whereby a lessee or tenant enters into a covenant, agreement or contract, by the use of any words whatsoever, the effect of which is to indemnify the lessor or landlord or hold the lessor or landlord harmless, or preclude or exonerate the lessor or landlord from any or all liability to the lessee or tenant, or to any other person, for any injury, loss, damage or liability arising from any omission, fault, negligence or other misconduct of the lessor or landlord on or about the leased or rented premises or on or about any elevators, stairways, hallways or other appurtenance used in connection therewith, shall be deemed to be against public policy and void.

Section 15A. Waiver of notices; lease or rental agreement provisions; validity.

Any provision of a lease or other rental agreement relating to residential real property whereby a lessee or tenant enters into a covenant, agreement or contract, by the use of any words whatsoever, the effect of which is to waive the notices required under section eleven or twelve, shall be deemed to be against public policy and void.

Section 15B. Entrance of premises prior to termination of lease; payments; receipts; interest; records; security deposits.

(1) (a) No lease relating to residential real property shall contain a provision that a lessor may, except to inspect the premises, to make repairs thereto or to show the same to a prospective tenant, purchaser, mortgagee or its agents, enter the premises before the termination date of such lease. A lessor may, however, enter such premises:

(i) in accordance with a court order;

(ii) if the premises appear to have been abandoned by the lessee; or

(iii) to inspect, within the last thirty days of the tenancy or after either party has given notice to the other of intention to terminate the tenancy, the premises for the purpose of determining the amount of damage, if any, to the premises which would be cause for deduction from any security deposit held by the lessor pursuant to this section.

(b) At or prior to the commencement of any tenancy, no lessor may require a tenant or prospective tenant to pay any amount in excess of the following:

(i) rent for the first full month of occupancy; and,

(ii) rent for the last full month of occupancy calculated at the same rate as the first month; and,

(iii) a security deposit equal to the first month's rent provided that such security deposit is deposited as required by subsection (3) and that the tenant is given the statement of condition as required by subsection (2); and,

(iv) the purchase and installation cost for a key and lock.

(c) No lease or other rental agreement shall impose any interest or penalty for failure to pay rent until thirty days after such rent shall have been due.

(d) No lessor or successor in interest shall at any time subsequent to the commencement of a tenancy demand rent in advance in excess of the current month's rent or a security deposit in excess of the amount allowed by this section. The payment in advance for occupancy pursuant to this section shall be binding upon all successors in interest.

(e) A security deposit shall continue to be the property of the tenant making such deposit, shall not be commingled with the assets of the lessor, and shall not be subject to the claims of any creditor of the lessor or of the lessor's successor in interest, including a foreclosing mortgagee or trustee in bankruptcy; provided, however, that the tenant shall be entitled to only such interest as is provided for in subsection (3)(b).

(2)(a) Any lessor or his agent who receives, at or prior to the commencement of a tenancy, rent in advance for the last month of the tenancy from a tenant or prospective tenant shall give to such tenant or prospective tenant at the time of such advance payment a receipt indicating the amount of such rent, the date on which it was received, its intended application as rent for the last month of the tenancy, the name of the person receiving it and, in the case of an agent, the name of the lessor for whom the rent is received, and a description of the rented or leased premises, and a statement indicating that the tenant is entitled to interest on said rent payment at the rate of five per cent per year or other such lesser amount of interest as has been received from the bank where the deposit has been held payable in accordance with the provisions of this clause, and a statement indicating that the tenant should provide the lessor with a forwarding address at the termination of the tenancy indicating where such interest may be given or sent.

Any lessor or his agent who receives said rent in advance for the last month of tenancy shall, beginning with the first day of tenancy, pay interest at the rate of five per cent per year or other such lesser amount of interest as has been received from the bank where the deposit has been held. Such interest shall be paid over to the tenant each year as provided in this clause; provided, however, that in the event that the tenancy is terminated before the anniversary date of such tenancy, the tenant shall receive all accrued interest within thirty days of such termination. Interest shall not accrue for the last month for which rent was paid in advance. At the end of each year of tenancy, such lessor shall give or send to the tenant from whom rent in advance was collected a statement which shall indicate the amount payable by such lessor to the tenant. The lessor shall at the same time give or send to such tenant the interest which is due or shall notify the tenant that he may deduct the interest from the next rental payment of such tenant. If, after thirty days from the end of each year of the tenancy, the tenant has not received said interest due or said notice to deduct the interest from the next rental payment, the tenant may deduct from his next rent payment the interest due.

If the lessor fails to pay any interest to which the tenant is then entitled within thirty days after the termination of the tenancy, the tenant upon proof of the same in an action against the lessor shall be awarded damages in an amount equal to three times the amount of interest to which the tenant is entitled, together with court costs and reasonable attorneys fees.

(b) Any lessor or his agent who receives a security deposit from a tenant or prospective tenant shall give said tenant or prospective tenant at the time of receiving such security deposit a receipt indicating the amount of such security deposit, the name of the person receiving it and, in the case of an agent, the name of the lessor for whom such security deposit is received, the date on which it is received, and a description of the premises leased or rented. Said receipt shall be signed by the person receiving the security deposit.

(c) Any lessor of residential real property, or his agent, who accepts a security deposit from a tenant or prospective tenant shall, upon receipt of such security deposit, or within ten days after commencement of the tenancy, whichever is later, furnish to such tenant or prospective tenant a separate written statement of the present condition of the premises to be leased or rented. Such written statement shall also contain a comprehensive listing of any damage then existing in the premises, including, but not limited to, any violations of the state sanitary or state building codes certified by a local board of health or building official or adjudicated by a court and then existing in the premises. Such statement shall be signed by the lessor or his agent and contain the following notice in twelve-point bold-face type at the top of the first page thereof:

"This is a statement of the condition of the premises you have leased or rented. You should read it carefully in order to see if it is correct. If it is correct you must sign it. This will show that you agree that the list is correct and complete. If it is not correct, you must attach a separate signed list of any damage which you believe exists in the premises. This statement must be returned to the lessor or his agent within fifteen days after you receive this list or within fifteen days after you move in, whichever is later. If you do not return this list, within the specified time period, a court may later view your failure to return the list as your agreement that the list is complete and correct in any suit which you may bring to recover the security deposit."

If the tenant submits to the lessor or his agent a separate list of damages, the lessor or his agent shall, within fifteen days of receiving said separate list, return a copy of said list to the tenant with either such lessor's signed agreement with the content thereof or a clear statement of disagreement attached.

(d) Every lessor who accepts a security deposit shall maintain a record of all such security deposits received which contains the following information:--

(i) a detailed description of any damage done to each of the dwelling units or premises for which a security deposit has been accepted, returned to any tenant thereof or for which the lessor has brought suit against any tenant;

(ii) the date upon which the occupancy of the tenant or tenants charged with such damage was terminated; and

(iii) whether repairs were performed to remedy such damage, the dates of said repairs, the cost thereof, and receipts therefor.

Said record shall also include copies of any receipt or statement of condition given to a tenant or prospective tenant as required by this section.

Said record shall be available for inspection upon request of a tenant or prospective tenant during normal business hours in the office of the lessor or his agent. Upon a wrong-ful failure by the lessor or his agent to make such record available for inspection by a tenant or prospective tenant, said tenant or prospective tenant shall be entitled to the immediate return of any amount paid in the form of a security deposit together with any interest which has accrued thereon.

The lessor or his agent shall maintain said record for each dwelling unit or premises for which a security deposit was accepted for a period of two years from the date of termination of the tenancy or occupancy upon which the security deposit was conditioned.

(3) (a) Any security deposit received by such lessor shall be held in a separate, interest-bearing account in a bank, located within the commonwealth under such terms as will place such deposit beyond the claim of creditors of the lessor, including a foreclosing mortgagee or trustee in bankruptcy, and as will provide for its transfer to a subsequent owner of said property. A receipt shall be given to the tenant within thirty days after such deposit is received by the lessor which receipt shall indicate the name and location of the bank in which the security deposit has been deposited and the amount and account number of said deposit. Failure to comply with this paragraph shall entitle the tenant to immediate return of the security deposit.

(b) A lessor of residential real property who holds a security deposit pursuant to this section for a period of one year or longer from the commencement of the term of the tenancy shall, beginning with the first day of the tenancy, pay interest at the rate of five per cent per year, or other such lesser amount of interest as has been received from the bank where the deposit has been held payable to the tenant at the end of each year of the tenancy. Such interest shall be paid over to the tenant each year as provided in this clause, provided, however, that in the event that the tenancy is terminated before the anniversary date of the tenancy, the tenant shall receive all accrued interest within thirty days of such termination. Such interest shall be beyond the claims of such lessor, except as provided for in this section. At the end of each year of a tenancy, such lessor shall give or send to the tenant from whom a security deposit has been received a statement which shall indicate the name and address of the bank in which the security deposit has been placed, the amount of the deposit, the account number, and the amount of interest payable by such lessor to the tenant. The lessor shall at the same time give or send to each such tenant the interest which is due or shall include with the statement required by this clause a notification that the tenant may deduct the interest from the tenant's next rental payment. If, after thirty days from the end of each year of the tenancy, the tenant has not received such notice or payment, the tenant may deduct from his next rent payment the interest due.

(4) The lessor shall, within thirty days after the termination of occupancy under a tenancy-at-will or the end of the ten-

ancy as specified in a valid written lease agreement, return to the tenant the security deposit or any balance thereof; provided, however, that the lessor may deduct from such security deposit for the following:

(i) any unpaid rent which has not been validly withheld or deducted pursuant to the provisions of any special or general law and

(ii) any unpaid increase in real estate taxes which the tenant is obligated to pay pursuant to a tax escalation clause which conforms to the requirements of section fifteen C; and

(iii) a reasonable amount necessary to repair any damage caused to the dwelling unit by the tenant or any person under the tenant's control or on the premises with the tenant's consent, reasonable wear and tear excluded. In the case of such damage, the lessor shall provide to the tenant within such thirty days an itemized list of damages, sworn to by the lessor or his agent under pains and penalties of perjury, itemizing in precise detail the nature of the damage and of the repairs necessary to correct such damage, and written evidence, such as estimates, bills, invoices or receipts, indicating the actual or estimated cost thereof. No amount shall be deducted from the security deposit for any damage to the dwelling unit which was listed in the separate written statement of the present condition of the premises which was required to be given to the tenant prior to the execution of the lease or creation of the tenancy pursuant to clause (c) of subsection (2) or any damages listed in any separate list submitted by the tenant and signed by the lessor or his agent pursuant to said clause (c), unless the lessor subsequently repaired or caused to be repaired said damage and can prove that the renewed damage was unrelated to the prior damage and was caused by the tenant or by any person under the tenant's control or on the premises with the tenant's consent. Nothing in this section shall limit the right of a landlord to recover from a tenant, who wilfully or maliciously destroys or damages the real or personal property of said landlord, to the forfeiture of a security deposit, when the cost of repairing or replacing such property exceeds the amount of such security deposit. No deduction may be made from the security deposit for any purpose other than those set forth in this section.

(5) Whenever a lessor who receives a security deposit transfers his interest in the dwelling unit for which the security deposit is held, whether by sale, assignment, death, appointment of a receiver or trustee in bankruptcy, or otherwise, the lessor shall transfer such security deposit together with any interest which has accrued thereon for the benefit of the tenant who made such security deposit to his successor in interest, and said successor in interest shall be liable for the retention and return of said security deposit in accordance with the provisions of this section from the date upon which said transfer is made; provided however, that the granting of a mortgage on such premises

shall not be a transfer of interest. The successor in interest shall, within forty-five days from the date of said transfer, notify the tenant who made such security deposit that such security deposit was transferred to him and that he is holding said security deposit. Such notice shall also contain the lessor's name, business address, and business telephone number, and the name, business address, and business telephone number of his agent, if any. Said notice shall be in writing.

Upon such transfer, the lessor or his agent shall continue to be liable with respect to the provisions of this section until:

(a) there has been a transfer of the amount of the security deposit so held to the lessor's successor in interest and the tenant has been notified in writing of the transfer and of the successor in interest's name, business address, and business telephone number;

(b) there has been compliance with this clause by the successor in interest; or

(c) the security deposit has been returned to the tenant.

In the event that the lessor fails to transfer said security deposit to his successor in interest as required by this subsection the successor in interest shall, without regard to the nature of the transfer, assume liability for payment of the security deposit to the tenant in accordance with the provisions of this section; provided, however, that if the tenant still occupies the dwelling unit for which the security deposit was given, said successor in interest may satisfy such obligation by granting the tenant free use and occupancy of the dwelling unit for a period of time equivalent to that period of time for which the dwelling unit could be leased or occupied if the security deposit were deemed to be rent. The liability imposed by this paragraph shall not apply to a city or town which acquires title to property pursuant to chapter sixty or to a foreclosing mortgagee or a mortgagee in possession which is a financial institution chartered by the commonwealth or the United States. The term "rent", as used in the preceding sentence, shall mean the periodic sum paid by the tenant for the use and occupation of the dwelling unit in accordance with the terms of his lease or other rental agreement.

(6) The lessor shall forfeit his right to retain any portion of the security deposit for any reason, or, in any action by a tenant to recover a security deposit, to counterclaim for any damage to the premises if he:

(a) fails to deposit such funds in an account as required by subsection (3);

(b) fails to furnish to the tenant within thirty days after the termination of the occupancy the itemized list of damages, if any, in compliance with the provisions of this section;

(c) uses in any lease signed by the tenant any provision which conflicts with any provision of this section and attempts to enforce such provision or attempts to obtain from the tenant or prospective tenant a waiver of any provision of this section.

(d) fails to transfer such security deposit to his successor in interest or to otherwise comply with the provisions of subsection (5) after he has succeeded to an interest in residential real property; or;

(e) fails to return to the tenant the security deposit or balance thereof to which the tenant is entitled after deducting therefrom any sums in accordance with the provisions of this section, together with any interest thereon, within thirty days after termination of the tenancy.

(7) If the lessor or his agent fails to comply with clauses (a), (d), or (e) of subsection 6, the tenant shall be awarded damages in an amount equal to three times the amount of such security deposit or balance thereof to which the tenant is entitled plus interest at the rate of five per cent from the date when such payment became due, together with court costs and reasonable attorney's fees.

(7A) Whenever a lessor who receives rent in advance for the last month of tenancy transfers his interest in the dwelling unit for which the rental advance was received, whether by sale, assignment, death, appointment of a receiver or trustee in bankruptcy, or otherwise, the lessor shall credit an amount equal to such rental advance together with any interest which has accrued thereon for the benefit of the tenant who made such rental advance, to the successor in interest of such lessor, and said successor in interest shall be liable for crediting the tenant with such rental advance, and for paying all interest accrued thereon in accordance with the provisions of this section from the date upon which said transfer is made; provided, however, that the granting of a mortgage on such premises shall not be deemed a transfer of interest. The successor in interest shall, within forty-five days from the date of said transfer, notify the tenant who made such rental advance that such rental advance was so credited, and that such successor has assumed responsibility therefor pursuant to the foregoing provision. Such notice shall also contain the lessor's name, business address, and business telephone number, and the name, business address, and business telephone number of his agent, if any. Said notice shall be in writing.

Upon such transfer, the lessor or his agent shall continue to be liable with respect to the provisions of this section until: (a) there has been a credit of the amount of the rental advance so held to the lessor's successor in interest and the tenant has been notified in writing of the transfer and of the successor in interest's name, business address, and business telephone number; (b) there has been compliance with this clause by the successor in interest; or (c) the rental advance has been credited to the tenant and all accrued interest has been paid thereon.

In the event that the lessor fails to credit said rental advance to his successor in interest as required by this subsection, the successor in interest shall, without regard to the nature of the transfer, assume liability for crediting of the rental advance, and payment of all interest thereon to the tenant

in accordance with the provisions of this section; provided, however, that if the tenant still occupies the dwelling unit for which the rental advance was given, said successor in interest may satisfy such obligation by granting the tenant free use and occupancy of the dwelling unit for a period of time equivalent to the period of time covered by the rental advance. The liability imposed by this subsection shall not apply to a city or town which acquires title to property pursuant to chapter sixty or to a foreclosing mortgagee or a mortgagee in possession which is a financial institution chartered by the commonwealth or by the United States.

(8) Any provision of a lease which conflicts with any provision of this section and any waiver by a tenant or prospective tenant of any provision of this section shall be deemed to be against public policy and therefore void and unenforceable.

(9) The provisions of this section shall not apply to any lease, rental, occupancy or tenancy of one hundred days or less in duration which lease or rental is for a vacation or recreational purpose.

Section 15C. Residential real estate, lease payments based on real estate tax increases.

No lease relating to residential real estate shall contain a provision which obligates a lessee to make payments to the lessor on account of an increased real estate tax levied during the term of the lease, unless such provision expressly sets forth (1) that the lessee shall be obligated to pay only that proportion of such increased tax as the unit leased by him bears to the whole of the real estate so taxed, (2) the exact percentage of any such increase which the lessee shall pay, and (3) that if the lessor obtains an abatement of the real estate tax levied on the whole of the real estate of which the unit leased by the lessee is a part, a proportionate share of such abatement, less reasonable attorney's fees, if any, shall be refunded to said lessee. Any provision of a lease in violation of the provisions of this section shall be deemed to be against public policy and void.

If the exact percentage of any such increased tax contained in such a provision is found to exceed that proportion of such increased tax as the lessee's unit bears to the whole of the real estate so taxed, then the lessor shall return to the lessee that amount of the tax payment collected from the lessee which exceeded the lessee's proportionate share of the increased tax, plus interest calculated at the rate of five per cent per year from the date of collection.

Section 15D. Oral agreement to execute lease; delivery of lease copy; penalty; waiver.

A lessor who has agreed orally to execute a lease and obtains the signature of the lessee shall, within thirty days thereafter, deliver a copy of said lease to the lessee, duly signed and executed by said lessor. Whoever violates any provision of this section shall be punished by a fine of not more than three hundred dollars. Any waiver of this provision in any lease or other rental agreement shall be void and unenforceable.

Section 15E. Action against owner; injuries due to defects violating building code; defense; waiver.

An owner of a building shall be precluded from raising as a defense in an action brought by a lessee, tenant or occupant of said building who has sustained an injury caused by a defect in a common area, that said defect existed at the time of the letting of the property, if said defect is at the time of the injury a violation of the building code of the city or town wherein the property is situated. Any waiver of this provision in any lease or other rental agreement shall be void and unenforceable.

Section 15F. Residential leases or rental agreements restricting litigation or landlord liability; ouster of tenant; remedies.

Any provision of a lease or other rental agreement relating to residential real property whereby the tenant agrees to waive his right to trial by jury in any subsequent litigation with the landlord, or agrees that no action or failure to act by the landlord shall be construed as a constructive eviction, shall be deemed to be against public policy and void. If a tenant is removed from the premises or excluded therefrom by the landlord or his agent except pursuant to a valid court order, the tenant may recover possession or terminate the rental agreement and, in either case, recover three months' rent or three times the damages sustained by him, and the cost of suit, including reasonable attorney's fees.

Any agreement or understanding between a landlord and a tenant which purports to exempt the landlord from any liability imposed by this section shall be deemed to be against public policy and void.

Section 16. Leases or rental agreements restricting occupancy of children.

Any provision of a lease or other rental agreement relating to real property whereby a lessee or tenant enters into a covenant, agreement or contract, by the use of any words whatsoever, the effect of which is to terminate, or to provide that the lessor or landlord may terminate, such lease or agreement if the tenant has or shall have a child or children, who shall occupy the premises covered by such lease or agreement, shall be deemed to be against public policy and void.

Section 17. Occupancy constituting tenancy at will; termination.

For the purposes of this chapter, chapter one hundred and eleven and chapter two hundred and thirty-nine, occupancy of a dwelling unit within premises licensed as a rooming house or lodging house, except for fraternities, sororities and dormitories of educational institutions, for three consecutive months shall constitute a tenancy at will; provided, however, that if the rent for occupancy in such premises is payable either daily or weekly, seven days written notice to the occupant shall be sufficient to terminate the tenancy where the tenant is committing or permitting to exist a nuisance in or is causing substantial damage to the rental unit, or is creating substantial damage to the rental unit, or is creating a substantial interference with the comfort, safety, or enjoyment of the landlord or other occupants of the accommodation; and provided, further, that the notice shall specify the nuisance or interference. Occupancy of a dwelling unit within a rooming house or lodging house, except for fraternities, sororities and dormitories of educational institutions, for more than thirty consecutive days and less than three consecutive months, or within a fraternity, sorority or dormitory of an educational institution for any length of time, may only be terminated by seven days' notice in writing to the occupant by the operator of such dwelling unit.

Section 17A. Residential care and services; housing facility providers; eviction; hearing; jurisdiction.

(a) Section 18 of chapter 184, section 17 of this chapter and chapter 239 shall apply to a lawful housing occupant who is a client in a program of residential care and services licensed, funded or operated by the department of mental health and who: (1) pays the program for such residential care and services; (2) receives care and services from the program in a housing unit equipped with a kitchen and bathroom; and (3) occupies the unit either alone or with the occupant's family, as defined in the regulations of the department.

(b) Said section 18 of said chapter 184 and said section 17 of this chapter and said chapter 239 shall not apply to an occupant in a program of residential care and services which does not satisfy the conditions established in subsection (a) if, before eviction, the occupant received the procedural protections contained in subsection (c).

(c) (1) A provider of a program of residential care and services which does not satisfy the conditions established in subsection (a) shall post in each residence of the program a clearly visible notice which explains in plain and simple language the rights of occupants under this subsection.

(2) Any such provider who seeks the eviction of an occupant shall provide to the occupant and to the department written notice of the grounds of the proposed eviction, including reasons, relevant facts and the sources of those facts. The notice shall contain a reference to this section and shall advise the occupant that he has the right to a hearing, to be represented at such hearing by a lawyer or other person of his own choosing. At the request of the occupant, the provider shall afford the occupant, or his representative, reasonable access to review and copy his file before the hearing, including any document intended to be used against him at the hearing.

(3) Upon receipt of notice from the provider, the department shall immediately assign an impartial hearing officer to conduct a hearing on the propriety of the proposed eviction. The hearing officer shall select a hearing location convenient to the provider and occupant and shall conduct the hearing not less than 4 business days and not later than 14 business days after receipt of the proposed eviction notice, unless the

provider and occupant jointly request an alternate date. The provider and the occupant may be represented by an attorney or other person and shall be afforded the opportunity to present evidence, to examine adverse evidence and to examine and cross examine witnesses.

(4) The provider shall have the burden of proving, by a preponderance of evidence, the propriety of the proposed eviction, but all such evidence shall be within the scope of the reasons for eviction set forth in the notice required by paragraph (2). An eviction under this section shall be deemed proper if the occupant has substantially violated an essential provision of a written agreement containing the conditions of occupancy or if the occupant is likely, in spite of reasonable accommodation, to impair the emotional or physical well being of other occupants, program staff or neighbors.

(5) Within 10 days after the conclusion of the hearing, the hearing officer shall prepare a written decision containing findings of fact and conclusions of law based on the evidence received at the hearing and shall submit copies of the decision, together with a notice of appeal rights, to the occupant and provider. The decision may be appealed to the superior court pursuant to section 14 of chapter 30A.

(6) Before the receipt of a written decision involving a client in a program funded or operated by the department, the provider may request that the department provide additional staffing or other assistance to protect the emotional or physical well being of other occupants, program staff or neighbors. Upon receipt of such request, the department shall provide timely assistance as it deems reasonable and appropriate.

(7) Upon receipt of a hearing officer's decision confirming the propriety of a proposed eviction of a client of the department who would otherwise become homeless, the department shall take steps to assist the client to secure alternative housing in the least restrictive setting that is appropriate and available.

(d) Nothing in this section shall: (1) restrict a provider from initiating an eviction proceeding under chapter 239 if the department fails to conduct a timely hearing pursuant to paragraph (3) of subsection (c); (2) apply to any facility for the care and treatment of mentally ill or mentally retarded persons or to restrict the temporary removal of an occupant under section 12 of chapter 123; (3) apply to a continuing care facility as defined in paragraph (u) of section 1 of chapter 40D or a facility as provided in section 71 of chapter 111; (4) diminish the rights of a lawful occupant of an assisted living facility; or (5) diminish or alter any other occupant rights or privileges not specifically set forth in this section.

(e) The superior court, housing court and district court departments shall have jurisdiction to enforce this section and the department may be made a party to an action brought pursuant to this section.

Section 18. Reprisal for reporting violations of law or for tenant's union activity; damages and costs; notice of termination, presumption; waiver in leases or other rental agreements prohibited.

Any person or agent thereof who threatens to or takes reprisals against any tenant of residential premises for the tenant's act of, commencing, proceeding with, or obtaining relief in any judicial or administrative action the purpose of which action is to obtain damages under, or otherwise enforce, any federal, state or local law, regulation, by-law or ordinance, which has as its objective the regulation of residential premises; or exercising the tenant's rights pursuant to section one hundred and twenty-four D of chapter one hundred and sixty-four; or reporting to the board of health or, in the city of Boston to the commissioner of housing inspection or to any other board having as its objective the regulation of residential premises a violation or a suspected violation of any health or building code or of any other municipal by-law or ordinance, or state or federal law or regulation which has as its objective the regulation of residential premises; or reporting or complaining of such violation or suspected violation in writing to the landlord or to the agent of the landlord; or for organizing or joining a tenants' union or similar organization, or for making or expressing an intention to make, a payment of rent to an organization of unit owners pursuant to paragraph (c) of section six of chapter one hundred and eighty-three A shall be liable for damages which shall not be less than one month's rent or more than three month's rent, or the actual damages sustained by the tenant, whichever is greater, and the costs of the suit, including a reasonable attorney's fee.

The receipt of any notice of termination of tenancy, except for nonpayment of rent, or, of increase in rent, or, of any substantial alteration in the terms of tenancy within six months after the tenant has commenced, proceeded with, or obtained relief in such action, exercised such rights, made such report or complaint, or organized or joined such tenants' union or within six months after any other person has taken such action or actions on behalf of the tenant or in, or relating to, the building in which the tenant resides, shall create a rebuttable presumption that such notice or other action is a reprisal against the tenant for engaging in such activities. Such presumption shall be rebutted only by clear and convincing evidence that such person's action was not a reprisal against the tenant and that such person had sufficient independent justification for taking such action, and would have in fact taken such action, in the same manner and at the same time the action was taken, regardless of tenants engaging in, or the belief that tenants had engaged in, activities protected under this section.

Any waiver of this provision in any lease or other rental agreement shall be void and unenforceable.

Section 19. Notice to landlord of unsafe condition; tort actions for injuries resulting from uncorrected condition.

A landlord or lessor of any real estate except an owner-occupied two- or three-family dwelling shall, within a reasonable time following receipt of a written notice from a tenant forwarded by registered or certified mail of an unsafe condition, not caused by the tenant, his invitee, or any one occupying through or under the tenant, exercise reasonable care to correct the unsafe condition described in said notice except that such notice need not be given for unsafe conditions in that portion of the premises not under control of the tenant. The tenant or any person rightfully on said premises injured as a result of the failure to correct said unsafe condition within a reasonable time shall have a right of action in tort against the landlord or lessor for damages. Any waiver of this provision in any lease or other rental agreement shall be void and unenforceable. The notice requirement of this section shall be satisfied by a notice from a board of health or other code enforcement agency to a landlord or lessor of residential premises not exempted by the provisions of this section of a violation of the state sanitary code or other applicable by-laws, ordinances, rules or regulations.

Section 20. Attorneys' fees and expenses; residential lease provisions; implied covenant; waiver.

Whenever a lease of residential property shall provide that in any action or summary proceeding the landlord may recover attorneys' fees and expenses incurred as the result of the failure of the tenant to perform any covenant or agreement contained in such lease, or that amounts paid by the landlord therefor shall be paid by the tenant as additional rent, there shall be implied in such lease a covenant by the landlord to pay to the tenant the reasonable attorneys' fees and expenses incurred by the tenant as the result of the failure of the landlord to perform any covenant or agreement on its part to be performed under the lease or in the successful defense of any action or summary proceeding commenced by the landlord against the tenant arising out of the lease, and an agreement that such fees and expenses may be recovered as provided by law in an action commenced against the landlord or by way of counterclaim in any action or summary proceeding commenced by the landlord against the tenant. Any waiver of this section shall be void as against public policy.

Section 21. Disclosure of insurance information by lessor; violations; waiver.

The landlord or lessor of any residential or commercial property, upon the written request of any tenant or lawful occupant, of any code or other law enforcement official or of any official of the municipality in which the property is situated, shall disclose in writing within fifteen days of such request the name of the company insuring the property against loss or damage by fire and the amount of insurance provided by each such company and the name of any person who would receive payment for a loss covered by such insurance. Whoever violates the provisions of this section shall be punished by a fine of not more than five hundred dollars. A waiver of this section in any lease or other rental agreement shall be void and unenforceable.

Chapter 239. Summary Process for Possession of Land. Section 1. Persons entitled to summary process.

If a forcible entry into land or tenements has been made, if a peaceable entry has been made and the possession is unlawfully held by force, if the lessee of land or tenements or a person holding under him holds possession without right after the determination of a lease by its own limitation or by notice to quit or otherwise, or if a mortgage of land has been foreclosed by a sale under a power therein contained or otherwise, or if a person has acquired title to land or tenements by purchase, and the seller or any person holding under him refuses to surrender possession thereof to the buyer, or if a tax title has been foreclosed by decree of the land court, or if a purchaser, under a written agreement to purchase, is in possession of land or tenements beyond the date of the agreement without taking title to said land as called for by said agreement, the person entitled to the land or tenements may recover possession thereof under this chapter. A person in whose favor the land court has entered a decree for confirmation and registration of his title to land may in like manner recover possession thereof, except where the person in possession or any person under whom he claims has erected buildings or improvements on the land, and the land has been actually held and possessed by him or those under whom he claims for six years next before the date of said decree or was held at the date of said decree under a title which he had reason to believe good.

Section 1A. Land or tenements used for residential purposes; action by lessor under this chapter to recover possession; conditions and restrictions.

A lessor of land or tenements used for residential purposes may bring an action under this chapter to recover possession thereof before the determination of the lease by its own limitation, subject to the following conditions and restrictions. The tenancy of the premises at issue shall have been created for at least six months duration by a written lease in which a specific termination date is designated, a copy of which, signed by all parties, shall be annexed to the summons. No such action may be initiated before the latest date permitted by the lease for either party to notify the other of his intention to renew or extend the rental agreement, or in any case before thirty days before the designated termination date of the tenancy. The person bringing the action shall notify all defendants by registered mail that he has done so, which notification shall be mailed not later than twenty-four hours after the action is initiated. The person bringing the action shall demonstrate substantial grounds upon which the court could reasonably conclude that the defendant is likely to continue in possession of the premises at issue without right after the designated termination date, which grounds shall be set forth in the writ. No execution for possession may issue in any such action before the day next following the designated termination date of the tenancy. Any action brought pursuant to this section shall conform to and be governed by the provisions of this chapter in all other respects and no remedy or procedure otherwise available to any party, including any stay of execution which the court has discretion to allow, shall be denied solely because the action was brought pursuant to this section.

Section 2. Jurisdiction; venue; form of writ.

Such person may bring an action in the superior court in the county, or in the district court in the judicial district, in which the land lies, by a writ in the form of an original summons to the defendant to answer to the claim of the plaintiff that the defendant is in possession of the land or tenements in question, describing them, which he holds unlawfully against the right of the plaintiff, and, if rent and use and occupation is claimed, that the defendant owed rent and use and occupation in the amount stated; provided, however, subject to the approval of the supreme judicial court, the judge of the housing court of the city of Boston shall determine the form of said writ in said actions brought in his court. Failure to claim rent and use and occupation in said action shall not bar a subsequent action therefor.

Section 2A. Reprisal for reporting violations of law or for tenant's union activity; defense; presumption.

It shall be a defense to an action for summary process that such action or the preceding action of terminating the tenant's tenancy, was taken against the tenant for the tenant's act of commencing, proceeding with, or obtaining relief in any judicial or administrative action the purpose of which action was to obtain damages under or otherwise enforce, any federal, state or local law, regulation, by-law, or ordinance, which has as its objective the regulation of residential premises, or exercising rights pursuant to section one hundred and twenty-four D of chapter one hundred and sixty-four, or reporting a violation or suspected violation of law as provided in section eighteen of chapter one hundred and eighty-six, or organizing or joining a tenants' union or similar organization or making, or expressing an intention to make, a payment of rent to an organization of unit owners pursuant to paragraph (c) of section six of chapter one hundred and eighty-three A. The commencement of such action against a tenant, or the sending of a notice to quit upon which the summary process action is based, or the sending of a notice, or performing any act, the purpose of which is to materially alter the terms of the tenancy, within six months after the tenant has commenced, proceeded with or obtained relief in such action, exercised such rights, made such report, organized or joined such tenants' union, or made or expressed an intention to make a payment of rent to an organization of unit owners, or

within six months after any other person has taken such action or actions on behalf of the tenant or relating to the building in which such tenant resides, shall create a rebuttable presumption that such summary process action is a reprisal against the tenant for engaging in such activities or was taken in the belief that the tenant had engaged in such activities. Such presumption may be rebutted only by clear and convincing evidence that such action was not a reprisal against the tenant and that the plaintiff had sufficient independent justification for taking such action, and would have in fact taken such action, in the same manner and at the same time the action was taken, even if the tenant had not commenced any legal action, made such report or engaged in such activity.

Section 3. Judgment and execution; costs; appeal.

Except as hereinafter provided, if the court finds that the plaintiff is entitled to possession, he shall have judgment and execution for possession and costs, and, if rent is claimed as provided in section two and found due, the judgment and execution shall include the amount of the award. If the plaintiff becomes nonsuit or fails to prove his right to possession, the defendant shall have judgment and execution for costs.

At least forty-eight hours prior to serving or levying upon an execution issued on a judgment for the plaintiff for possession of land or tenements rented or leased for dwelling purposes, the officer serving or levying upon the execution shall give the defendant written notice that at a specified date and time he will serve or levy upon the execution and that at that time he will physically remove the defendant and his personal possessions from the premises if the defendant has not prior to that time vacated the premises voluntarily.

Said notice shall contain the signature, full name, full business address and business telephone number of the officer, and the name of the court and the docket number of the action, and shall be served in the same manner as the summary process summons and complaint.

No execution for possession of premises rented or leased for dwelling purposes shall be served or levied upon after five o'clock p.m. or before nine o'clock a.m., nor on a Saturday, Sunday, or legal holiday.

If the underlying money judgment in any summary process action for nonpayment of rent in premises rented or leased for dwelling purposes has been fully satisfied, together with any use and occupancy accruing since the date of judgment, the plaintiff shall be barred from levying on any execution for possession that has issued and shall return the execution to the court fully satisfied. If no execution has issued, the plaintiff shall notify the court of the satisfaction of judgment and no execution shall issue thereafter. If the underlying money judgment has been fully satisfied and use and occupancy fully paid, the defendant shall be considered a lawful tenant and may enforce this right through judicial process, including injunctions barring the issuance of or levying upon the execution and motions to supersede or recall the execution. Notwithstanding this paragraph, the plaintiff shall not be required to accept full satisfaction of the money judgment. Any refusal by the plaintiff to accept full satisfaction of the money judgment under this paragraph shall not be a bar to the enforcement of said judgment in any lawful manner.

In case of appeal from the district court on either or both issues involved or on any counterclaim, the appeal shall be to the superior court under section five of this chapter and section ninety-seven of chapter two hundred and thirty-one.

Section 4. Storage of property removed; liens and enforcement.

If an officer, serving an execution issued on a judgment for the plaintiff for possession of land or tenements, removes personal property, belonging to a person other than the plaintiff, from the land or tenements and places it upon the sidewalk, street or way on which the land or tenements abut, he may forthwith, and before the expiration of the time limited in any ordinance or by-law for the removal of obstructions in the street, remove such property and cause it to be stored for the benefit of the owners thereof. Whoever accepts the same on storage from such officer shall have a lien thereon for reasonable storage fees and for reasonable expenses of removing it to the place of storage, but such lien shall not be enforced by sale of the property until it has been kept on storage for at least six months. If the owner of such property is present and claims it when it is so removed from the land or tenements, the officer shall not remove and store it, and his act of placing it upon the sidewalk or street shall be deemed the act of the owner, who alone shall be held to answer therefor.

Section 5. Appeal; bond; actions thereon; waiver; appeal of waiver or periodic payments.

If either party appeals from a judgment of the superior court, a housing court, or a district court in an action under this chapter, including a judgment on a counterclaim, such party shall file a notice of appeal with said court within ten days after the entry of said judgment. No execution upon a judgment rendered pursuant to section three shall issue until the expiration of ten days after the entry of said judgment.

In an appeal of a judgment of a district court, other than an appeal governed by the provisions of the next paragraph, the appellant shall, before any appeal under this section is allowed, file in the district court a bond payable to the appellee in the penal sum of one hundred dollars, with such surety or sureties as approved by the court, or secured by cash or its equivalent deposited with the clerk, conditioned to satisfy any judgment for costs which may be entered against such appellant in the superior court within thirty days after the entry thereof.

Except as provided in section six, the defendant shall, before any appeal under this section is allowed from a judgment of the superior court, a housing court, or a district court, rendered for the plaintiff for the possession of the land or tenements demanded in a case in which the plaintiff continues at the time of establishment of bond to seek to recover possession, give bond in such sum as the court orders, payable to the plaintiff, with sufficient surety or sureties approved by the court, or secured by cash or its equivalent deposited with the clerk, in a reasonable amount to be fixed by the court. In an appeal from a judgment of a district court such bond shall be conditioned to enter the action in the superior court at the return day next after the appeal is taken. In an appeal from a judgment of the superior court or a housing court such bond filed shall be conditioned to enter the action in the appeals court. Appeals from judgments of the superior court or a housing court shall otherwise be governed by the Massachusetts Rules of Appellate Procedure. Such bond shall also be conditioned to pay to the plaintiff, if final judgment is in plaintiff's favor, all rent accrued at the date of the bond, all intervening rent, and all damage and loss which the plaintiff may sustain by the withholding of possession of the land or tenements demanded and by any injury done thereto during such withholding, with all costs, until delivery of possession thereof to such plaintiff.

In appeals from a district court the deposit shall be transmitted by the clerk of the district court with the papers to the clerk of the superior court, who shall thereupon deliver a receipt therefor to such clerk of the district court, but in such appeals from a judgment of the superior court or a housing court the deposit shall not be transmitted to the appeals court unless specifically requested by said appeals court. The superior court or a housing court may give directions as to the manner of keeping such deposit. Upon final judgment for the plaintiff, all money then due to him may be recovered in an action on the bond provided for in the third paragraph of this section.

A party may make a motion to waive the appeal bond provided for in this section if he is indigent as provided in section twenty-seven A of chapter two hundred and sixty-one. Such motion shall, together with a notice of appeal and any supporting affidavits, be filed within the time limits set forth in this section. The court shall waive the requirement of such bond or security if it is satisfied that the person requesting the waiver has any defense which is not frivolous and that he is indigent as provided in section twenty-seven A of chapter two hundred and sixty-one. The court shall require any person for whom the bond or security provided for in the third paragraph has been waived to pay in installments as the same becomes due, pending appeal, all or any portion of any rent which shall become due after the date of such waiver. No court shall require any such person to make any other payments or deposits. The court shall forthwith make a decision on the motion. If such motion is made, no execution shall issue until the expiration of six days from the court's decision on the motion or until the expiration of the time specified in this section for the taking of appeals, whichever is later.

Any party aggrieved by the denial of a motion to waive the bond or who wishes to contest the amount of periodic payments required by the court may seek review of such decision as hereinafter provided. If such motion was made in the superior court or a housing court, the request for review shall be to the single justice of the appeals court at the next sitting thereof. If such motion was made in any district or municipal court, the request for review shall be to the superior court then sitting in the same county or, if not so sitting, to the superior court sitting in the nearest county or in Suffolk county. The court receiving the request shall review the findings, the amount of bond or deposit, if any, and the amount of periodic payment required, if any, as if it were initially deciding the matter, and said court may withdraw or amend any finding or reduce or rescind any amount of bond, deposit or periodic payment when in its judgment the facts so warrant.

Any party to the action may file a request for such review with the clerk of the court originally hearing the request to waive bond within the time period provided in this section for filing notice of appeal, or within six days after receiving notice of the decision of the court on the motion to waive bond, whichever is the later. Said court shall then forward the motion, the court's findings and any other documents relevant to the appeal to the clerk of the court reviewing such decision who, upon receipt thereof, shall schedule a speedy hearing thereon and send notice thereof to the parties. Any request for review filed pursuant to this section shall be heard upon statements of counsel, memoranda and affidavits submitted by the parties. Further testimony shall be taken if the reviewing court shall find that the taking of further testimony would aid the disposition of the review.

Upon the rendering of a decision on review, the reviewing court shall give notice of the decision to the parties and the defendant shall comply with the requirements of such decision within five days after receiving notice thereof. If the defendant fails to file with the clerk of the court rendering the judgment, the amount of bond, deposit or periodic payment required by the decision of the reviewing court within five days from receipt of notice of said decision, the appeal from the judgment shall be dismissed. Where a defendant seeks review pursuant to this section, no execution shall issue until the expiration of five days from the date defendant has received notice of the decision of the reviewing court.

Section 6. Condition of bond in action for possession after foreclosure of mortgage; after purchase.

If the action is for the possession of land after foreclosure of a mortgage thereon, the condition of the bond shall be for the entry of the action and payment to the plaintiff, if final judgment is in his favor, of all costs and of a reasonable amount as rent of the land from the day when the mortgage was foreclosed until possession of the land is obtained by the plaintiff. If the action is for possession of land after purchase, the condition of the bond shall be for the entry of the action and payment to the plaintiff, if final judgment is in his favor, of all costs and of a reasonable amount as rent of the land from the day that the purchaser obtained title to the premises until the delivery of possession thereof to him, together with all damage and loss which he may sustain by withholding of possession of the land or tenement demanded, and by any injury done thereto during such withholding with all costs. Upon final judgment for the plaintiff, all money then due to him may be recovered in an action on the bond.

Section 6A. Condition of bond after foreclosure of tax title.

If the action is for the possession of land after foreclosure of a tax title thereon, the condition of the bond shall be for the entry of the action and payment to the plaintiff, if final judgment is in his favor, of all costs and of a reasonable amount as rent of the land from the day when the tax title was foreclosed until possession of the land is obtained by the plaintiff, and of all damage and loss which he may sustain by the withholding of possession of the land or tenements demanded and by any injury done thereto during such withholding.

Section 7. Judgments; effect.

The judgment in an action under this chapter shall not be a bar to any action thereafter brought by either party to recover the land or tenements in question, or to recover damages for any trespass thereon; but the amount recovered for rent under section five shall be deducted in any assessment of damages in such subsequent action by the original plaintiff.

Section 8. Three years quiet possession; effect.

There shall be no recovery under this chapter of any land or tenements of which the defendant, his ancestors or those under whom he holds the land or tenements have been in quiet possession for three years next before the commencement of the action unless the defendant's estate therein is ended.

Section 8A. Rent withholding; grounds; amount claimed; presumptions and burden of proof; procedures.

In any action under this chapter to recover possession of any premises rented or leased for dwelling purposes, brought pursuant to a notice to quit for nonpayment of rent, or where the tenancy has been terminated without fault of the tenant or occupant, the tenant or occupant shall be entitled to raise, by defense or counterclaim, any claim against the plaintiff relating to or arising out of such property, rental, tenancy, or occupancy for breach of warranty, for a breach of any material provision of the rental agreement, or for a violation of any other law. The amounts which the tenant or occupant may claim hereunder shall include, but shall not be limited to, the difference between the agreed upon rent and the fair value of the use and occupation of the premises, and any amounts reasonably spent by the tenant or occupant pursuant to section one hundred and twenty-seven L of chapter one hundred and eleven and such other damages as may be authorized by any law having as its objective the regulation of residential premises.

Whenever any counterclaim or claim of defense under this section is based on any allegation concerning the condition of the premises or the services or equipment provided therein, the tenant or occupant shall not be entitled to relief under this section unless: (1) the owner or his agents, servants, or employees, or the person to whom the tenant or occupant customarily paid his rent knew of such conditions before the tenant or occupant was in arrears in his rent; (2) the plaintiff does not show that such conditions were caused by the tenant or occupant or any other person acting under his control; except that the defendant shall have the burden of proving that any violation appearing solely within that portion of the premises under his control and not by its nature reasonably attributable to any action or failure to act of the plaintiff was not so caused; (3) the premises are not situated in a hotel or motel, nor in a lodging house or rooming house wherein the occupant has maintained such occupancy for less than three consecutive months; and (4) the plaintiff does not show that the conditions complained of cannot be remedied without the premises being vacated; provided, however, that nothing in this clause shall be construed to deprive the tenant or occupant of relief under this section when the premises are temporarily vacated for purposes of removal or covering of paint, plaster, soil or other accessible materials containing dangerous levels of lead pursuant to section one hundred and ninety-seven of chapter one hundred and eleven.

Proof that the premises are in violation of the standard of fitness for human habitation established under the state sanitary code, the state building code, or any other ordinance, by-law, rule or regulation establishing such standards and that such conditions may endanger or materially impair the health, safety or well-being of a person occupying the premises shall create a presumption that conditions existed in the premises entitling the tenant or occupant to a counterclaim or defense under this section. Proof of written notice to the owner or his agents, servants, or employees, or to the person to whom the tenant or occupant customarily paid his rent, of an inspection of the premises, issued by the board of health, or in the city of Boston by the commissioner of housing inspection, or by any other agency having like powers of inspection relative to the condition of residential premises, shall create a presumption that on the date such notice was received, such person knew of the conditions revealed by such inspection and mentioned in such notice. A copy of an inspection

report issued by any such agency, certified under the penalties of perjury by the official who inspected the premises, shall be admissible in evidence and shall be prima facie evidence of the facts stated therein.

There shall be no recovery of possession pursuant to this chapter pending final disposition of the plaintiff's action if the court finds that the requirements of the second paragraph have been met. The court after hearing the case may require the tenant or occupant claiming under this section to pay to the clerk of the court the fair value of the use and occupation of the premises less the amount awarded the tenant or occupant for any claim under this section, or to make a deposit with the clerk of such amount or such installments thereof from time to time as the court may direct, for the occupation of the premises. In determining said fair value, the court shall consider any evidence relative to the effect of any conditions claimed upon the use and occupation of residential premises. Such funds may be expended for the repair of the premises by such persons as the court after a hearing may direct, including if appropriate a receiver appointed as provided in section one hundred and twenty-seven H of chapter one hundred and eleven. When all of the conditions found by the court have been corrected, the court shall direct that the balance of funds, if any, remaining with the clerk be paid to the landlord. Any tenant or occupant intending to invoke the provisions of this section may, after commencement of an action under this chapter by the landlord, voluntarily deposit with the clerk any amount for rent or for use and occupation which may be in dispute, and such payments shall be held by the clerk subject to the provisions of this paragraph.

There shall be no recovery of possession under this chapter if the amount found by the court to be due the landlord equals or is less than the amount found to be due the tenant or occupant by reason of any counterclaim or defense under this section. If the amount found to be due the landlord exceeds the amount found to be due the tenant or occupant, there shall be no recovery of possession if the tenant or occupant, within one week after having received written notice from the court of the balance due, pays to the clerk the balance due the landlord, together with interest and costs of suit, less any credit due the tenant or occupant for funds already paid by him to the clerk under this section. In such event, no judgment shall enter until after the expiration of the time for such payment and the tenant has failed to make such payment. Any such payment received by the clerk shall be held by him subject to the provisions of the preceding paragraph.

Any provision of any rental agreement purporting to waive the provisions of this section shall be deemed to be against public policy and void. The provisions of section two A and of section eighteen of chapter one hundred and eighty-six shall apply to any tenant or occupant who invokes the provisions of this section.

Section 9. Stay of proceedings.

In an action of summary process to recover possession of premises occupied for dwelling purposes, other than a room in a hotel, or a dwelling unit in a lodging house or rooming house wherein the occupant has maintained such occupancy for less than three consecutive months, where a tenancy has been terminated without fault of the tenant, either by operation of law or by act of the landlord, except by a notice to quit for nonpayment of rent as provided in section twelve of chapter one hundred and eighty-six, a stay or stays of judgment and execution may be granted, as hereinafter provided, for a period not exceeding six months or for periods not exceeding six months in the aggregate, or, for a period not exceeding twelve months or for periods not exceeding twelve months in the aggregate in the case of premises occupied by a handicapped person or an individual sixty years of age or older, as the court may deem just and reasonable, upon application of the tenant or the surviving spouse, parent or child of a deceased tenant if such spouse, parent or child occupied said premises for dwelling purposes at the time when said tenancy was terminated and such occupancy was not in violation of the terms of the tenancy; provided, however, that a stay or stays of judgment and execution in the case of premises occupied by an employee of a farmer conditioned upon his employment by such farmer and which employment has been legally terminated shall not be granted for a period exceeding two months or for periods exceeding two months in the aggregate. For the purpose of this section, the words "handicapped person" shall mean a person who:

(a) has a physical or mental impairment which substantially limits such person's ability to care for himself, perform manual tasks, walk, see, hear, speak, breathe, learn or work; or

(b) has a physical or mental impairment which significantly limits the housing appropriate for such person or which significantly limits such person's ability to seek new housing; or

(c) would be eligible for housing for handicapped persons under the provisions of chapter one hundred and twenty-one B.

Section 10. Stay of proceedings; hearings.

Upon application for such a stay of proceedings, the court shall hear the parties, and if upon the hearing it appears that the premises of which possession is sought to be recovered are used for dwelling purposes; that the applicant cannot secure suitable premises for himself and his family elsewhere within the city or town in a neighborhood similar to that in which the premises occupied by him are situated; that he has used due and reasonable effort to secure such other premises; that his application is made in good faith and that he will abide by and comply with such terms and provisions as the court may prescribe; or that by reason of other facts such action will be warranted, the court may grant a stay as provided in the preceding section, on condition that the terms upon which such stay is granted be complied with.

In any action to recover possession of premises occupied for dwelling purposes brought pursuant to this chapter in which a stay or stays of execution have been granted, by the court or by agreement of the parties, or in any such action where there is an agreement for judgment that grants the tenant a right to reinstate the tenancy, no execution shall issue prior to the expiration of the period of such stay or stays or such reinstatement period unless the plaintiff shall first bring a motion for the issuance of the execution and the court after a hearing shall determine that the tenant or occupant is in substantial violation of a material term or condition of the stay or a material term of the agreement for judgment.

Section 11. Stay of proceedings; deposit of applicant.

Such stay shall be granted and continue effective only upon the condition that the applicant shall make a deposit in court of the entire amount, or such installments thereof from time to time, as the court may direct, for the occupation of the premises for the period of the stay, at the rate to which he was liable as rent for the month immediately prior to the expiration of his term or tenancy plus such additional amount, if any, as the court may determine to be reasonable. The deposit shall also include all rent unpaid prior to the period of the stay. The amount of the deposit shall be determined by the court at the hearing upon the application for the stay, and such determination shall be final and conclusive in respect only to the amount of the deposit, and the amount thereof shall be paid into court, in such manner and in such installments, if any, as the court may direct. A separate account shall be kept of the amount to the credit of each proceeding, and all such payments shall be deposited by the clerk of the court, and paid over to the landlord or his duly authorized agent, in accordance with the terms of the stay or the further order of the court.

Section 12. Stay of proceedings; validity of waiver in lease.

Any provision of a lease whereby a lessee or tenant waives the benefits of any provision of sections nine to thirteen, inclusive, shall be deemed to be against public policy and void.

Section 13. Stay of proceedings; costs.

Costs recoverable under section three shall, in actions to which sections nine to eleven, inclusive, apply, include only legal costs covering actual disbursements and shall not include fictitious costs, so-called.

CODE OF MASSACHUSETTS REGULATIONS
Title 940: Office of the Attorney General
Chapter 10.00. Manufactured Housing Community Regulations
Section 10.07. Sale of Manufactured Home by Homeowner.

(1) General.

(a) An operator shall not limit a manufactured homeowners right to sell or encumber a manufactured home, or require a manufactured homeowner to remove a home from the manufactured community because of the sale of the home.

(b) An operator shall not condition its approval of residency of a purchaser on payment by the selling homeowner of monies lawfully withheld under M.G.L. c. 239, § 8A. An operator shall not charge or collect from a succeeding manufactured homeowner or resident any rent, taxes or other charges relating to a prior owner's ownership of the home or occupancy of the manufactured home site.

(c) An operator shall not make any false, deceptive, or misleading representation to discourage a potential buyer from purchasing a home from a homeowner in the community. Where the operator discloses that a notice of discontinuance has been issued to community residents, the operator must also disclose the existence of and nature of any legal challenge to the issuance of the notice, and any related judicial rulings that have attacked the validity of the notice.

(d) A licensee may have a lien upon a manufactured home as provided in M.G.L. c. 140, § 32J, upon a manufactured home and the contents thereof, as provided in M.G.L. c. 255, § 25A, or if otherwise authorized by a court of law, but it shall be an unfair or deceptive practice to fail to disclose to a prospective purchaser of a manufactured home the existence of a lien placed by or on behalf of an operator on such home.

(e) A licensee may require a homeowner to provide notice of an intended sale at least 30 days prior to its execution.

(2) Residency Application by Purchaser. Upon the sale or proposed sale of a manufactured home by the homeowner, the operator shall consent to entrance by the purchaser and members of the purchasers household if the purchaser meets the currently enforceable rules of the manufactured housing community and provides reasonable evidence of financial ability to pay the rent and other charges associated with the tenancy in question. An operator shall not reject the application or prohibit the sale because the applicant owns another home in the community or leases another site in the community. Any application for residency shall be deemed approved if the operator fails, within ten days of receipt of the application, to notify the applicant of its rejection of the application and the reasons for the rejection. If such application is not timely rejected, then the purchaser shall have the right to assume the obligations thereafter arising under any continuing occupancy agreement of a current resident then in effect or, if such occupancy agreement has expired, to enter into a new occupancy agreement on terms satisfactory to the operator and purchaser and not inconsistent with 940 CMR. 10.00.

(3) Broker. No operator or manufactured home dealer shall:

(a) require a resident to designate the operator, the manufactured home dealer, or any designee thereof, as broker or agent for any sale, sublease or lease assignment; or

(b) restrict the manufactured homeowner in undertaking such a transaction directly or through a broker or agent of the homeowner's choosing.

(4) Fees or Commissions. No operator, manufactured home dealer, or agent shall impose any fee (which is to be passed, directly or indirectly, to the operator) as a condition to the sale, lease or other transaction involving a manufactured home unless such person has entered into a separate written contract for, and rendered, brokerage services in connection with such transaction and the fee or change is reasonable in relation to the services provided. No commission or fee paid to an operator for the sale of a manufactured home shall exceed ten percent of the sale price.

(5) "For Sale" Signs. An operator shall not prohibit a homeowner from placing on their manufactured home or manufactured home site commercially reasonable "for sale" or "for lease" signs. An operator may not require that any such signs display the community logo or contain information directing an interested buyer to the community sales or management office, except pursuant to any exclusive brokerage contract the homeowner enters into with the operator for the sale of the home.

(6) Condition of Home on Sale. An operator shall not reject the application for residency of a prospective purchaser of a tenant's home:

(a) because of the age of the home; and

(b) because the home, if built before June 15, 1976, does not comply with federal standards for construction of manufactured housing that became effective on that date and are administered by the U.S. Department of Housing and Urban Development; or

(c) because the external condition of the home or site does not comply with community rules, unless before the home was offered for sale the operator specified in writing the area(s) of noncompliance with community rules and gave the homeowner a reasonable opportunity to bring the home into compliance and the homeowner failed to do so.

(7) Operator's Right of First Refusal. A right of first refusal granted to an operator or manufactured home dealer or designee thereof shall be enforceable only if:

(a) it is based on the full amount of the bona fide third-party offer;

(b) the operator must accept or reject the offer within 15 days;

(c) the sale will take place on the terms set forth in the third-party offer;

(d) if the operator fails to timely accept the offer and the third-party offer is not consummated, the selling homeowner shall not be required to submit a subsequent third-party offer made within one year and unless a price is materially reduced; and

(e) the right of first refusal shall not apply to any transfer to members of the homeowner's family, including, but not limited to, step-relatives and domestic partners.

APPENDIX B:
HIGHLIGHTS OF THE
STATE SANITARY CODE

Highlights of Chapter II of the Massachusetts Sanitary Code

Published by
William Francis Galvin
Secretary of the Commonwealth
Citizen Information Service
One Ashburton Place, Room 1611
Boston, Massachusetts 02108

Telephone: 617-727-7030
Toll-free: 800-392-6090 (in MA only)
Fax: 617-742-4528
Email: cis@sec.state.ma.us

The Massachusetts Department of Public Health establishes regulations detailing the standards that must be maintained by the occupants and owners of housing. These regulations protect the health, safety and well-being of Massachusetts citizens and are found in Chapter II of the Sanitary Code (105 Mass. Code. Reg. 410.000) entitled "Minimum Standards of Fitness for Human Habitation." The standards apply to every owner-occupied or rented dwelling, dwelling unit, mobile dwelling unit, or rooming house unit in Massachusetts that is used for living, sleeping, cooking and eating. Dwelling unit shall also mean a condominium unit. These regulations have the force of law. Local boards of health have the primary responsibility for their enforcement. This publication summarizes those regulations in Chapter II that pertain to essential living needs and describe enforcement procedures. Preceding each summary is a citation to the regulation number that is used in the Sanitary Code. For complete information, review Chapter II of the Sanitary Code and check with your local board of health.

Summary of Standards

410.180: Potable Water

The owner shall provide, for the occupant of every dwelling, dwelling unit, and rooming unit, a supply of water sufficient in quantity and pressure to meet the ordinary needs of the occupant, connected with the public water supply system, or with any other source that the board of health has determined does not endanger the health of any potential user. (See 105 CMR 410.350 through 410.352). Examination of the water system. shall. include an examination of the plumbing system and its actual performance. If possible, such examination shall occur at the times and under such conditions as the occupant has identified the system as being insufficient.

410.190: Hot Water

The owner shall provide and maintain in good operating condition the facilities capable of heating water. The owner shall also provide the hot water for use at a temperature of not less than 110°F (43°C) and in a quantity and pressure sufficient to satisfy the ordinary use of all plumbing fixtures which normally need hot water for their proper use and function, unless and to the extent the occupant is required to provide fuel for the operation of the facilities under a written letting agreement. The hot water shall not exceed 130°F (54°C). Inspection of the hot water system shall include an examination of the hot water system and its actual performance. If possible, such examination shall occur at the times and under such conditions as the occupant has identified the system to be insufficient.

410.200: Heating Facilities Required

(A) The owner shall provide and maintain in good operating condition the facilities for heating every habitable room and every room containing a toilet, shower or bathtub to such temperature as required under 105 CMR 410.201.(B) Portable space heaters, parlor heaters, cabinet heaters, room heaters and any similar heaters having a barometric fed fuel control and its fuel supply tank located less than 42 inches from the enter of the burner as well as the type of heating appliance adapted for burning kerosene, range oil or number one fuel oil and any portable wick type space heaters shall not be used and shall not meet the requirements of 105 CMR 410.200. (See M.G.L. c. 148, §§ 5A and 25B.)

410.201: Temperature Requirements

The owner shall provide heat in every habitable room and every room containing a toilet, shower, or bathtub to at least 68 °F 20 °C between 7:00 A.M. and 11:00 P.M. and at least 64 °F (17° C) between 11:01 P.M. and 6:59 A.M. every day other than during the period from June 15th to September 15th, both inclusive; in each year except and to the extent the occupant is required to provide the fuel under a written letting agreement. The temperature shall at no time exceed 78°F (25° C) during the beating season. The temperature may be read and the requirement shall be met at a height of five feet above floor level on a wall any point more than five feet from the exterior wall. The number of days per year during which heat must be provided in accordance 105 CMR 410.000 tray be increased or decreased through a variance granted in accordance with the provisions of 105 CMR 410.840 notwithstanding the prohibitions of the first clause of the first sentence of 105 CMR 410.840(A).

410.202: Venting

Space heaters and water heaters, except electrical ones, shall be properly vented to a chimney or vent leading to the outdoors.

410.250: Habitable Rooms other than Kitchen-Natural Light and Electrical Outlets

The owner shall provide for each habitable room other than a kitchen: (A) transparent or translucent glass which admits light from the outdoors and which is equal in area to no less than 8% of the entire floor area of that room.(B) two separate wall-type convenience outlets or one such outlet and one electric light fixture. The outlets shall be placed in practical locations and shall insofar as practicable, be on different walls and at least ten feet apart. (See 105 CMR 410.351.)

410.251: Kitchen Lighting and Electrical Outlets

The owner shall provide for each kitchen: (A) one electric light fixture; (B) two wall-type convenience outlets located in convenient locations; and (C) For each kitchen over 70 square feet, transparent or translucent glass which admits light from the outdoors and which is equal in area to no less than 8% of the entire floor area of that kitchen.

410.252: Bathroom Lighting and Electrical Outlets

The owner shall provide in each room containing a toilet, bathtub, or shower one electric light fixture. (See 105 CMR 410.150(A)(1) and 410.150(B).)

410.253: Light Fixtures Other than in Habitable Rooms or Kitchens

(A) The owner shall provide and so locate electric light switches and fixtures in good working order so that illumination may be provided for the safe and reasonable use of every laundry, pantry, foyer, hallway, stairway, closet, storage place, cellar, porch, exterior stairway and passageway. (B) The owner shall provide working incandescent light bulbs or fluorescent tubes in all required light fixtures in all common areas of any dwelling.

410.254: Light In Passageways, Hallways, and Stairways

(A) Except as allowed in 105 CMR 410.254(B), the owner shall provide light 24 hours per day so that illumination alone or in conjunction with natural lighting shall be at least one foot candle as measured at floor level, in every part of all interior passage ways, hallways, foyers and stairways used or intended for use by the occupants of more than one dwelling unit or rooming unit: (B) In a dwelling containing three or fewer dwelling units, the light fixtures used to illuminate a common hallway, passage way, foyer and/or stairway may be wired to the electric service serving an adjacent dwelling unit provided that if the occupant of such dwelling unit is responsible for paying for the electric service to such dwelling unit: (1) a written agreement shall state that the occupant is responsible for paying for light in the common hallway, passage way, foyer and/or stairway, and (2) the owner shall notify the occupants of the other dwelling units.

410.300: Sanitary Drainage System Required

The owner shall provide, for each dwelling, a sanitary drainage system connected to the public sewerage system, provided, that if, because of distance or ground conditions, connection to a public sewerage system is not practicable, the owner shall provide, and shall maintain in a sanitary condition, a means of sewage disposal which is in compliance with 310 CMR 15.00: Subsurface Disposal of Sanitary Sewage (Title V). (See 105 CMR 410.840.)

410.350: Plumbing Connections

(A) Every required kitchen sink, wash basin and shower or bathtub shall be connected to the hot and cold water lines of the water distribution system (See 105 CMR 410.180) and to a sanitary drainage system (See 105 CMR 410.300) in accordance with accepted plumbing standards. (B) Every provided toilet shall be connected to the water distribution system (See 105 CMR 410.180) and to a sanitary drainage system (See 105 CMR 410.300) in accordance with accepted plumbing standards.

410.351: Owners Installation and Maintenance Responsibilities

The owner shall install in accordance with accepted plumbing, gas fitting and electrical wiring standards, and shall maintain free from leaks, obstructions or other defects, the following: (A) all facilities and equipment which the owner is or may be required to provide including, but not limited to, all sinks, washbasins, bathtubs, showers, toilets, water heating facilities, gas pipes, heating equipment water pipes, owner installed stoves and ovens, catch basins, drains, vents and other similar supplied fixtures; the connections to water, sewer and gas lines; the subsurface sewage disposal system, if any, all electrical fixtures, outlets and wiring, and all heating and ventilating equipment and appurtenances thereto; and (B) all owner-installed optional equipment, including but not limited to, refrigerators, dishwashers, clothes washing machines and dryers, and garbage grinders.

410.352: Occupant's Installation and Maintenance Responsibilities

(A) The occupant shall install in accordance with accepted plumbing, heating, gas fitting, and electrical wiring standards, and shall maintain free from leaks, obstructions and other defects, all occupant owned and installed equipment such as, but not limited to, refrigerators, clothes washing machines and dryers, dishwashers, stoves, garbage grinders and electrical fixtures. (B) Every occupant of a dwelling unit shall keep all toilets, washbasins, sinks, showers, bathtubs, stoves, refrigerators and dishwashers in a clean and sanitary condition and exercise reasonable care in the proper use and operation thereof.

410.353: Asbestos Material

Every owner shall maintain all asbestos material in good repair, and free from any defects including, but not limited to, holes, cracks, tears or any looseness which may allow the release of asbestos dust, or any powdered, crumbled or pulverized asbestos material. Every owner shall correct any violation of 105 CMR 410.353 in accordance with the regulations of the Department of Environmental Protection appearing at 310 CMR 7.00 and in accordance with the regulations of the Department of Labor and Workforce Development appearing at 453 CMR 6.00 and with any other applicable statutes and regulations.

410.354: Metering of Electricity and Gas

(A) The owner shall provide the electricity and gas used in each dwelling unit unless (1) Such gas or electricity is metered through a meter which serves only the dwelling unit or other area under the exclusive use of an occupant of that dwelling unit, except as allowed by 105 CMR 410.254(B); and (2) A written letting agreement provides for payment by the occupant. (B) If the owner is required, by 105 CMR 410.000 or by a written letting agreement consistent with 105 CMR 410.000, to pay for the electricity or gas used in a dwelling unit, then such electricity or gas may be metered through meters which serve more than one dwelling unit.(C) If the owner is not required to pay for the electricity or gas used in a dwelling unit, then the owner shall install and maintain wiring and piping so that any such electricity or gas used in the dwelling unit is metered through meters which serve only such dwelling unit, except as allowed by 105 CMR 410.254(B).

410.355: Provision of Oil

The owner shall provide the oil used for heating and/or hot water in each dwelling unit unless such oil is provided through a separate oil tank which serves only that dwelling unit, provided however, that 105 CMR 410.000 shall only apply to tenancies created or renewed after July 1, 1994.

410.400: Minimum Square Footage

(A) Every dwelling unit shall contain at least 150 square feet of floor space for its first occupant, and at least 100 square feet of floor space for each additional occupant, the floor space to be calculated on the basis of total habitable room area. (B) In a dwelling unit, every room occupied for sleeping purposes by one occupant shall contain at least 70 square feet of floor space; every room occupied for sleeping purposes by more than one occupant shall contain at least 50 square feet of floor space for each occupant. (C) In a rooming unit, every room occupied for sleeping purposes by one occupant shall contain at least 80 square feet of floor space; every room occupied for sleeping purposes by more than one occupant shall contain at least 60 square feet for each occupant.

410.401: Ceiling Height

(A) No room shall be considered habitable if more than 3/4 of its floor area has a floor-to-ceiling height of less than seven feet. (B) In computing total floor area for the purpose of determining maximum permissible occupancy, that part of the floor area where the ceiling height is less than five feet shall not be considered.

410.402: Grade Level

No room or area in a dwelling may be used for habitation if more than 1/2 of its floor-to-ceiling height is below the average grade of the adjoining ground and is subject to chronic dampness.

410.430: Temporary Housing Allowed Only with Board of Health Permission

No temporary housing may be used except with the written permission of the board of health.

410.431: Any Exceptions to Minimum Standards Must Be Specified

All temporary housing shall be subject to the requirements of these minimum standards, except as the board of health may provide in its written permission. (See 105 CMR 410.840.)

410.450: Means of Egress

Every dwelling unit, and rooming unit shall have as many means of exit as will allow for the safe passage of all people in accordance with 780 CMR 104.0, 105.1, and 805.0 of the Massachusetts State Building Code.

410.451: Egress Obstructions

No person shall obstruct any exit or passageway. The owner is responsible for maintaining free from obstruction every exit used or intended for use by occupants of more than one dwelling unit or rooming unit. The occupant shall be responsible for maintaining free from obstruction all means of exit leading from his unit and not common to the exit of any other unit.

410.452: Safe Condition

The owner shall maintain all means of egress at all times in a safe, operable condition and shall keep all exterior stairways, fire escapes, egress balconies and bridges free of snow and ice, provided, however, in those instances where a dwelling has an independent means of egress, not shared with other occupants, and a written letting agreement so states, the occupant is responsible for maintaining free of snow and ice, the means of egress under his or her exclusive use and control. All corrodible structural parts thereof shall be kept painted or otherwise protected against rust and corrosion. All wood structural members shall be treated to prevent rotting and decay. Where these structural elements tie directly into the building structural system, all joints shall be sealed to prevent water from damaging or corroding the structural elements.

410.480: Locks

The owner shall provide. install and maintain locks so that:(A) Every dwelling unit shall be capable of being secured against unlawful entry. (B) Every door of a dwelling unit shall be capable of being secured from unlawful entry. (C) The main entry door of a dwelling containing more than three dwelling units shall be so designed or equipped so as to close and lock automatically with a lock, including a lock with an electrically-operated striker mechanism, a self-closing door and associated equipment. Every door of the main common entryway and every exterior door into said dwelling, other than the door of such main common entryway which is equipped as provided in the preceding sentence shall be equipped with an operating lock. (M.G.L. c. 143, § 3R.) (D) Every entry door of a dwelling unit or rooming unit shall be capable of being secured from unlawful entry. (E) Every openable exterior window shall be capable of being secured. (F) Locking devices shall comply with the requirements of 780 CMR 1017.4.1 to avoid entrapment in the building.

410.481: Posting of Name of Owner

An owner of a dwelling which is rented for residential use, who does not reside therein and who does not employ a manager or agent for such dwelling who resides therein, shall post and maintain or cause to be posted and maintained on such dwelling adjacent to the mailboxes for such dwelling or elsewhere in the interior of such dwelling in a location visible to the residents a notice constructed or durable material, not less than 20 square inches in size, bearing his name, address and telephone number. If the owner is a realty trust or partnership, the name, address and telephone number of the managing trustee or partner shall be posted. If the owner is a corporation, the name, address and telephone number of the president of the corporation shall be posted. Where the owner employs a manager or agent who does not reside in such dwelling, such manager or agent's name, address and telephone number shall also be included in the notice. (See M.G.L. c. 143, § 3S.)

410.482: Smoke Detectors

The owner of every dwelling that is required by any provision of the Massachusetts General Laws to be equipped with smoke detectors shall provide and maintain all such required smoke detectors in compliance with such provision and with any applicable regulation of the State Board of Fire Prevention (527 CMR) or of the State Fire Marshall. The board of health shall immediately notify the fire prevention official of the local fire department of any violation of 105 CMR. 410.482 which is observed during an inspection of any dwelling. If any dwelling is found by the local fire department to be adequately equipped with smoke detectors, the board of health shall not be authorized by 105 CMR. 410.482 to impose any additional or differing smoke detector requirement beyond that which has been found sufficient by the local fire department.

410.483: Auxiliary Emergency Lighting Systems and Exit Signs

The owner of every multiple dwelling of ten or more units shall provide such dwelling with an auxiliary emergency lighting system independent of the conventional lighting system, and with lighted signs indicating both a primary and secondary means of egress, by a diagram or signal so as to assure recognition by all persons regardless of their English speaking ability. Such lighting system signs shall be maintained in good working order in compliance with any applicable regulations promulgated by the Commissioner of Public Safety (See 780 CMR 1023.0, 780 CMR 1024.0 and M.G.L. c.143, § 21D).

410.484: Building, Identification

The owner shall affix to every building covered by 105 CMR 410.000, a number representing the address of such building. The number shall be of a nature and size and shall be situated on the building so that, to the extent practicable, it is visible from the nearest street providing vehicular access to such building (M.G.L. c. 148, § 59).

410.500: Owners Responsibility to Maintain Structural Elements

Every owner shall maintain the foundation, floors, walls, doors, windows, ceilings, roof, staircases, porches, chimneys, and other structural elements of his dwelling so that the dwelling excludes wind, rain and snow, and is rodent proof watertight and free from chronic dampness, weather tight, in good repair and in every way fit for the use intended. Further, he shall maintain every structural element free from holes, tracks, loose plaster, or other defect where such holes, cracks, loose plaster or defect renders the area difficult to keep clean or constitutes an accident hazard or an insect or rodent harborage.

410.501: Weather tight Elements

(A) A window shall be considered weather tight only if: (1) all panes of glass are in place, unbroken and properly caulked; and (2) the window opens and closes fully without excessive effort; and (3) exterior cracks between the prime window frame and the exterior wall are caulked; and (4) one of the following conditions is met: (a) a storm window is affixed to the prime window frame, with caulking installed so as to fill exterior cracks between the storm window frame and the prime window frame; or (b) weather stripping is applied such that the space between the window sash and the prime window frame is no larger than 1/16 inch at airy point on the perimeter of the sash, in the case of double hung windows and 1/32 inch in the case of casement windows; or (c) the window sash is sufficiently well-fitted such that, without weather stripping, the space between the window sash and the prime window frame is no larger than 1/16 inch at any point on the perimeter of the sash in the case of double hung windows and 1/8 inch in the case of casement windows. (B) An exterior door or a door leading from a dwelling unit to a common passageway shall be considered to be weather tight only if: (1) all panes of glass are in place, unbroken and properly caulked; and (2) the door opens and closes fully without excessive effort; and (3) exterior cracks between the prime door frame and the exterior wall are caulked; and (4) one of the following conditions is met:(a) a storm door is affixed to the prime door frame, with caulking installed so as to fill exterior cracks between the storm door frame and the prime door frame, or (b) weather stripping is applied such that the space between the door and the prime door frame is no larger than 1/16 inch at any point on the perimeter of the door or (c) the door is sufficiently well-fitted such that, without weather-stripping, the space between the door and the prime doorframe is no larger than 1/16 inch at any point on the sides of the door or 1/8 inch at any point on the top or bottom of the door. (C) A wall, floor, ceiling or other structural element shall be considered weather tight only if all cracks and spaces not part of heating, ventilating or air conditioning systems are caulked or filled in as to prevent infiltration of exterior air or moisture.

410.502: Use of Lead Paint Prohibited

No paint that contains lead shall be used in painting any surface of any dwelling. (See 105 CMR 460.000.)

410.503: Protective Railings and Walls

The owner of all dwellings shall provide: (A) A safe handrail for every stairway that is used or intended for use by the occupant as required by 780 CMR: Massachusetts State Building Code. (B) A wall or guardrail on the open side of all stairways no less than 30 inches in height. Any such guardrail replaced or constructed after August 28, 1997 (effective date of Massachusetts State Building Code, Sixth Edition) shall be not less than 34 inches in height (780 CMR 1022.2.2 and 3603.14.2.1). (C) A wall or guardrail at least 36 inches in height, enclosing every porch, balcony, mezzanine, landing, roof or similar place, which is 30 inches or more above the ground and that is used or intended for use by the occupants. Any such wall or guardrail for other than Use Group R-4 and along opens sided floor areas, mezzanines and landings in occupancies in Use Group R-3, replaced or constructed after August 28, 1997, shall not be less than 42 inches in height (780 CMR 102 and 3603.14). (D) Between all required guardrails and open handrails, balusters placed at intervals of no more than six inches, or any other ornamental pattern between the guardrail or handrail and floor or stair such that a sphere six inches in diameter can not passthrough the opening. Any balusters or ornamental work constructed or replaced after August 28, 1997 shall have no space greater than 41/2 inches and in all use groups other than R-4, shall not be constructed as to provide a ladder effect (780 CMR 1021 and 3603.14).

410.504: Non-absorbent Surfaces

The owner shall provide: (A) On the floor surfaces of every room containing a toilet, shower or bathtub and every kitchen and pantry, a smooth, noncorrosive, nonabsorbent and water proof covering. This shall not prohibit the use of carpeting in kitchens and bathrooms, nor the use of wood in the kitchen, provided they meet the following qualifications: (1) Carpeting must contain a solid, nonabsorbent, water repellent backing which will prevent the passage of moisture through it to the floor below; and (2) Wood flooring must have a water resistant finish and have no cracks to allow the accumulation of dirt and food, or the harborage of insects. (B) On the walls of every room containing a toilet, shower or bathtub up to a height of 48 inches, a smooth noncorrosive, nonabsorbent and waterproof covering. (C) On wall areas above built-in bathtubs having installed shower heads and in shower compartments up to height not less than six feet above the floor level, with a smooth, noncorrosive, nonabsorbent waterproof covering. Such wall shall form a water tight joint with each other and with either the tub, receptor or shower floor.

410.505: Occupant's Responsibility Respecting Structural Elements

The occupant shall exercise reasonable care in the use of the floors, walls, doors, windows, ceilings, roof, staircases, porches, chimneys, and other structural elements of the dwelling.

410.550: Extermination of Insects, Rodents and Skunks

(A) The occupant of a dwelling containing one dwelling unit shall maintain the unit free from all rodents, skunks, cockroaches and insect infestation, and shall be responsible for exterminating them, provided, however, that the owner shall maintain any screen, fence or other structural element necessary to keep rodents and skunks from entering the dwelling. (B) The owner of a dwelling containing two or more dwelling units shall maintain it and its premises free from all rodents, skunks, cockroaches and insect infestation and shall be responsible for exterminating them. (C) The owner of a rooming house shall maintain it and its premises free from all rodents, skunks, cockroaches and insect infestation, and shall be responsible for exterminating them. (D) Extermination shall be accomplished by eliminating the harborage places of insects and rodents, by removing or making inaccessible materials that may serve as their food or breeding ground, by poisoning, spraying, fumigating trapping or by any, other recognized and legal pest elimination method. All use of pesticides within the interior of a dwelling, dwelling unit, rooming house, or mobile home shall be in accordance with applicable laws and regulations of the Department of Food and Agriculture's Pesticide Board, including those appearing at 333 CMR 13.00, which provide, among other things, that pesticide applicators or their employers must give at least 48 hours pre-notification to occupants of all residential units prior to any routine commercial application of pesticides for the control of indoor household or structural indoor pests.

410.551: Screens for Windows

The owner shall provide screens for all windows designed to be opened on the first four floors opening directly to the outside from any dwelling unit or room unit provided, that in an owner-occupied unit, the owner need provide screens for only those windows used for ventilation. All new or replacement screens shall be of not less than 16 mesh per square inch. Said screens: (1) shall cover that part of the window that is designed to be opened but in no case less than the area as required in 105 CMR 410.280(A); and (2) shall be tight fitting as, to prevent the entrance of insects and rodents around the perimeter. (3) Expandable temporary screens shall not be deemed to satisfy the requirements of 105 CMR 410.551(1) or (2).

410.552: Screens for Doors

The owner shall provide a screen door for all doorways opening directly to the outside from any dwelling unit or rooming unit where the screen door will be permitted to slide to the side or open in an outward direction, provided, that in an owner occupied unit, the owner need provide screens only for those doorways used for ventilation. All new or replacement screens in screen doors shall be of not less that 16 mesh per square inch. Said screen door: (1) shall be equipped with a self-closing device except where the screen is designed to slide to the side; and (2) shall be tight-fitting as to prevent the entrance of insects and rodents around the perimeter.

410.553: Installation of Screens

The owner shall provide and install screens as required in 105 CMR 410.551 and 410.552 so that they shall be in place during the period between April first to October 30th, both inclusive, in each year.

410.600: Storage of Garbage and Rubbish

(A) Garbage or mixed garbage and rubbish shall be stored in watertight receptacles with tight-fitting covers. Said receptacles and covers shall be of metal or other durable, rodent-proof material. Rubbish shall be stored in receptacles of metal or other durable, rodent-proof material. Garbage and rubbish shall be put out for collection no earlier than the day of collection. (B) Plastic bags shall be used to store garbage or mixed rubbish and garbage only if used as a liner in watertight receptacles with tight-fitting covers as required in 105 CMR 410.600(A), provided that the plastic bags may be put out for collection except in those places where such practice is prohibited by local rule or ordinance or except in those cases where the Department of Public Health determines that such practice constitutes a health problem. For purposes of the preceding sentence, in making its determination the Department shall consider, among other things, evidence of strewn garbage, torn garbage bags, or evidence of rodents. (C) The owner of any dwelling that contains three or more dwelling units, the owner of any rooming house, and the occupant of any other dwelling place shall provide as many receptacles for the storage of garbage and rubbish as are sufficient to contain the accumulation before final collection or ultimate disposal, and shall locate them so as to be convenient to the tenant and so that no objectionable odors enter any dwelling. (D) The occupants of each dwelling, dwelling unit, and rooming unit shall be responsible for the proper placement of his garbage and rubbish in the receptacles required in 105 CMR 410.600(C) or at the point of collection by the owner.

410.601: Collection of Garbage and Rubbish

The owner of any dwelling that contains three or more dwelling units, the owner of any rooming house, and the occupant of any other dwelling place shall be responsible for the final collection or ultimate disposal or incineration of garbage and rubbish by means of: (A) the regular municipal collection system; or (B) any other collection system approved by the board of health; or (C) when otherwise lawful, a garbage grinder which grinds garbage into the kitchen sink drain finely enough to ensure its free passage, and which is otherwise maintained in a sanitary condition; or (D) when otherwise lawful, a garbage or rubbish incinerator located within the dwelling which is properly installed and which is maintained so as not to create a safety or health hazard; or (E) when otherwise lawful, by backyard composting of compostable material, provided that the composting operation does not attract rodents or other vectors and does not create a nuisance, and provided further that in the case of composting by an occupant, the occupant obtain the prior written permission of the owner. (F) any other method of disposal which does not endanger any person and which is approved in writing by the board of health.(See 105 CMR 410.840.)

410.602: Maintenance of Areas Free from Garbage and Rubbish

(A) Land. The owner of any parcel of land, vacant or otherwise, shall be responsible for maintaining such parcel of land in a clean and sanitary condition and free from garbage, rubbish or other refuse. The owner of such parcel of land shall correct any condition caused by or on such parcel or its appurtenance which affects the health or safety, and well-being of the occupants of any dwelling or of the general public. (B) Dwelling Units. The occupant of any dwelling unit shall be responsible for maintaining in a clean and sanitary condition and free of garbage, rubbish, other filth or causes of sickness that part of the dwelling which he exclusively occupies or controls. (C) Dwellings Containing Less than Three Dwelling Units. In a dwelling that contains less than three dwelling units, the occupant shall be responsible for maintaining in a clean and sanitary condition, free of garbage, rubbish, other filth or causes of sickness the stairs or stairways leading to his dwelling unit and the landing adjacent to his dwelling unit if the stairs, stairways or landing are not used by another occupant. (D) Common Areas. In any dwelling, the owner shall be responsible for maintaining in a clean and sanitary condition free of garbage, rubbish, other filth or causes of sickness that part of the dwelling which is used in common by the occupants and which is not occupied or controlled by one occupant exclusively. The owner of any dwelling abutting a private passageway or right-of-way owned or used in common with other dwellings or which the owner or occupants under his control have the right to use or are in fact using shall be responsible for maintaining in a clean and sanitary condition free of garbage, rubbish, other filth or causes of sickness that part of the passageway or right-of-way which abuts his property and which he or the occupants under his control have the right to use, or are in fact using, or which he owns.

410.620: Curtailment Prohibited

No owner or occupant shall cause any service, facility, equipment, or utility which is required to be made available by 105 CMR 410.000 to be removed from or shut off from any occupied dwelling except for such temporary period as may be necessary during actual repairs or alterations and where reasonable notice of curtailment of service is given to the occupant, or during temporary emergencies when curtailment of service is approved by the board of health. If any such service or facility that a person is required to provide by 105 CMR 410.000 or has agreed to supply by a written letting agreement becomes curtailed, that person shall take immediate steps to cause its restoration. (See M.G.L. c. 186, § 14.)

APPENDIX C:
ADDRESSES OF DISTRICT AND HOUSING COURTS

The following are the addresses of the District courts and Housing Courts where eviction cases are filed.

Barnstable County

Barnstable District Court
(For: Barnstable, Yarmouth, and Sandwich)
Court House
P.O. Box 427
Barnstable, MA 02630
508-362-2511

Falmouth District Court
161 Jones Road
Falmouth, MA 02540
508-495-1500
(For: Bourne, Falmouth, and Mashpee)

Orleans District Court
(For: Provincetown, Truro, Wellfleet, Eastham, Orleans, Brewster, Chatham, Harwich, and Dennis)
Court House
237 Rock Harbor Road
Orleans, MA 02653
508-255-4700

Berkshire County

Pittsfield District Court
(For: Pittsfield, Hancock, Lanesborough, Peru, Hinsdale, Dalton, Washington, Richmond, Lenox, Becket, and Windsor)
24 Wendell Avenue, P.O. Box 875
Pittsfield, MA 01201
413-499-0558

Northern Berkshire District Court
(For: Adams, North Adams, Williamstown, Clarksburg, Florida, New Ashford, Chesire, Savoy, Hancock, and Windsor)
City Hall
10 Main Street
North Adams, MA 01247
413-663-5339

Southern Berkshire District Court
(For: Sheffield, Great Barrington, Egremont, Alford, Mount Washington, Monterey, New Malborough, Stockbridge, West Stockbridge, Sandisfield, Lee, Tyringham, Otis, Lenox, and Becket)
9 Gilmore Avenue
Great Barrington, MA 01230
413-528-3520

Bristol County

Housing Court: Southeast Division
(For: All of Bristol and Plymouth Counties)
289 Rock Street, 2nd Floor
Fall River, MA 02720-3246
508-677-1505

Attleboro District Court
(For: Attleboro, North Attleborough, Mansfield, and Norton)
Courthouse
88 N. Main Street
Attleboro, MA 02703
508-222-5900

Fall River District Court
(For: Fall River, Freetown, Somerset, Swansea, and Westport)
45 Rock Street
Fall River, MA 02720
508-679-8161

New Bedford District Court
(For: New Bedford, Freetown, Fairhaven, Acushnet, Dartmouth, and Westport)
75 N. Sixth Street
New Bedford, MA 02740
508-999-9700

Taunton District Court
(For: Berkley, Easton, Dighton, Raynham, Rehoboth, Seekonk, and Taunton)
15 Court Street
Taunton, MA 02780
508-824-4033

Dukes County

Edgartown District Court
(For: Martha's Vineyard, Gosnold, and Elizabeth Islands)
Court House
81 Main Street
P.O. Box 1284
Edgartown, MA 02539
508-627-3751

Essex County

Housing Court: Northeast Division
(For: All of Essex County, and Lowell, Billerica, Chelmsford, Dracut, Dunstable, Groton, Pepperell, Shirley, Tewksbury, Tyngsborough and Westford)
Fenton Judicial Center
2 Appleton Street
Lawrence, MA 01840
978-689-7833

Gloucester District Court
(For: Essex, Rockport and Gloucester)
197 Main Street
Gloucester, MA 01915
978-283-2620

Haverhill District Court
(For: Haverhill, Groveland, Georgetown, West Newbury and Boxford)
J.P. Ginty Boulevard
P.O. Box 1389
Haverhill, MA 01831
978-373-4151

Ipswich District Court
(For: Hamilton, Ipswich, Topsfield, and Wenham)
30 S. Main Street
P.O. Box 246
Ipswich, MA 01938
978-356-2681

Lawrence District Court
(For: Andover, Lawrence, Methuen, and North Andover)
Fenton Judicial Center
2 Appleton Street
Lawrence, MA 01840-1525
978-687-7184

Lynn District Court
(For: Lynn, Marblehead, Nahant, Saugus, and Swampscott)
580 Essex Street
Lynn, MA 01901
781-598-5200

Newburyport District Court
(For: Amesbury, Merrimac, Newburyport, Newbury, Rowley, West Newbury and Salisbury)
188 State Road
Route 1 Traffic Circle
Newburyport, MA 01950-6637
978-462-2652

Peabody District Court
(For: Peabody, Lynnfield)
1 Lowell Street
P.O. Box 666
Peabody, MA 01960
978-532-3100

Salem District Court
(For: Salem, Beverly, Danvers, Middleton, Manchester)
65 Washington Street
Salem, MA 01970
978-744-1167

Franklin County

Greenfield District Court
(For: Ashfield, Bernardston, Buckland, Charlemont, Colrain, Conway, Deerfield, Gill, Greenfield, Hawley, Heath, Leverett, Leyden, Monroe, Montague, Northfield, Rowe, Shelburne, Shutesbury, Sunderland, and Whately)
425 Main Street
Greenfield, MA 01301
413-774-5533

Orange District Court
(For: Erving, New Salem, Orange, Warwick, Wendell and Athol)
1 Court Square
Orange, MA 01364
978-544-8277

Hampden County

Housing Court: Western Division
(For: Hampden, Berkshire, Franklin, and Hampshire)
37 Elm Street
Springfield, MA 01103
413-748-7838

Chicopee District Court
(For: Chicopee)
30 Church Street
Chicopee, MA 01020
413-598-0099

Holyoke District Court
(For: Holyoke)
20 Court Plaza
Holyoke, MA 01040
413-538-9710

Palmer District Court
(For: Palmer, Brimfield, Hampden, Monson, Holland, Wales,
Wilbraham, and Ludlow)
235 Sykes Street
Palmer, MA 01069
413-283-8916

Springfield District Court
(For: Springfield, West Springfield, Agawam, Longmeadow, and
East Longmeadow)
50 State Street
P.O. Box 2421
Springfield, MA 01101-2421
413-748-8600

Westfield District Court
(For: Westfield, Chester, Granville, Russell, Southwick, Blandford,
Tolland, and Montgomery)
224 Elm Street
Westfield, MA 01085
413-568-8946

Hampshire County

Northhampton District Court
(For: Amherst, Chesterfield, Cummington, Easthampton, Goshen,
Hadley, Hatfield, Huntington, Middlefield, Northhampton,
Pelham, Plainfield, Southhampton, South Hadley, Westhampton,
Williamsburg, and Worthington.)
15 Gothic Street
Northhampton, MA 01060
413-584-7400

Ware District Court
(For: Ware, Belchertown, and Granby, all of MDC Quabbin
Reservoir and Watershed area)
71 South Street
P.O. Box 300
Ware, MA 01082
413-967-3301

Middlesex County

Housing Court: Northeast Division
(For: Essex County, plus Lowell, Billerica, Chelmsford, Dracut,
Dunstable, Groton, Pepperell, Shirley, Tewksbury, Tyngsborough,
and Westford)
Fenton Judicial Center
2 Appleton Street
Lawrence, MA 01840
978-689-7833

Ayer District Court
(For: Ashby, Ayer, Boxborough, Dunstable, Littleton, Groton,
Pepperell, Shirley, Townsend, and Westford)
25 East Main Street
Ayer, MA 01432
978-772-2100

Cambridge District Court
(For: Cambridge, Arlington, and Belmont)
40 Thorndike Street
East Cambridge, MA 02141
617-494-4310

Concord District Court
(For: Acton, Bedford, Carlisle, Concord, Lexington, Lincoln,
Maynard, and Stow)
305 Walden Street
Concord, MA 01742-3616
978-369-0500

Framingham District Court
(For: Framingham, Ashland, Holliston, Hopkinton, Sudbury, and
Wayland)
600 Concord Street
P.O. Box 1969
Framingham, MA 01701
508-875-7461

Lowell District Court
(For Lowell, Billerica, Chelmsford, Dracut, Tewksbury, and
Tyngsborough)
41 Hurd Street
Lowell, MA 01852
978-459-4101

Malden District Court
(For: Malden, Melrose, Everett, and Wakefield)
89 Summer Street
Malden, MA 02148
781-322-7500

Malborough District Court
(For: Malborough and Hudson)
45 Williams Street
Malborough, MA 01752
508-485-3700

Natick District Court
(For: Natick and Sherborn)
117 East Central Street
Natick, MA 01760
508-653-8100

Newton District Court
(For: Newton)
1309 Washington Street
West Newton, MA 02465-2011
617-494-0102

Somerville District Court
(For: Somerville and Medford)
175 Fellsway
Somerville, MA 02145
617-666-8000

Waltham District Court
(For: Waltham, Watertown, and Weston)
38 Linden Street
Waltham, MA 02453
781-894-4500

Woburn District Court
(For: Reading, North Reading, Woburn, Winchester, Burlington, Wilmington, and Stoneham)
Courthouse
30 Pleasant Street
Woburn, MA 01801
781-935-4000

Nantucket County

Nantucket District Court
(For: Nantucket)
Town and County Building
16 Broad Street
P.O. Box 1800
Nantucket, MA 02554
508-228-0460

Norfolk County

Brookline District Court
(For: Brookline)
360 Washington Street
Brookline, MA 02445
617-232-4660

Dedham District Court
(For: Dedham, Dover, Norwood, Westwood, Medfield, Needham, and Wellesley)
631 High Street
Dedham, MA 02026
781-329-4777

Quincy District Court
(For: Randolph, Braintree, Cohasset, Weymouth, Quincy, Holbrook, and Milton)
One Dennis F. Ryan Parkway.
Quincy, MA 02169
617-471-1650

Stoughton District Court
(For: Stoughton, Canton, Avon, Sharon)
1288 Central Street
Stoughton, MA 02072
781-344-2131

Wrentham District Court
(For: Wrentham, Walpole, Franklin, Foxborough, Medway, Millis, Norfolk, and Plainville)
Courthouse
60 East Street
Wrentham, MA 02093
508-384-3106

Plymouth County

Housing Court-Southeast Division
(For: All of Bristol and Plymouth Counties)
289 Rock Street, 2nd Floor
Fall River, MA 02720-3246
508-677-1505

Brockton District Court
(For: Brockton, Bridgewater, West Bridgewater, East Bridgewater, Abington and Whitman)
215 Main Street
Brockton, MA 02301
Mailing Address:
P.O. Box 7610
Brockton, MA 02303-7610
508-587-8000

Hingham District Court
(For: Rockland, Hingham, Hull, Hanover, Scituate, and Norwell)
28 George Washington Boulevard
Hingham, MA 02043
781-749-7000

Plymouth District Court
(For: Plymouth, Kingston, Plympton, Pembroke, Duxbury, Marshfield, Halifax, and Hanson)
South Russell Street
Plymouth, MA 02360
508-747-0500

Wareham District Court
(For: Wareham, Marion, Mattapoisett, Middleboro, Carver, Rochester, and Lakeville)
Courthouse
2200 Cranberry Highway.
West Wareham, MA 02576
508-295-8300

Suffolk County

Housing Court: Boston Division
(For: the City of Boston)
Edward W. Brooke
24 New Chardon Street
Boston, MA 02114
617-788-8485

Boston Municipal Court
(For: Boston proper)
John W. McCormack P.O. & Ct.
16th Floor
90 Devonshire St.
Boston, MA 02109
617-788-8700

Brighton District Court
(For: Brighton)
52 Academy Hill Road
Brighton, MA 02135
617-782-6521

Charlestown District Court
(For: Charlestown)
3 City Square
Charlestown, MA 02129
617-242-5400

Chelsea District Court
(For: Chelsea and Revere)
120 Broadway
Chelsea, MA 02150
617-660-9200

Dorchester District Court
(For: Dorchester)
510 Washington Street
Dorchester, MA 02124
617-288-9500

East Boston District Court
(For: East Boston and Winthrop)
37 Meridian Street
East Boston, MA 02128
617-569-7550

Roxbury District Court
(For: Roxbury)
85 Warren Street
Roxbury, MA 02119
617-427-7000

South Boston District Court
(For: South Boston)
535 East Broadway
South Boston, MA 02127
617-268-9292

West Roxbury District Court
(For West Roxbury)
Courthouse
445 Arborway
Jamaica Plain, MA 02130
617-522-4710

Worcester County

Housing Court: Worcester Division
(For: Worcester County towns plus Bellingham, Ashby, and Townsend)
2 Main Street
Room 101
Worcester, MA 01608
508-792-0800

Clinton District Court
(For: Clinton, Berlin, Bolton, Boylston, Harvard, Lancaster, and Sterling)
Rates 62 & 70
300 Boylston Street
Clinton, MA 01510
978-368-7811

Dudley District Court
(For: Sturbridge, Southbridge, Charlton, Dudley, Oxford, and Webster)
P.O. Box 100
West Main Street
Dudley, MA 01571
508-943-7123

East Brookfield District Court
(For: Brookfield, East Brookfield, Hardwick, Leicester, New Parcarthel, N. Brookfield, Spencer, Warner, W. Brookfield)
544 East Main Street
East Brookfield, MA 01515-1701
508-885-6305

Fitchburg District Court
(For: Fitchburg, Ashburnham, and Lunenburg)
100 Elm Street
Fitchburg, MA 01420
978-345-2111

Gardner District Court
(For: Gardner, Hubbardston, Petersham, Phillipston, Royalston, Templeton, and Westminster)
108 Matthews Street
Gardner, MA 01440-0040
978-632-2373

Leominster District Court
(For: Leominster and Princeton)
25 School Street
Leominster, MA 01453
978-537-3722

Milford District Court
(For: Milford, Mendon, Upton, Hopedale, and Bellingham)
161 West Street
Milford, MA 01757
508-473-1260

Orange District Court
(For: Athol, Erving, New Salena, Orange, Warwick, and Wendell)
1 Ct. Sq., Suite 1
Orange, MA 01364
978-544-8277

Uxbridge District Court
(For: Blackstone, Millville, Uxbridge, Douglas, Northbridge, and
Sutton)
261 South Main Street
Uxbridge, MA 01569-1690
508-278-2454

Westborough District Court
(For: Westborough, Southborough, Northborough, Grafton, and
Shrewsbury)
175 Milk Street
Westborough, MA 01581
508-366-8266

Winchendon District Court
(For: Winchendon)
80 Central Street
P.O. Box 309
Winchendon, MA 01475
978-297-0156

Worcester District Court
(For: Worcester, Auburn, Barre, Holden, Millbury, Oakham,
Paxton, Rutland, West Boylston, and Worcester)
50 Harvard Street
Worcester, MA 01608
508-757-8350

APPENDIX D:
EVICTION PROCESS
SAMPLE FORMS

This appendix takes you through the eviction process, referred to as Summary Process, by providing sample forms for you to review. The forms are not included as blank forms in Appendix E because you will either obtain the form from the clerk's office or they are forms that the tenant will prepare. However, by reviewing forms that the tenant may serve on you as discovery or as a defense and counterclaim will be better prepared to respond to a tenant's claims against you.

This appendix begins with an *Eviction Flowchart in Massachusetts* so you may review the process from beginning to end. It is followed by a sample *Summary Process Summons & Complaint* that you will file. Next are four documents that the tenant may serve on you. The first is a *Summary Process Answer and Counterclaim*. This is where the tenant may make claims against you. By reviewing the form you will be prepared to address issues the tenant may raise to the judge. The other three forms, the *Defendant/Tenant's Interrogatories to be Answered by the Plaintiff/Landlord under Oath*, the *Defendant/Tenant's Request for the Production of Documents to the Plaintiff/Landlord*, and the *Defendant/Tenant's Request for Admission by the Plaintiff/Landlord*, are discovery documents a tenants may serve on you. Lastly, a *Notice of Entry of Summary Process Judgement* is provided. This document details what the judge ordered as a result of the hearing.

Review Chapter 10 for an in-depth discussion of these forms and the eviction process.

Eviction Flowchart in Massachusetts

Start Here:

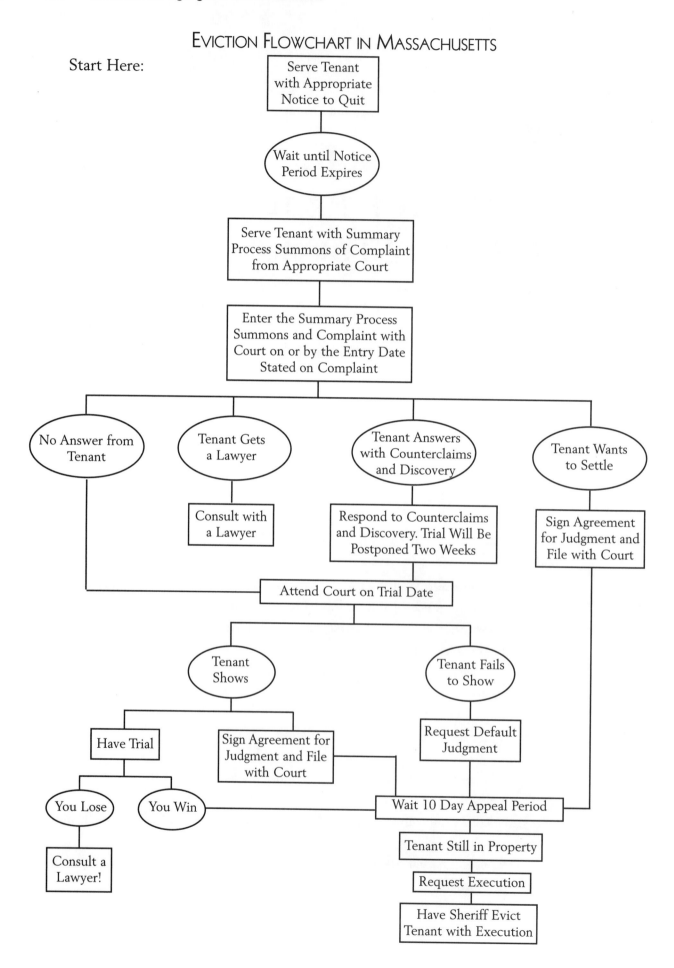

Commonwealth of Massachusetts

The Trial Court

SUMMARY PROCESS SUMMONS & COMPLAINT

Worchester_____, SS

No. SP_____(Summary Process Waived)

Entered **April 14, 2004**

Entry Fee_____

DISTRICT COURT DEPARTMENT
MILFORD DIVISION

IMPORTANT!   THIS IS A COURT NOTICE OF A PROCEEDING TO EVICT YOU.
PLEASE READ IT CAREFULLY.

IMPORTANTE!   ESTE DOCEMENTO ES UNA NOTICIA DE UNA CORTE, RESPECTO
A PROCEDIENTES PARA DESALOJARLE.

To:___**Eric and Mariah Tenant**_____   Of:___**123 Main Street Apt. #2**___
   (name)   (address)

___**Milford, MA**_____   You are hereby summoned to appear for a hearing

hearing before the Judge of the court sitting at_____**Milford District Court**_____

On Thursday,____**April 24, 2004**_____at 9:30 A.M., to answer the complaint of

_____**Susie Landlord**_____landlord/owner

_____of 123 Main Street #1, Milford, MA_____, that you occupy the premises

_____of 123 Main Street #2, Milford, MA_____, being within the

judicial district of this court, unlawfully and against the right of said landlord/owner because: ___**you**___

were duly served with a 14 Day Notice to Quit for

Nonpayment on March 25, 2004, and you have failed to

duly pay and/or vacate premises

and further, that rent is owed by you in the amount of $_____**$1,000.00**_____
according to the following account:

LEAH W. SPRAGUE

Presiding Justice

Louise K. Calplair

Clerk/Magistrate
   April 2, 2004

Date

ACCOUNT ANNEXED
   March, 2000 = $500.00

   April, 2000 = $500.00

Susie Landlord

Signature of Plaintiff or Attorney

Notice to Occupants: At the hearing on_____**April 24, 2004**_____ , you (or your attorney)
must appear in person to present your defense. You (or your attorney) must also file a written
answer to this complaint. (Answer form 2 is available in the clerk's office.) You must file (deliver
or mail) the answer with the court clerk and serve (deliver or mail) a copy on the landlord (or
landlord's attorney) at the address shown on the back of this form. The answer must be received
by the court clerk and received by the landlord (or the landlord's attorney) no later than the
Monday___**April 21, 2004**___before the hearing date. If the landlord does not file a copy of
this form in court on or before the entry date on the back of this form, the court will not schedule
the case for trial.

IF YOU DO NOT FILE AND SERVE AN ANSWER, OR IF YOU DO NOT DEFEND AT THE TIME OF THE
HEARING, JUDGMENT MAY BE ENTERED AGAINST YOU FOR POSSESSION AND THE RENT AS
REQUESTED IN THIS COMPLAINT.

NOTIFICATION PARA LAS PERSONAS DE HABLA HISPANA: SI USTED NO PUEDE LEER INGLES
TENGE ESTE DOCUMENTO LEGAL TRADUCIDO CUANTO ANTES.

To the Sheriffs of our several Counties, or their Deputies, or any Constable of any City or Town within said Commonwealth, GREETINGS: We command you to summon the within named defendant (tenant/occupant) to appear as herein ordered:

WITNESS.   **LEAH W. SPRAGUE**

_____
Presiding Justice

Louise K. Caplain
_____
Clerk/Magistrate

Date: _____ April 2, 2004 _____   _____ April 14, 2004 _____
Entry Date

Officer's Return

_____ Worchester _____, SS: City/Town _____ Milford _____ Date _04/04/04_

By virtue of the Writ, I this day served the within-named defendant (tenant or occupant) and summoned him/her as herein directed, by giving in hand to

_____

_____ or by leaving it at _____

_____

the last and usual place of abode. A copy of this summons was mailed first class to the defendant (tenant/occupant) at this address on _____ Eric Tenant _____

_____

Officer: _____ Harry Constable _____   FEES: Service _____ $30.00 _____
Copy _____
Travel _____
Use of Car _____
L & U Mailing _____

➡ ➡ ➡

NAME AND ADDRESS OF LANDLORD (OR ATTORNEY) MAKING THIS COMPLAINT:

Name _____ Susie Landlord _____

Street _____ 123 Main Street #1 _____

City _____ Milford _____ Zip _____ 01757 _____

Telephone _____ (508) 555-1234 _____

NOTICE TO LANDLORD/OWNER:

Have the officer complete the Officer's Return section above. Service must be made on the defendant no later than the seventh day and not earlier than the thirtieth day before the Monday entry day.

This form must be filed in court no later than the close of business on the scheduled Monday entry day In appropriate cases, proper evidence of notice to quit must be provided this court upon the filing of the complaint. See Rule 2(b). According to Rule 2(c), the hearing date is the second Thursday   after the entry day.

COMMONWEALTH OF MASSACHUSETTS

SUFFOLK, SS

BOSTON HOUSING COURT
C.A. No. 97-12345

LUCILLE LANDLORD,

        Plaintiff

v.

JIM TENANT,

      Defendant

SUMMARY PROCESS ANSWER AND COUNTERCLAIMS*

Facts

1. My name is *Jim Tenant*

2. I live at: *123 Main Street #3, Boston MA*. I moved in on: September 1, 2003

3. My rent is $ 650.00 per month. I do not have a written lease.

4. My rent when I moved in was $650.00 per month.

5. (X) I deny that I live in my home unlawfully and against the rights of the landlord.

6. (X) I deny that I owe the amount of money listed in the landlord's complaint.

Defense: My landlord Did Not Terminate My Tenancy

7. ( ) I have a written lease which has not ended and the landlord has not given me a valid Notice to Quit.

8. (X) I do not have a written lease and I have not received a valid Notice to Quit.

9. ( ) If I ever owed the landlord rent, I paid or offered to pay it within the time allowed by law. (This includes an offer of emergency assistance from the Welfare Department.)

10. ( ) Even if my tenancy was terminated, I have a new tenancy because my landlord has accepted rent without reservation of rights.

Defense: My Landlord Has Not Brought This Case Properly

11. I was not properly notified of this case because my landlord did not do at least one of the following:

    (X) a) Have the Summons and Complaint handed to me, or

    (X) b) Have the Summons and Complaint both left and mailed to my home

12. ( ) The landlord started this case before the Notice to Quit expired.

13.( ) The complaint does not state the reasons for and facts supporting my eviction.

14.( ) I am not the tenant and this case should not have been brought against me. My name is:

15.( ) There is another ongoing eviction against me.

Defense: Public and Subsidized Housing

16.(X) I am a tenant in public or subsidized housing and my landlord did not terminate my tenancy as required by the lease or program rules.

17.(X) I am a tenant in public or subsidized housing and my landlord does not have a good cause to evict me as required by the lease or program rules.

18.(X) I am a tenant in public or subsidized housing and my landlord did not grant me my right to a grievance hearing or conference as required by the lease or program rule.

Defense: Rent COntrol and Condominium Conversion

19.( ) My landlord has failed to comply with local rent control and vacancy decontrol laws.

20.( ) My landlord has failed to comply with condominium conversion eviction laws.

Defense & Counterclaim: Bad Conditions in My Home

21.(X) I have a defense and counterclaim because of the following problems in mt home that my landlord knew or should have known about:
The plumbing in the kitchen sink is defective and the sink's drain has been plugged up. In addition, there are loose tiles in the bathroom.

( ) The Board of Health has inspected my home on:

( ) I have pictures of the problems in my home taken on:

(X) Because my home is not up to code, I should recover the extra rent I paid above what my home was worth. This defense and counterclaim entitles me to have my rent reduced or returned in an amount to be decided by the judge.

Defense & Counterclaim: Security Deposit

22.(X) My landlord is holding a security deposit of $650.00.

23.The Landlord violated the security deposit law by:

(X) a. Not putting it in an "escrow" bank account entitling me to:

1. Return of the security deposit, and	1. *$ 650.00*
2. Three times the deposit	2. *$1,950.00*

( ) b. Not paying or deducting from my rent 5% yearly interest entitling me to:

3. Three times the interest owed	3.$

( ) c. Not giving me the required receipts and statements of conditions entitling me to:

    4. Minimum damages of $25 per violation   4. $

    d. **Total**   *$2,600.00*

Defense & Counterclaim: Last Month's Rent

24.(X) My landlord is holding the last month's rent of $650.00 and my landlord has not paid me 5% yearly interest of given me rent credit for this interest.

25.(X) For this defense and counterclaim, I am entitled to three times the amount of interest owed for a total of $97.50.

Defense & Counterclaim: Interference with Use and Quiet Enjoyment

26.   The landlord did the following and therefore I am entitled to at least three months rent for each violation:

( ) a. Failed to provide adequate heat $ _____ (3 months rent)

( ) b. Failed to provide adequate hot water $ _____ (3 months rent)

( ) c. Cut off my utilities $ _____ (3 months rent)

( ) d. Locked me out of my apartment $ _____ (3 months rent)

( ) e. Put my possessions out without court order $ _____ (3 months rent)

( ) f. Interfered with my right to enjoy my home by:

_____

_____ $ _____ (3 months rent)

27.( ) Therefore, I am entitled to a total of $_____ for all violations checked in number 26.

28.( ) I have been billed for heat and/or hot water and the landlord and I did not have a written agreement requiring me to pay for these utilities. This defense and counterclaim entitles me to be paid back for all heat and/or hot water bills I have paid since I moved in or three months rent, whichever is greater.

29.( ) I am being billed for gas and electricity that do not go to my apartment. This defense and counterclaim entitles me to be paid back for all gas and electricity bills I have paid since I moved in or three months rent, whichever is greater.

Defense & Counterclaim: Retaliation

30. The landlord is trying to evict me because:
   ( ) I withheld rent because of bad conditions $ _____ (3 months rent)
   ( ) I reported bad conditions to the Board of Health

                                                      $ _____ (3 months rent)
   ( ) I joined a tenant's union $ _____ (3 months rent)
   ( ) Other _____ $ _____ (3 months rent)

31. ( ) Each of these defenses and counterclaims entitled me to three times the rent for a total of $_____.

Defense & Counterclaim: Rent Control Overcharges

32. ( ) The landlord charged me more rent than Rent Control allows, and therefore I am entitled to the return of the extra rent paid for up to four years, plus any penalties allowed by law for my defense and counterclaim. The amount I am entitled to is:

_____

Defense & Counterclaim: Consumer Protection

33. The Landlord acted in the following unfair or deceptive ways:
   ( ) a. not repairing bad conditions in my home
   ( ) b. other: _____

_____

34. ( ) Therefore, under Chapter 93A, I am entitled to:
   a. Damages in an amount of $_____ or an amount to be decided by the judge;
   b. Triple my actual damages or triple whatever the judge decides because my landlord's conduct was intentional.

WHAT I WANT THE COURT TO DO

The Court should allow me to stay in my home.

35. (X) The defenses listed above entitle me to possession and to remain in my home.

36. (X) The Counterclaims listed above are greater than the amount of rent owed thereby entitling me to keep possession of my home. This applies to both nonpayment and no fault evictions.

The Court Should Allow Me to Pay Any Balance Within 7 Days

37. (X) I request that the court tell me how much I owe for purposes of cure. If the court finds that I owe the landlord more rent than he/she owes me for my counterclaims, I claim my right to keep possession of my home by paying the court clerk this amount within one week of receiving notice of the amount die from the court.

The Court Should Find I Was Not at Fault

38.( ) The court should find that the landlord has not proven that I was at fault. This is a fault eviction case in which the landlord claimed I did something wrong other than nonpayment of rent. The landlord did not prove that I did anything serious enough to justify eviction, therefore the court should award me possession of my home.

The Court Should Order the Landlord to Make Repairs

39.( ) I request the court to order that defective conditions be corrected. If the court finds that bad conditions exist in my home, I request permission to pay the fair value for use of my home minus the amount awarded on my counterclaims to the court clerk. Also, I request that the court order my landlord to use those funds to repair the bad conditions in my home.

The Court Should Allow Me More Time to Move

40.(X) I need time to move because I cannot find another place to live. The court may award up to six months for all tenants and up to one year for elderly or disabled tenants.

41.(X) I hereby certify that I delivered or mailed (circle which one) a copy of this Answer to my landlord or his/her lawyer on _____ (date).

Jim Tenant
Signature of Tenant

Jim Tenant
Tenant's Name (print)

123 Main Street #3
Address

Boston , *MA*   *02108*
City   State   Zip

(617) 555-1234
Telephone Number

---

* This is a simplified Answer and Counterclaim form similar to that supplied by the Housing Court and tenant organizations. When a tenant is represented by an attorney, the answer and counterclaim is usually more formal and legalistic, yet still achieves the same general purpose.

```
                COMMONWEALTH OF MASSACHUSETTS
ESSEX, SS                            LAWRENCE DISTRICT COURT
                                     SUMMARY PROCESS
                                     C.A. NO. 97 SP 1234


RONALD LANDLORD,
                 Plaintiff
v.

LAURA TENANT,
            Defendant
```

DEFENDANT/ TENANT'S INTERROGATORIES TO BE ANSWERED BY THE PLAINTIFF/ LANDLORD UNDER OATH*

A. You are required by law to answer these interrogatories truthfully and fully, under the pains and penalties of perjury.

B. As the defendant/tenant has files these discovery requests, the hearing/trial in this action is automatically postponed two weeks until October 16, 2004.

C. The court and the defendant must receive your answers to these Interrogatories no later than 10 days after you receive them.

<u>INTERROGATORIES</u>

1. What is the name, address, telephone number, and occupation of the person answering there interrogatories?

2. When did the tenant/defendant move into the home?

3. Please give a description of the exact premises leased to the defendant?

4. Please give the initial rental amount, and if the rent has since changed, please give the new rate(s) and the date the new rate(s) became effective.

5. Please state the type of tenancy entered into with the tenant.

6. Please list each and every reason for your evicting the tenant. If the eviction is for fault, other than nonpayment, please specifically describe the reason(s).

7. Please state the type of notice to quit relied on in this action, the nature of service, by whom it was served, the date it was served, and who received said notice.

8. If you have ever received a security deposit or last month's rent from the defendant/tenant, please state:

    a) whether it was a security deposit or last month's rent;
    b) the amount of said deposit;
    c) the date the deposit was taken;
    d) whether you gave the defendant a receipt for said deposit;
    e) whether you gave the defendant a statement of condition (if said deposit is a security deposit);
    f) Whether you deposited it into a separate, interest-bearing account protected from creditors; and

      g) the dates and amount of any interest paid to the defendant on the deposit.

9. Please state any and all repairs requested by the defendant since the date of her commencement of occupancy and the date of said request.

10. Please state any and all repairs made by you or someone on your behalf to the defendant's premises, the date of said repair, the person who performed said repair, and the cost of said repair.

11. If you believe the tenant has caused any damage to the premises since his commencement of occupancy, please state specifically the nature of the damage, the date you believe it was caused, when and how you learned of said damage, and the cost or expected cost of said repair.

12. Have you ever learned or tried to discover the existence of lead paint in the tenant's premises? If so, please state:

    a) the date you first learned or tried to learn of the existence of lead paint, and

    b) what, if anything, you did to remove the lead paint, including dates, and names of contractors.

13. State whether there is a written agreement requiring the tenant to pay for heat or hot water, the date of said agreement, and which utilities are separately metered for each apartment.

14. Within the six months prior to the date of the Notice to Quit, has the tenant contacted the Board of Health or any other agency regarding the premises or joined a tenant's organization to your knowledge?

15. If you own any other residential units, please state the total number of units you own, their addresses, and the period of time for which you owned them.

16. For each witness you intend to call at the hearing/trial of this action, please state his/her name, address, and summary of testimony to be given.

                        Defendant,
                        Laura Tenant

                        Laura Tenant
                        Laura Tenant

* Note: Either party is entitled to serve interrogatories on the other. However, because the filing of discovery postpones the eviction hearing for two weeks, it is more common for the tenant or her attorney to file. Also, a party is allowed to ask only thirty (30) interrogatories. If served with interrogatories, it is wise to hire an attorney for representation, if you have not already.

COMMONWEALTH OF MASSACHUSETTS

SUFFOLK, SS

EAST BOSTON DISTRICT COURT
SUMMARY PROCESS
C.A. NO. 97 SP 1234

BARBARA LANDLORD,
         Plaintiff

v.

ELAINE TENANT,
         Defendant

DEFENDANT/ TENANT'S REQUEST FOR THE PRODUCTION OF DOCUMENTS TO THE PLAINTIFF/ LANDLORD*

A. The Court and the Defendant must receive copies of the requested documents no later than 10 days after you receive this Request.

B. As discovery requests have been filed, the trial/ hearing in this case is automatically postponed for two weeks until October 16, 2004.

DOCUMENTS REQUESTED:

1. Any lease or any other written agreement between the parties.

2. The notice to quit relied on in this action.

3. Any other notices to quit served by the plaintiff on the defendant since the commencement of occupancy.

4. A copy of the receipt given for any security deposit taken by the plaintiff from the defendant.

5. A copy of the receipt given for any last month's rent taken by the plaintiff from the defendant.

6. A copy of any executed statement of condition form for the defendant's premises.

7. Any and all documents received by the plaintiff from the defendant or on the defendant's behalf regarding the tenancy at issue.

8. Any and all documents sent by the plaintiff or the plaintiff's behalf to the defendant regarding the tenancy at issue.

9. Any and all written documents and reports concerning condition in the defendant's premises, including complaints, code reports, and requests for repairs by the defendant.

10. Any documents concerning who is responsible for heat and hot water and shutoff or reconnection of utilities.

11. A copy of any and all other documents you intend to introduce as evidence at time of trial/ hearing in this action.

12. A copy of the certificate of occupancy issued for the defendant's premises.

13. Copies of any and all documents evidencing payment or nonpayment by the defendant from the commencement of occupancy to the present.

14. All written records regarding the repairs done to the defendant's premises.

                    The Defendant
                    Elaine Tenant,

                    Elaine Tenant
                    Elaine Tenant

Note: Unlike the Interrogatories, Massachusetts law does not limit the number of document requests a party can have.

COMMONWEALTH OF MASSACHUSETTS

NORFOLK, SS   QUINCY DISTRICT COURT
                                               SUMMARY PROCESS
                                               C.A. NO. 97 SP 1234

MARK LANDLORD,
            Plaintiff

v.

JOSEPH TENANT,
        Defendant

DEFENDANT/ TENANT'S REQUEST FOR ADMISSIONS BY
THE PLAINTIFF/ LANDLORD*

A. The Court and the Defendant must receive copies of the answers to admissions no later than 10 days after you receive this Request.

B. As discovery requests have been filed, the trial/ hearing in this case is automatically postponed for two weeks until October 16, 2002.

REQUESTS FOR ADMISSIONS:

1. You are the owner of the premises in which the defendant is a tenant.

2. You own other residential units, besides the defendant's, in which you rent.

3. You at no time received an occupancy permit from the building inspector in which the defendant resides.

4. You know that lead paint exists in defendant's premises.

5. You have taken rent money from the defendant since the serving of the notice to quit.

6. The defendant has complained to you on at least one occasion of problems with insects, the lack of hot water, and the non-existence of smoke detectors among other problems.

7. You never hired a professional exterminator to remedy the insect situation in the defendant's premises.

                                    The Defendant
                                    Joseph Tenant

                                    Joseph Tenant
                                    Joseph Tenant

* Note: Requests for Admissions are limited to 30 under Massachusetts law.

COMMONWEALTH OF MASSACHUSETTS

WORCESTER, SS.   HOUSING COURT DEPARTMENT
                                        WORCHESTER COUNTY DIVISION

Case No. 04-SP-01548

 Ralph and Jessica Shultz   , PLAINTIFF

V.

  Cedric LeBuerre   , DEFENDANT

NOTICE OF ENTRY OF SUMMARY PROCESS JUDGMENT

    This action came on for hearing before the Court, Judge John
G. Martin presiding, and the issues having been duly heard and
findings having been duly rendered, it is ORDERED and ADJUDGED
under Rule 10 of the Uniform Summary Process Rules, that judgment
enter this day for the Plaintiff for possession of the premises
and money damages as follows:

RENT owed through 07/31/04	$	1500.00
COSTS	$	148.00
PLAINTIFF'S ATTORNEY'S FEES	$	0.00
TOTAL JUDGMENT	$	1648.00

Date of Judgment: 07/21/04

James A. Bisceglia

JAMES A. BISCEGLIA
CLERK MAGISTRATE

APPENDIX E: BLANK FORMS

Use of the forms in this appendix is either described in the text or should be self-explanatory. If you do not understand any aspect of a form, you should seek advice of an attorney.

LICENSE: Some of the forms in this book are official government forms, which are in the public domain and may be copied by anyone. Other forms have been created by the author. Although this book is copyrighted, purchasers of the book are granted a license to copy the forms created by the author for their own personal use or use in their law practice.

Table of Forms

Publisher's Note: Forms 8, 9, and 10 are provided courtesy of the Greater Boston Real Estate Board and reflect the most current version of the forms at the time this book was published.

RENTAL APPLICATION

Date: _____

Applicant: _____ Work Phone #: _____

Social Security #: _____ Home Phone #: _____

Present Address: _____ How Long: _____

Former Address: _____ How Long: _____

Applying for Apartment No._____ at _____

Rent $_____ per month, (_____), payable in advance beginning_____, _____

How many to occupy:_____ How many children:_____ ____Ages:_____

Present Employer: _____ Salary $: _____

Employer Address: _____ Phone #: _____

Previous Employer: _____ Phone #: _____

Present Landlord: _____ Phone #: _____

Landlord's Address: _____

Previous Landlord: _____ Phone #: _____

Previous Landlord Address: _____

References: (Give three **credit** and two **social**)

	Name	Address	Phone Number
1.			
2.			
3.			
4.			
5.			

In case of emergency notify: (List 2)

	Name	Address	Phone Number
1.			
2.			

Bank References: Bank Name: _____ Savings Account #: _____

Bank Name: _____ Checking Account #: _____

Remarks: _____

Deposit $ _____ (to be refunded only if this application is declined by owner or his agent)

Dogs and cats not allowed without consent of the owner or agent in writing. Subletting of this apartment is not allowed without the consent of the owner in writing. This application is submitted subject to clearance with The Credit Bureau and satisfactory reports from references listed above. The applicant must produce receipts for payment of rent for the past two years.

Being obligated by law to give at least 30 days notice before a rent day of my intention to vacate this apartment, I agree to show the apartment to prospective tenants on request of the owner or his agent.

Neither the owner or the Management is responsible for the loss of personal belongings caused by fire, theft, smoke, water or otherwise. Proper tenant insurance should be purchased.

Automobile: Make & Year: _____ Registration (State & No.)_____

The undersigned warrants and represents all statements herein are true

_____ _____

Applicant's Signature   Initial if over
                                                    18 years of age

This page intentionally left blank.

do certain other deleading and interim control work. Owners and workers must have special training to perform the deleading tasks they may do. After the work is done, the lead inspector or risk assessor checks to home. He or she may take dust samples to test for lead, to make sure the home has been properly cleaned up. If everything is fine, he or she may give the owner a Letter of Compliance or Letter of Interim Control. After getting one of these letters, the owner must take care of the home and make sure there is no peeling paint.

What is a Letter of Compliance?

It is a legal letter that says either that there are no lead paint hazards or that the home has been deleaded. The letter is signed and dated by a licensed lead inspector.

What is a letter of Interim Control?

It is a legal letter that says work necessary to make the home temporarily safe from lead hazards has been done. The letter is signed and dated by a licensed risk assessor. It is good for one year, but can be renewed for one more year. The owner must fully delead the home and get a Letter of Compliance before the end of the second year.

Where can I learn more about lead poisoning?

Massachusetts Department of Public Health Childhood Lead Poisoning Prevention Program (CLPPP) (For more copies of this form, as well as a full range of information on lead poisoning prevention, tenant's rights and responsibilities under the MA Lead Law, how to clean lead dust and chips, healthy foods to protect your children, financial help for owners, safe deleading and renovation work, and soil testing.)

Massachusetts Department of Labor and Workforce Development
(List of licensed deleaders)
617-969-7177, 1-800-425-0004

Your local lead poisoning prevention program or your local Board of Health

U.S. Consumer Product Safety Commission (Information about lead in consumer products) 1-800-638-2772

U.S. Environmental Protection Agency, REgion I (Information about federal laws on lead) 617-565-3420

National Lead Information Center (General lead poisoning information) 1-800-LEAD-FYI

This page intentionally left blank.

Tenant Certification Form

Required Federal Lead Warning Statement

Housing built before 1978 may contain lead-based paint. Lead from paint, paint chips, and dust can pose health hazards if not managed properly. Lead exposure is especially harmful to young children and pregnant women. Before renting pre-1978 housing, lessors must disclose the presence of known lead-based paint and/or lead-based paint hazards in the dwelling. Lessees must also receive a federally approved pamphlet on lead poisoning prevention. The Massachusetts Tenant Lead Law Notification and Certification Form is for compliance with state and federal lead notification requirements.

Owner's Disclosure

(a) Presence of lead-based paint and/or lead-based paint hazards (check (i) or (ii) below):

(i)_____ Known lead-based paint and/or lead-based paint hazards are present in the housing (explain).

_____

(ii)_____ Owner/Lessor has no knowledge of lead-based paint and/or lead-based paint hazards in the housing.

(b) Records and reports available to the owner/lessor (Check (i) or (ii) below):

(i)_____ Owner/Lessor has provided the tenant with all available records and reports pertaining to lead-based paint and/or lead-based paint hazards in the housing (circle documents below).

Lead Inspection Report;   Risk Assessment Report;   Letter of Interim Control;   Letter of Compliance

(ii)_____ Owner/Lessor has no reports or records pertaining to lead-based paint and/or lead-based paint hazards in the housing.

Tenant's Acknowledgement (initial)

(c)_____ Tenant has received copies of all documents circled above.

(d) _____ Tenant has received no documents listed above.

(e)_____ Tenant has received the Massachusetts Tenant Lead Law Notification.

Agent's Acknowledgement (initial)

(f)_____ Agent has informed the owner/lessor of the owner's/lessor's obligations under federal and state law for lead-based paint disclosure and notification and is aware of his/her responsibility to ensure compliance.

Certification of Accuracy

The following parties have reviewed the information above and certify, to the best of their knowledge, that the information they have provided is true and accurate.

Owner/Lessor	Date	Owner/Lessor	Date
Tenant	Date	Tenant	Date
Agent	Date	Agent	Date

Owner/Managing Agent Information (Please Print):

Name	Street	Apt.
City/Town	Zip	Telephone

____I (owner/managing agent) certify that I provided the Tenant Lead Law Notification/Tenant Certification Form and any existing Lead Law documents to the tenant, but the tenant refused to sign this certification.

The tenant gave the following reason: _____

The Massachusetts Lead Law prohibits rental discrimination, including refusing to rent to families with children or evicting families with children because of lead paint.

Contact the Childhood Lead Poisoning Prevention Program for information on the availability of this form in other languages.

Tenant and owner must each keep a completed and signed copy of this form.

This page intentionally left blank.

Prior Landlord and Credit Report Authorization Letter

Landlord's Name: _____

Address: _____

City, State, Zip: _____

Rental Property: _____

      I hereby give the above landlord the right to obtain a credit report, criminal background check, and any other information regarding me and I release from all liability all persons, companies and corporations supplying such information. I indemnify the above landlord against any liability which might result from making such investigation.

      I understand that any false answers, statements, or implications made by me in this application or other required documents shall be considered sufficient cause for denial of this rental lease application.

Applicant's Name: _____

Second Applicant's Name: _____

Address: _____

City, State, Zip: _____

Applicant: SSN#_____   D.O.B. _____

2nd Applicant: SSN#_____   D.O.B. _____

Signed By:

_____   _____

Applicant   **Date**

_____   _____

Second Applicant   **Date**

Witnessed By:

_____

This page intentionally left blank.

STATEMENT OF CONDITION

NOTE: This is a statement of the condition of the premises you have leased or rented. You should read it carefully in order to see if it is correct. If it is correct, you must sign it. If it is not correct, you must attach a separate signed list of any damage which you believe exists in the premises. This statement must be returned to the lessor or his agent within fifteen (15) days after you receive this list or within fifteen (15) days after you move in, whichever is later. If you do not return this list within the specified time period, a court may later view your failure to return the list as your agreement that the list is complete and correct in any suit which you may bring to recover the security deposit.

To:

Upon examination of the above premises, the lessor has found the premises to be in good condition and without defect except as to the existence of the following conditions:

Date:

_____
Landlord's Signature

This statement is correct, agrees and assented to:

_____   _____
Lessee   Lessee

Date: Date:

This page intentionally left blank.

RECEIPT FOR SECURITY DEPOSIT AND LAST MONTH'S RENT DEPOSIT
Required by M.G.L. c. 186 Section 15B(2)(b)

1. Premises: _____

          street   city   state

_____

    floor   apartment number   number of rooms

2. Landlord(s): _____

                name(s)

_____

    street   city   state   zip

3. Tenant(s): _____

           name(s)

_____

    street   city   state   zip

4. Deposits

Receipts of $_____ is hereby acknowledged to be applied as follows:

    First month's rent for _____ (month): $_____
    Last month's rent for deposit:: $_____
    Security Deposit:: $_____
    Purchase/installation of new lock/key: $_____

Tenant(s) will be notified within 30 days of the name and location of the bank where this payment is deposited, and the account number. The tenant is entitled to interest on the security deposit and the last month's rent deposit as required by law. Interest is payable to a tenant at the end of each year of a tenancy. Upon termination of the tenancy, interest shall be prorated. The tenant shall provide the landlord with a forwarding address at the termination of the tenancy indicating where such interest may be given or sent.

Additional, subsequent amounts may be requested and shall be paid by Tenant(s) when, as and if the rent is increased. The amount of each subsequent, additional payment shall not exceed the amount of each monthly rental increase.

_____

                          Landlord

This page intentionally left blank.

STATEMENT DOCUMENTING DEPOSIT OF SECURITY DEPOSIT
[Required by M.G.L. c. 186 Section 15B(2)(b)]

To: _____

_____

_____

As required by law, the security deposit is presently held in a separate, interest-bearing account at:

Name of bank: _____

Address: _____

City: _____ Zip: _____

Account No.: _____

Sincerely,

_____

This page intentionally left blank.

This form has been made available through the courtesy of the Greater Boston Real Estate Board and is protected by copyright laws.

TENANCY AT WILL
2003 EDITION

Date: _____

_____ rents and the

LANDLORD: _____

(Name, Address and Telephone Number)

TENANT: _____

hires the PREMISES at: _____

consisting of _____

at a RENT of $_____ per_____ payable on the _____ day of each _____ in advance,

the rental period commencing on _____

Landlord rents to tenant the premises at the specified rent from rental period to rental period. This tenancy may be terminated by a written notice given by either party to the other before the first day of any rental period and shall be effective on the last day of that rental period, or thirty days after such notice has been given, whichever is longer; provided, however, that in the event of any breach by Tenant of this agreement, Landlord shall be entitled to pursue any and all remedies provided or recognized by applicable law. This tenancy shall be under the following conditions:

1. CARE OF PREMISES – The Tenant shall not paint, decorate or otherwise embellish and/or change and shall not make nor suffer any additions or alterations to be made in or to the premises without the prior written consent of the Landlord, nor make nor suffer any strip or waste, nor suffer the heat or water to be wasted, and at termination shall deliver up the premises and all property belonging to the Landlord in good, clean and tenantable order and condition, reasonable wear and tear excepted. No washing machine, air-conditioning unit, space heater, clothes dryer, television or other aerials, or other like equipment shall be installed without the prior written consent of the Landlord. No waterbeds shall be permitted in the premises.

2. MAINTENANCE – For maintenance, if other than Landlord contact:

_____

(Name)	(Address)	(Telephone Number)

3. CLEANLINESS – Tenant shall maintain the premises in a clean condition and shall not sweep, throw, or dispose of nor permit to be swept, thrown, or disposed of, from said premises nor from any doors, windows, balconies, porches or other parts of said building, any dirt, waste, rubbish, or other substance or article into any other parts of said building or the land adjacent thereto, except in proper receptacles and except in accordance with the rules of the Landlord.

4. DISTURBANCE, ILLEGAL USE – Neither the Tenant nor his family, friends, relatives, invitees, visitors, agents or servants shall make or suffer any unlawful, noisy or otherwise offensive use of the premises, nor commit or permit any nuisance to exist thereon, nor cause damage to the premises, nor create any substantial interference with the rights, comfort, safety or enjoyment of the Landlord or other occupants of the same or any other apartment, nor make any use whatsoever thereof than as and for a private residence. No articles shall be hung or shaken from the windows, doors, porches, balconies, or placed upon the exterior windowsills.

5. COMMON AREAS – No receptacles, vehicles, baby carriages or other articles of obstructions shall be placed in the halls or other common areas or passageways.

6. HEAT AND OTHER UTILITIES - The Tenant shall pay, as they become due, all bills for electricity and other utilities, whether they are used for furnishing heat or other purposes, that are furnished to the premises and presently separately metered. The Landlord agrees that he will furnish reasonably hot and cold water and reasonable heat (except to the extent that such water and heat are furnished through utilities metered to the premises as stated above) during regular heating season, all in accordance with the applicable laws, but the failure of the Landlord to provide any of the foregoing items to any specific degree, quantity, quality or character due to any causes beyond the reasonable control of the Landlord, such as accident, restriction by City, State or Federal regulations, or during necessary repairs to the apparatus shall not (subject to applicable law) form a basis of any claim for damages against the Landlord. *This section governs utility payments. Be sure to discuss with the Landlord those payments which will be required of you for this apartment.*

7. KEY AND LOCKS – Landlord shall, within a reasonable period of time following receipt of notice from Tenant of such condition, repair or replace any defective exterior locks. Locks shall not be changed, altered, or replaced nor shall new locks be added by Tenant without written permission of Landlord. Any locks so permitted to be installed shall become the property of Landlord and shall not be removed by Tenant. Tenant shall promptly give duplicate key to any such changed, altered, replaced or new lock to the Landlord.

COPYRIGHT© 1978
GREATER BOSTON REAL ESTATE BOARD
FN:RH220   PD 01/03-5000

EQUAL HOUSING
OPPORTUNITY

8. LOSS OR DAMAGE – Tenant agrees to indemnify and save Landlord harmless from all liability, loss or damage arising from any nuisance made or suffered on the premises by Tenant, his family, friends, relatives, invitees, visitors, agents, or servants or from any carelessness, neglect, or improper conduct of any such persons. Subject to the provisions of applicable law, Landlord shall not be liable for damage to or loss of property of any kind while on the premises or in any storage space in the building nor for any personal injury, unless caused by negligence of Landlord.

9. PARKING – Parking on the premises of Landlord is prohibited unless written consent is given by Landlord.

10. PETS – No dogs or other animals, birds, or pets shall be kept in or upon the premises without Landlord's written consent; and consent so given may be revoked at any time.

11. PLUMBING - Water closets, disposals, and waste pipes shall not be used for any other purposes than those for which they were constructed, nor shall any sweepings, rubbish, rags, or any other improper articles be thrown into same.

12. REPAIRS – Tenant shall at all times keep and maintain the premises and all equipment and fixtures therein or used therewith repaired, whole and of the same kind, quality, and description and in such good repair, order and condition as at the commencement of occupancy, or as may be put in thereafter, reasonable wear and tear and damage by unavoidable casualty only excepted. Landlord and Tenant agree to comply with any responsibility which either may have under applicable law to perform repairs upon the premises. If Tenant fails within a reasonable time to make such repairs, then and in any such event, Landlord may (but shall not be obligated to) make such repairs and Tenant shall reimburse Landlord for the reasonable cost of such repairs in full, upon demand.

13. RIGHT OF ENTRY - The Landlord may enter upon the leased premises in case of emergency, to make repairs thereto, to inspect the premises, or to show the premises to prospective tenants, purchasers, or mortgagees. The Landlord may also enter upon the said premises if same appear to have been abandoned by the Tenant or as otherwise permitted by law.

14. OCCUPANCY OF PREMISES – Tenant shall not assign or underlet any part or the whole of the premises, nor shall permit the premises to be occupied for a period longer than a temporary visit by anyone except the individuals specifically named in the first paragraph of this tenancy, their spouses, and any children born to them hereafter, without first obtaining on each occasion the assent in writing of Landlord.

15. NOTICES – Written notice from the Landlord to the Tenant shall be deemed to have been properly given if mailed by registered or certified mail, postage prepaid, return receipt requested to the Tenant at the address of the premises, or if delivered or left in or on any part thereof, provided that if so mailed, the receipt has been signed, or if so delivered or left, that such notice has been delivered to or left with the Tenant or anyone expressly or impliedly authorized to receive messages for the Tenant, or by any adult who resides with the Tenant in the premises. Written notice from the Tenant to the Landlord shall be deemed to have been properly given if mailed by registered or certified mail, postage prepaid, return receipt requested, to the Landlord at his address set forth in the first paragraph of this agreement, unless the Landlord shall have notified the Tenant of a change of the Landlord's address, in which case such notice shall be so sent to such changed address of the Landlord, provided that the receipt has been signed by the Landlord or anyone expressly or impliedly authorized to receive messages for the Landlord. *Notwithstanding the foregoing, notice by either party to the other shall be deemed adequate if given in any other manner authorized by law.*

16. TRUSTEE – In the event that the Landlord is a trustee or a partnership, no such trustee nor any beneficiary nor any shareholder of said trust and no partner, General or Limited, or such partnership shall be personally liable to anyone under any term, condition, covenant, obligation, or agreement expressed herein or implied hereunder or for any claim of damage or cause at law or in equity arising out of the occupancy of said premises, the use or the maintenance of said building or its approaches and equipment.

17. COPY OF AGREEMENT – Landlord shall deliver a copy of the agreement, duly executed by Landlord or his authorizing agent, to Tenant within thirty (30) days after a copy hereof, duly executed by Tenant, has been delivered to Landlord.

18. REPRISALS PROHIBITED – Landlord acknowledges that provisions of applicable law forbid a landlord from threatening to take or taking reprisals against any tenant for seeking to assert his legal rights.

19. ATTACHED FORMS - The forms, if any, attached hereto are incorporated herein by reference.

20. ADDITIONAL PROVISIONS –

TENANT – Subject to applicable law, the Landlord will provide insurance for up to $750 in benefits to cover the actual costs of relocation of the Tenant if displaced by fire or damage resulting from fire.

IN WITNESS WHEREOF, the said parties hereunto and to another instrument of like tenor, have set their hands and seals on the day and year first above written.

_____
Landlord

_____
Tenant

_____
Tenant

form 9 ◆ **213**

This form has been made available through the courtesy of the Greater Boston Real Estate Board and is protected by copyright laws.

RHA
Rental Housing Association

STANDARD FORM APARTMENT LEASE
(FIXED TERM)
2003 EDITION

Date_____

_____
(Name)

_____
(Address)   (Telephone No.)

Lessor, hereby leases to _____
         (Name)   (Address)   (Telephone No.)

_____ Lessee, who hereby hires

the following premises, viz: (Apartment)   (Suite) _____ at _____
                                                                 (Street)

_____ MA Zip _____ (consisting of) _____
         (City or Town)

_____

for the term of _____, beginning_____

and terminating on _____. The rent to be paid by the Lessee for the leased premises shall be as follows:

RENT:

TENANT:
This section governs rent payments. In some cases, rent payments may increase during the lease term. Please be sure that you carefully read and understand this section. Please initial here when you are certain that you understand and agree with this section.
Lessee's initials:

_____

_____

A: The term rent shall be $_____, payable, except as herein otherwise provided, in installments of $_____, on the _____ day of every month, in advance, so long as this lease is in force and effect;

B: However, if in any tax year commencing with the fiscal year _____ the real estate taxes on the land and buildings, of which the leased premises are a part, are in excess of the amount of the real estate taxes thereon for the fiscal year _____, (herein called the "Base Year", and being the most recent year in which the Lessor has actually received a real estate tax bill for the leased premises) Lessee will pay to Lessor as additional rent hereunder, when and as designated by notice in writing by Lessor, _____ per cent of such excess that may occur in each year of the term of this Lease or any extension or renewal thereof and proportionately for any part of a fiscal year. The Lessor represents to the Lessee that the term rent set forth in the immediately preceding paragraph (A) does not reflect any real estate tax increase subsequent to the said Base Year. Notwithstanding anything contained herein to the contrary, the Lessee shall be obligated to pay only that proportion of such increased tax as the unit leased him bears to the whole of the real estate so taxed, and if the Lessor obtains an abatement of the real estate tax levied on the whole of the real estate of which the unit leased by Lessee is a part, a proportionate share of such abatement, less reasonable attorney's fees, if any, shall be refunded to said Lessee.

LESSOR AND LESSEE FURTHER COVENANT AND AGREE:

1.   **MAINTENANCE –** For maintenance, if other than lessor, contact:

_____
    (Name)   (Address)   (Telephone No.)

2.   **ADDITIONAL PROVISIONS –**

EQUAL HOUSING OPPORTUNITY
COPYRIGHT © 1978

Form ID: RH201 PD: 08/03 10,000

13. COMMON AREAS

No receptacles, vehicles, baby carriages or other articles or obstructions shall be placed in the halls or other common areas or passageways.

14. INSURANCE

Lessee understands and agrees that it shall be Lessee's own obligation to insure his personal property.

15. KEYS AND LOCKS

Upon expiration or termination of the lease, the Lessee shall deliver the keys of the premises to the landlord. Delivery of keys by the Lessee to the Lessor, or to anyone on his behalf, shall not constitute a surrender or acceptance of surrender of the leased premises unless so stipulated in writing by the Lessor. In the event that the exterior door lock or locks in the leased premises are not in normal working order at any time during the term thereof, and if the Lessee reports such condition to the Lessor, then and in that event the Lessor shall, within a reasonable period of time following receipt of notice from the Lessee of such condition, repair or replace such lock or locks. Locks shall not be changed, altered, or replaced nor shall new locks be added by the Lessee without the written permission of the Lessor. Any locks so permitted to be installed shall become the property of the Lessor and shall not be removed by the Lessee. The Lessee shall promptly give a duplicated key to any such changed, altered, replaced or new lock to the Lessor.

16. LOSS OR DAMAGE

The Lessee agrees to indemnify and save the Lessor harmless from all liability, loss or damage arising from any nuisance made or suffered on the leased premises by the Lessee, his family, friends, relatives, invitees, visitors, agents, or servants or from any carelessness, neglect or improper conduct of any such persons. All personal property in any part of the building within the control of the Lessee shall be at the sole risk of the Lessee. Subject to provisions or applicable law the Lessor shall not be liable for damage to or loss of property of any kind which may be lost or stolen, damaged or destroyed by fire, water, steam, defective refrigeration, elevators, or otherwise, while on the leased premises or in any storage space in the building or for any personal injury unless caused by the negligence of the Lessor.

17. NOTICES

Written notice from the Lessor to the Lessee shall be deemed to have been properly given if mailed by registered or certified mail postage prepaid, return receipt requested to the Lessee at the address of the leased premises, or if delivered or left in or on any part thereof, provided that if so mailed, the receipt has been signed, or if so delivered or left, that such notice has been delivered to or left with, the Lessee or anyone expressly or impliedly authorized to receive messages for the Lessee, or by any adult who resides with the Lessee in the leased premises. Written notice from the Lessee to the Lessor shall be deemed to have been properly given if mailed by registered or certified mail, postage prepaid, return receipt requested to the Lessor at his address set forth in the first paragraph of this lease, unless the Lessor shall have notified the Lessee of a change of the Lessor's address, in which case such notice shall be so sent to such changed address of the Lessor, provided that the receipt has been signed by the Lessor or anyone expressly or impliedly authorized to receive messages for the Lessor. *Notwithstanding the foregoing, notice by either party to the other shall be deemed adequate if given in any other manner authorized by law.*

18. OTHER REGULATIONS

The Lessee agrees to conform to such lawful rules and regulations which are reasonably related to the purpose and provisions of this lease, as shall from time to time be established by the Lessor in the future for the safety, care, cleanliness, or orderly conduct of the leased premises and the building of which they are a part, and of the benefit, safety, comfort and convenience of all the occupants of said building.

19. PARKING

Parking on the premises of the Lessor is prohibited unless written consent is given by the Lessor.

20. PETS

No dogs or other animals, birds or pets shall be kept in or upon the leased premises without the Lessor's written consent, and consent so given may be revoked at any time.

21. PLUMBING

The water closets, disposals, and waste pipes shall not be used for any purposes other than those for which they were constructed, nor shall any sweepings, rubbish, rags, or any other improper articles be thrown into same, and any damage to the building caused by the misuse of such equipment shall be borne by the Lessee by whom or upon whose premises shall have been caused unless caused by the negligence of the Lessor, or by the negligence of an independent contractor employed by the Lessor.

22. REPAIRS

The Lessee agrees with the Lessor that, during this lease and for such further time as the Lessee shall hold the leased premises or any part thereof, the Lessee will at all times keep and maintain the leased premises and all equipment and fixtures therein or used therewith repaired, whole and of the same kind, quality and description and in such good repair, order and condition as the same are at the beginning of, or may be put in during the term or any extension or renewal thereof, reasonable wear and tear and damage by unavoidable casualty only excepted. The Lessor and the Lessee agree to comply with any responsibility which either may have under applicable law to perform repairs upon the leased premises. If Lessee fails within a reasonable time, or improperly makes such repairs, then and in any such event or events, the Lessor may (but shall not be obligated to) make such repairs and the Lessee shall reimburse the Lessor for the reasonable cost of such repairs in full, upon demand.

23. RIGHT OF ENTRY

The Lessor may enter upon the leased premises to make repairs thereto, to inspect the premises, or to show the premises to prospective tenants, purchasers, or mortgagees. The Lessor may also enter upon the said premises if same appear to have been abandoned by the Lessee or as otherwise permitted by law.

24. NON-PERFORMANCE OR BREACH BY LESSEE

If the Lessee shall fail to comply with any lawful term, condition, covenant, obligation, or agreement expressed herein or implied hereunder, or if the Lessee shall be declared bankrupt, or insolvent according to law or if any assignment of the Lessee's property shall be made for the benefit of creditors, or if the premises appear to be abandoned then, and in any of the said cases and notwithstanding any license or waiver of any prior breach of any of the said terms, conditions, covenants, obligations, or agreements the Lessor, without necessity or requirement of making any entry may (subject to the Lessee's rights under applicable law) terminate this lease by:

1. a seven (7) day written notice to the Lessee to vacate said leased premises in case of any breach except only for non-payment of rent, or
2. a fourteen (14) day written notice to the Lessee to vacate said leased premises upon the neglect or refusal of the Lessee to pay the rent as herein provided.

Any termination under this section shall be without prejudice to any remedies which might otherwise be used for arrears of rent or preceding breach of any of the said terms, conditions, covenants, obligations or agreements.

25. LESSEE'S COVENANTS IN EVENT OF TERMINATION

The Lessee covenants that in case of any termination of this lease, by reason of the default of the Lessee, then at the option of Lessor:

(A) the Lessee will forthwith pay to the Lessor as damages hereunder a sum equal to the amount by which the rent and other payments called for hereunder for the remainder of the term or any extension or renewal thereof exceed the fair rental value of said premises for the remainder of the term or any extension or renewal thereof; and

(B) the Lessee covenants that he will furthermore indemnify the Lessor from and against any loss and damage sustained by reason of any termination caused by the default of, or the breach by, the Lessee. Lessor's damages hereunder shall include, but shall not be limited to any loss of rents; reasonable broker's commissions for the re-letting of the leased premises; advertising costs; the reasonable cost incurred in cleaning and repainting the premises in order to re-let the same; and moving and storage charges incurred by Lessor in moving Lessee's belongings pursuant to eviction proceedings.

13. COMMON AREAS

No receptacles, vehicles, baby carriages or other articles or obstructions shall be placed in the halls or other common areas or passageways.

14. INSURANCE

Lessee understands and agrees that it shall be Lessee's own obligation to insure his personal property.

15. KEYS AND LOCKS

Upon expiration or termination of the lease, the Lessee shall deliver the keys of the premises to the landlord. Delivery of keys by the Lessee to the Lessor, or to anyone on his behalf, shall not constitute a surrender or acceptance of surrender of the leased premises unless so stipulated in writing by the Lessor. In the event that the exterior door lock or locks in the leased premises are not in normal working order at any time during the term thereof, and if the Lessee reports such condition to the Lessor, then and in that event the Lessor shall, within a reasonable period of time following receipt of notice from the Lessee of such condition, repair or replace such lock or locks. Locks shall not be changed, altered, or replaced nor shall new locks be added by the Lessee without the written permission of the Lessor. Any locks so permitted to be installed shall become the property of the Lessor and shall not be removed by the Lessee. The Lessee shall promptly give a duplicated key to any such changed, altered, replaced or new lock to the Lessor.

16. LOSS OR DAMAGE

The Lessee agrees to indemnify and save the Lessor harmless from all liability, loss or damage arising from any nuisance made or suffered on the leased premises by the Lessee, his family, friends, relatives, invitees, visitors, agents, or servants or from any carelessness, neglect or improper conduct of any such persons. All personal property in any part of the building within the control of the Lessee shall be at the sole risk of the Lessee. Subject to provisions or applicable law the Lessor shall not be liable for damage to or loss of property of any kind which may be lost or stolen, damaged or destroyed by fire, water, steam, defective refrigeration, elevators, or otherwise, while on the leased premises or in any storage space in the building or for any personal injury unless caused by the negligence of the Lessor.

17. NOTICES

Written notice from the Lessor to the Lessee shall be deemed to have been properly given if mailed by registered or certified mail postage prepaid, return receipt requested to the Lessee at the address of the leased premises, or if delivered or left in or on any part thereof, provided that if so mailed, the receipt has been signed, or if so delivered or left, that such notice has been delivered to or left with, the Lessee or anyone expressly or impliedly authorized to receive messages for the Lessee, or by any adult who resides with the Lessee in the leased premises. Written notice from the Lessee to the Lessor shall be deemed to have been properly given if mailed by registered or certified mail, postage prepaid, return receipt requested to the Lessor at his address set forth in the first paragraph of this lease, unless the Lessor shall have notified the Lessee of a change of the Lessor's address, in which case such notice shall be so sent to such changed address of the Lessor, provided that the receipt has been signed by the Lessor or anyone expressly or impliedly authorized to receive messages for the Lessor. *Notwithstanding the foregoing, notice by either party to the other shall be deemed adequate if given in any other manner authorized by law.*

18. OTHER REGULATIONS

The Lessee agrees to conform to such lawful rules and regulations which are reasonably related to the purpose and provisions of this lease, as shall from time to time be established by the Lessor in the future for the safety, care, cleanliness, or orderly conduct of the leased premises and the building of which they are a part, and of the benefit, safety, comfort and convenience of all the occupants of said building.

19. PARKING

Parking on the premises of the Lessor is prohibited unless written consent is given by the Lessor.

20. PETS

No dogs or other animals, birds or pets shall be kept in or upon the leased premises without the Lessor's written consent, and consent so given may be revoked at any time.

21. PLUMBING

The water closets, disposals, and waste pipes shall not be used for any purposes other than those for which they were constructed, nor shall any sweepings, rubbish, rags, or any other improper articles be thrown into same, and any damage to the building caused by the misuse of such equipment shall be borne by the Lessee by whom or upon whose premises shall have been caused unless caused by the negligence of the Lessor, or by the negligence of an independent contractor employed by the Lessor.

22. REPAIRS

The Lessee agrees with the Lessor that, during this lease and for such further time as the Lessee shall hold the leased premises or any part thereof, the Lessee will at all times keep and maintain the leased premises and all equipment and fixtures therein or used therewith repaired, whole and of the same kind, quality and description and in such good repair, order and condition as the same are at the beginning of, or may be put in during the term or any extension or renewal thereof, reasonable wear and tear and damage by unavoidable casualty only excepted. The Lessor and the Lessee agree to comply with any responsibility which either may have under applicable law to perform repairs upon the leased premises. If Lessee fails within a reasonable time, or improperly makes such repairs, then and in any such event or events, the Lessor may (but shall not be obligated to) make such repairs and the Lessee shall reimburse the Lessor for the reasonable cost of such repairs in full, upon demand.

23. RIGHT OF ENTRY

The Lessor may enter upon the leased premises to make repairs thereto, to inspect the premises, or to show the premises to prospective tenants, purchasers, or mortgagees. The Lessor may also enter upon the said premises if same appear to have been abandoned by the Lessee or as otherwise permitted by law.

24. NON-PERFORMANCE OR BREACH BY LESSEE

If the Lessee shall fail to comply with any lawful term, condition, covenant, obligation, or agreement expressed herein or implied hereunder, or if the Lessee shall be declared bankrupt, or insolvent according to law or if any assignment of the Lessee's property shall be made for the benefit of creditors, or if the premises appear to be abandoned then, and in any of the said cases and notwithstanding any license or waiver of any prior breach of any of the said terms, conditions, covenants, obligations, or agreements the Lessor, without necessity or requirement of making any entry may (subject to the Lessee's rights under applicable law) terminate this lease by:

1. a seven (7) day written notice to the Lessee to vacate said leased premises in case of any breach except only for non-payment of rent, or
2. a fourteen (14) day written notice to the Lessee to vacate said leased premises upon the neglect or refusal of the Lessee to pay the rent as herein provided.

Any termination under this section shall be without prejudice to any remedies which might otherwise be used for arrears of rent or preceding breach of any of the said terms, conditions, covenants, obligations or agreements.

25. LESSEE'S COVENANTS IN EVENT OF TERMINATION

The Lessee covenants that in case of any termination of this lease, by reason of the default of the Lessee, then at the option of Lessor:

(A) the Lessee will forthwith pay to the Lessor as damages hereunder a sum equal to the amount by which the rent and other payments called for hereunder for the remainder of the term or any extension or renewal thereof exceed the fair rental value of said premises for the remainder of the term or any extension or renewal thereof; and

(B) the Lessee covenants that he will furthermore indemnify the Lessor from and against any loss and damage sustained by reason of any termination caused by the default of, or the breach by, the Lessee. Lessor's damages hereunder shall include, but shall not be limited to any loss of rents; reasonable broker's commissions for the re-letting of the leased premises; advertising costs; the reasonable cost incurred in cleaning and repainting the premises in order to re-let the same; and moving and storage charges incurred by Lessor in moving Lessee's belongings pursuant to eviction proceedings.

(C) At the option of the Lessor, however, Lessor's cause of action under this article shall accrue when a new tenancy or lease term first commences subsequent to a termination under this lease, in which event Lessor's damages shall be limited to any and all damages sustained by him prior to said new tenancy or lease date.

Lessor shall also be entitled to any and all other remedies provided by law. All rights and remedies are to be cumulative and not exclusive.

26. REMOVAL OF GOODS
Lessee further covenants and agrees that if Lessor shall remove Lessee's goods or effects, pursuant to the terms hereof or of any Court order, Lessor shall not be liable or responsible for any loss of or damage to Lessee's goods or effects and the Lessor's act of so removing such goods or effects shall be deemed to be the act of and for the account of Lessee, provided, however, that if the Lessor removes the Lessee's goods or effects, he shall comply with all applicable laws, and shall exercise due care in the handling of such goods to the fullest practical extent under the circumstances.

27. NON-SURRENDER
Neither the vacating of the premises by the Lessee, nor the delivery of keys to the Lessor shall be deemed a surrender or an acceptance of surrender of the leased premises, unless so stipulated in writing by Lessor.

28. SUBLETTING, NUMBER OF OCCUPANTS
The Lessee shall not assign nor underlet any part of the whole of the leased premises, nor shall permit the leased premises to be occupied for a period longer than a temporary visit by anyone *except the individuals specifically named in the first paragraph of this lease*, their spouses, and any children born to them during the term of this lease or any extension or renewal thereof without first obtaining on each occasion the assent in writing of the Lessor.

29. TRUSTEE
In the event that the Lessor is a trustee or a partnership, no such trustee nor any beneficiary nor any shareholder of said trust and no partner, General or Limited, of such partnership shall be personally liable to anyone under any term, condition, covenant, obligation, or agreement expressed herein or implied hereunder or for any claim of damage or cause at law or in equity arising out of the occupancy of said leased premises, the use or the maintenance of said building or its approaches or equipment.

30. WAIVER
The waiver of one breach of any term, condition, covenant, obligation, or agreement of this lease shall not be considered to be a waiver of that or any other term, condition, covenant, obligation, or agreement or of any subsequent breach thereof.

31. SEPARABILITY CLAUSE
If any provision of this lease or portion of such provision or the application thereof to any person or circumstance is held invalid, the remainder of the lease (or the remainder of such provision) and the application thereof to other persons or circumstances shall not be effected thereby.

32. COPY OF LEASE
The Lessor shall deliver a copy of this lease, duly executed by Lessor or his authorized agent, to the Lessee within thirty (30) days after a copy hereof, duly executed by the Lessee, has been delivered to the Lessor.

33. REPRISALS PROHIBITED
The Lessor acknowledges that provisions of applicable law forbid a landlord from threatening to take or taking reprisals against any tenant for seeking to assert his legal rights.

34. OTHER PROVISIONS

IN WITNESS WHEREOF, the said parties hereunto and to another instrument of like tenor, have set their hands and seals on the day and year first above written; and Lessee as an individual states under the pains and penalties of perjury that said Lessee is over the age of 18 years.

_____
Lessee

_____

_____

_____
Lessor

_____
Trustee or Agent

TENANT: SUBJECT TO APPLICABLE LAW, THE LANDLORD WILL PROVIDE INSURANCE FOR UP TO $750 IN BENEFITS TO COVER THE ACTUAL COSTS OF RELOCATION OF THE TENANT IF DISPLACED BY FIRE OR DAMAGE RESULTING FROM FIRE.

TENANT: MAKE SURE TO RECEIVE A SIGNED COPY OF THIS LEASE.

GUARANTY

In consideration of the execution of the within lease by the Lessor at the request of the undersigned and of one dollar paid to the undersigned by the Lessor, the undersigned hereby, jointly and severally, guarantee the Lessor, and the heirs, successors, and assigns of the Lessor, the punctual performance by the Lessee and the legal representatives, successors and assigns of the Lessee of all the terms, conditions, covenants, obligations, and agreements in said lease on the Lessee's or their part to be performed or observed, demand and notice of default being hereby waived. The undersigned waive all surety-ship defenses and defenses in the nature thereof and assent to any and all extensions and postponements of the time of payment and all other indulgences and forbearances which may be granted from time to time to the Lessee.

WITNESS the execution hereof under seal by the undersigned the day and year first written in said lease.

_____

_____

_____

_____

_____

_____

This form has been made available through the courtesy of the Greater Boston Real Estate Board and is protected by copyright laws.

From the Office of:

SINGLE FAMILY VACATION DWELLING LEASE
(for term of 31 days or less)

FOR RESIDENTIAL PROPERTY CONSTRUCTED PRIOR TO 1978 TENANT(S) WITH CHILDREN UNDER SIX YEARS OF AGE MUST ALSO RECEIVE A SHORT TERM VACATION RENTAL LEAD PAINT NOTIFICATION FORM

Date: _____ 20____

1. PARTIES

In consideration of the mutual promises, obligations and agreements herein set forth, the parties hereto agree as follows:

_____
(Name)   (Address)   (Telephone No.)

hereinafter called "Landlord", hereby leases to:

_____
(Name)   (Address)   (Telephone No.)

hereinafter called "Tenant", and Tenant hereby hires from Landlord, the Leased Premises described in Paragraph 2.

2. LEASED PREMISES

The Leased Premises consist of the land and the buildings thereon now known as and numbered

_____
(Street)

_____ , Massachusetts _____
(City or Town)   (Zip Code)

3. TERM

This Lease shall be for a term of _____ days, beginning on _____ , 20____ and ending on

_____ , 20____.

4. RENT

Landlord acknowledges payment of rent for the term hereof in the amount of ($).

5. CLEANLINESS

Tenant shall keep the Leased Premises in a clean condition. Tenant shall be responsible for the proper storage and the final collection or ultimate disposal of all garbage and rubbish, all in accordance with the regular municipal collection system. Tenant shall not permit the Leased Premises to be overloaded, damaged, stripped or defaced, nor suffer any waste, and shall obtain the written consent of Landlord before erecting any sign on the Leased Premises. The toilets and pipes shall not be used for any purpose other than those for which they were constructed.

6. PETS

No dogs, birds or other animals or pets shall be kept in or upon the Leased Premises without Landlord's prior written consent obtained in each instance.

7. GROUNDS

Tenant shall be responsible for normal grounds maintenance during the Term of this lease. Without limiting the generality of the foregoing language, Tenant shall promptly remove snow and ice from the driveway, walks and steps of the Leased Premises, and shall keep the lawn and all shrubbery neatly trimmed, healthy and of good appearance.

8. INSURANCE

Tenant understands and agrees that it shall be Tenant's own obligation to insure Tenant's personal property.

9. COMPLIANCE WITH LAWS

Tenant shall not make or permit any use of the Leased Premises which will be unlawful, improper, or contrary to any applicable law or municipal ordinance (including without limitation all zoning, building or sanitary statutes, codes, rules, regulations, or ordinances), or which will make voidable or increase the cost of any insurance maintained on the Leased Premises by Landlord.

10. ADDITIONS OR ALTERATIONS

Tenant shall not make any additions or alterations to the Leased Premises without Landlord's prior written consent obtained in each instance.

11. SUBLETT-ING, NUMBER OF OCCUPANTS

Tenant shall not assign or sublet any part or the whole of the Leased Premises, nor shall Tenant permit the Leased Premises to be occupied by any one *except the individuals specifically named in the first paragraph of this Lease*, and their spouses without first obtaining on each occasion the consent in writing of Landlord. Notwithstanding any such consent, Tenant shall remain unconditionally and principally liable to Landlord for the payment of all rent and for the full performance of the covenants and conditions of this Lease.

12. ENTRY

Tenant shall permit Landlord to enter the Leased Premises prior to the termination of this Lease to inspect the same, to make repairs thereto (although nothing contained in this Paragraph shall be construed to require Landlord to make any such repairs), or to show the same to prospective tenants, purchasers, or mortgagees. Landlord shall also be entitled to enter the Leased Premises if they appear to have been abandoned by Tenant or otherwise, as permitted by law. Any person entitled to enter the Leased Premises in accordance with this Paragraph may do so through a duly-authorized representative. Wherever possible, Tenant shall be informed in advance of any proposed entry hereunder. Landlord may affix to any suitable part of the Leased Premises a notice for letting or selling the same and keep such notice so affixed without hindrance or molestation.

13. KEYS AND LOCKS

Locks shall not be changed, altered, or replaced nor shall new locks be added by Tenant without the written permission of Landlord. Any locks so permitted to be installed shall become the property of Landlord and shall not be removed by Tenant. Tenant shall promptly give a duplicate key to any such changed, altered, replaced or new lock to Landlord, and upon termination of this Lease, Tenant shall deliver all keys to the Leased Premises to Landlord.

14. REPAIRS

Subject to applicable law, Tenant shall keep and maintain the Leased Premises and all equipment and fixtures thereon or used therewith repaired, whole and of the same kind, quality and description and in such good repair, order and condition as the same are at the beginning of the Term of this Lease or may be put in thereafter, reasonable and ordinary wear and tear and damage by fire and other unavoidable casualty only excepted. If Tenant fails within a reasonable time to make such repairs, or makes them improperly, then and in any such event or events, Landlord may (but shall not be obligated to) make such repairs and Tenant shall reimburse Landlord for the reasonable cost of such repairs in full, as additional rent, upon demand. For maintenance, contact the Landlord or Landlord's agent:_____

                   (NAME)   (ADDRESS)   (TELEPHONE)

15. LOSS OR DAMAGE

Tenant shall indemnify Landlord against all liabilities, damages and other expenses, including reasonable attorney's fees, which may be imposed upon, incurred by, or asserted against Landlord by reason of (a) any failure on the part of Tenant to perform or comply with any covenant required to be performed or complied with by Tenant under this Lease, or (b) any injury to person or loss of or damage to property sustained or occurring on the Leased Premises on account of or based upon the act, omission, fault, negligence or misconduct of any person whomsoever other than Landlord.

16. CASUALTY AND EMINENT DOMAIN

Should a substantial portion of the Leased Premises be substantially damaged by fire or other casualty, or if the Leased Premises or any part thereof, shall be taken for any purpose by exercise of the power of eminent domain or condemnation or shall receive any direct or consequential damage for which Landlord or Tenant shall be entitled to compensation by reason of anything lawfully done in pursuance of any public authority, then this Lease shall terminate at the option of Landlord or Tenant. If this Lease is not so terminated, then a just and proportionate abatement of rent shall be made.

17. DEFAULT

If Tenant shall fail to comply with any lawful term, condition, covenant, obligation, or agreement expressed herein or implied hereunder or if the Leased Premises appear to be abandoned, then Landlord may (subject to the Tenant's rights under applicable law) terminate this Lease and recover possession of the Leased Premises without prejudice to any remedies which might otherwise be used for arrears of rent or proceeding breach of any of the said terms, conditions, covenants, obligations or agreements.

18. SURRENDER

Upon the termination of this Lease, Tenant shall deliver up the Leased Premises in as good order and condition as the same were in at the commencement of the Term, reasonable and ordinary wear and tear and damage by fire and other unavoidable casualty only excepted. Neither the vacating of the Leased Premises by Tenant, nor the delivery of keys to Landlord shall be deemed a surrender or an acceptance of surrender of the Leased Premises, unless so stipulated in writing by Landlord.

19. ATTACHED FORMS

The forms, if any, attached hereto are incorporated herein by reference.

20. NOTICES

Notice from one party to the other shall be deemed to have been properly given if mailed by registered or certified mail, postage prepaid, return receipt requested, to the other party (a) in the case of Landlord, at the address set forth in the first paragraph in this agreement or any other address of which Tenant has been notified, and (b) in the case of Tenant, at the Leased Premises, or if said notice is delivered or left in or on any part thereof, provided that there is actual or presumptive evidence that the other party or someone on his behalf received said notice. *Notwithstanding the foregoing, notice by either party to the other shall be deemed adequate if given in any other manner provided or recognized by law.*

21. LIABILITY   In the event that Landlord is a trustee or partner, no such trustee or partner nor any beneficiary nor any shareholder of said trust nor any partner of such partnership shall be personally liable to anyone under any term, condition, obligation or agreement expressed herein or implied hereunder or for any claim of damage or cause at law or in equity arising out of the occupancy of the Leased Premises, the use or maintenance of said building or its approaches and equipment.

22. DEFINITIONS   The words "Landlord" and "Tenant" as used herein shall include their respective heirs, legatees, devisees, executors, administrators, successors, personal representatives and assigns; and the words "he", "his", and "him", where applicable shall apply to Landlord or Tenant regardless of sex, number, corporate entity, trust or other body. If more than one party signs as Landlord or Tenant hereunder, the conditions and agreements herein of Landlord or Tenant shall be joint and several obligations of each such party.

23. WAIVER   The waiver of one breach of any term, condition, covenant, obligation, or agreement of this Lease shall not be considered to be a waiver of that or any other Term, condition, covenant, obligation, or agreement or of any subsequent breach thereof.

24. SEP-ARABILITY CLAUSE   If any provision of this Lease or portion of such provision or the application thereof to any person or circumstance is held invalid, the remainder of the lease (or the remainder of such provision) and the application thereof to other persons or circumstances shall not be affected thereby.

25. ADDITIONAL PROVISIONS

EXECUTED as an instrument under seal in duplicate on the day and date first written above, and Tenant as an individual states under penalty of perjury that Tenant is at least eighteen (18) years of age.

_____	_____
Witness	Landlord
_____	_____
Witness	Landlord
_____	_____
Witness	Tenant
_____	_____
Witness	Tenant

TENANT: REMEMBER TO OBTAIN A SIGNED COPY OF THIS LEASE.

GUARANTEE: In consideration of the execution of the within Lease by Landlord at the request of the undersigned and of one dollar paid to the undersigned by Landlord, the undersigned hereby, jointly and severally, guarantee to Landlord, and the heirs, successors, and assigns of Landlord, the punctual performance by Tenant and the legal representatives, successors, and assigns of Tenant of all the terms, conditions, covenants, obligations and agreements in said Lease on Tenant's or their part to be performed or observed, demand and notice of default being hereby waived. The undersigned waive all suretyship defenses and defenses in the nature thereof and assent to any and all extensions and postponements of the time of payment and all other indulgences and forbearances which may be granted from time to time to Tenant.

WITNESS the execution hereof under seal by the undersigned the day and year first written in said Lease.

_____	_____
_____	_____
_____	_____

COMMERCIAL LEASE

[Parties.]

LEASE dated as of the _____ day of _____, _____ by and between _____ and _____ of _____ _____, LESSOR, which expression shall include heirs, successors, assigns and nominees and _____, with an address at _____, LESSEE, which expression shall include successors, executors, administrators, and assigns where the context so admits.

WITNESSETH:

[Demise, Term, and Rent.]

1. LESSOR hereby leases to LESSEE and LESSEE leases from LESSOR, upon the terms and conditions set forth, the land and the commercial building known and numbered as _____.

To have and to hold the said premises unto the lessee, his executors, administrators, and assigns, for the term of _____ years from the _____ day of _____, _____, to the _____ day of _____, _____.

Yielding and paying as rent therefor the sum of _____ yearly, payable at the residence of the LESSOR in the said town of _____, in equal monthly installments (in advance) of _____ on the _____ day of each month, the first payment to be made on or by the _____ day of _____, _____.

[Security Deposit.]

2. LESSEE hereby agrees to pay to the LESSOR a security deposit in the sum equivalent to one month's rent. This deposit will be held as security for LESSEE's performance as herein provided and refunded to the LESSEE at the end of this lease subject to the LESSEE's satisfactory compliance with the conditions hereof. LESSEE shall not be entitled to interest payment of security deposit and such deposit shall not be used in lieu of payment and the last month's rent. LESSOR agrees to allow the LESSOR to pay said security deposit on or before _____, _____.

[Rent Adjustment.]

3. (a) [Tax Escalation.] If in any tax year commencing with the fiscal year _____, the real estate taxes on the land and buildings, of which the leased premises are a part, are in excess of the amount of the real estate taxes thereon for the fiscal year _____ (hereinafter called the "Base Year"), LESSEE will pay to LESSOR as additional rent hereunder, when and as designated by notice in writing by LESSOR, 100% of such excess that may occur in each year of the term of this lease or any extension or renewal thereof and proportionately for any part of a fiscal year. If the LESSOR obtains an abatement, less the reasonable fees and costs incurred in obtaining the same, shall be refunded to the LESSEE.

(b) [Consumer Price Escalation.] The LESSEE agrees that in the event the "Consumer Price Index for Urban Wage Earners and Clerical Workers, U.S. City Average, All items (1967=100)" (Hereinafter referred to as the "Price Index") published by the Bureau of Labor Statistics of the U.S. Department of Labor, or any comparable successor or substitute index designated by LESSOR appropriately adjusted, reflects an increase in the cost of living over and above the cost of living as reflected by the Price Index for the month of _____, _____ (hereinafter called the "Base Price Index"), the Basic Rent shall be adjusted in accordance with the following sub-paragraph.

Commencing as of the first anniversary of the Term Commencement Date, there shall be an adjustment (hereinafter referred to as "Adjustment") in the Basic Rent calculated by multiplying the Basic Rent by a fraction, the numerator of which shall be the Price Index for the Term Commencement Anniversary month (_____) and the denominator of which (for each such fraction) shall be the Base Price Index; PROVIDED, HOWEVER, no adjustment shall reduce the Basic Rent as previously payable in accordance with this lease.

In the event the Price Index ceases to use the 1967 average of 100 as the basis of calculation, or if a substantial change is made in the terms or number of items contained in the Price Index, then the Price Index shall be adjusted to the figure that would have been arrived at had the manner of computing the Price Index in effect at the date of this lease not been changed.

[Lessee's Covenants.]

4. The LESSEE, for himself, his heirs, executors, administrators, and assigns, does hereby covenant with the LESSOR, their successors and assigns:

(a) [To Pay Rent.] That the LESSEE will pay the said rent at the times and in the manner aforesaid, except only in the case of fire or other unavoidable casualty as hereinafter provided.

(b) [To Pay Taxes.] That he will pay the general real estate taxes which shall be assessed and levied upon the demised premises during said term as they shall fall due.

(c) [To Insure Against Fire.] That LESSEE shall maintain with respect to the leased premises and the property of which the leased premises are a part comprehensive public liability insurance in the amount of $500,000.00 with property damage insurance in limits of $100,000.00/$300,000.00 in responsible companies qualified to do business in Massachusetts and in good standing therein insuring the LESSOR as well as LESSEE against injury to persons or damage to property as provided. The LESSEE shall deposit with the LESSOR certificates for such insurance at or prior to the commencement of the term, and thereafter within thirty (30) days prior to the expiration of any such policies. All such insurance certificates shall provide that such policies shall not be cancelled without at least ten (10) days prior written notice to each assured named therein.

(d) [To Pay Light and Water Rates.] That he will promptly pay all gas, electric light, and water rates or charges which may become payable during the continuance of this lease for gas, electric light, and water used on the said premises.

(e) [To Keep in Repair and Replace Glass Broken.] That he will keep all and singular the said building and premises, including the plumbing and heating plant, in such repair as the same are at the commencement of the said term or may be put in during the continuance thereof, reasonable wear and tear and damage by fire or other unavoidable casualty only excepted, and will promptly replace all glass thereof broken during the said term by other of the same size and quality.

(f) [Not to Injure or Overload.] That he will not injure, overload, or deface or suffer to be injured, overloaded, or defaced the premises or any part thereof.

(g) [To Indemnify against Accidents and Negligence- Snow and Ice.] That he will save harmless the LESSOR from and against all loss, liability, or expense that may be incurred by reason of any accident with the machinery, gas or water or other pipes, or from any damage, neglect, or misadventure arising from or in any way growing out of the pipes, or from any neglect in the use of coalholes and covers, or in not removing snow and ice from the sidewalks or from the roof of the building, unless caused by the negligence of the LESSOR.

(h) [Note to Suffer Unlawful Use, or to Endanger Insurance, etc.] That he will not make or suffer any unlawful, improper, or offensive use of the premises, or any use or occupancy thereof contrary to any law of the state or any ordinance of the Town of _____ now or hereafter made, or which shall be injurious to any person or property, or which shall be liable to endanger or affect any insurance on the said building or to increase the premium thereof.

(i) [Not to Make Alterations, Place Signs, etc.] Not to make any alterations or additions in or to the premises without the written consent of the LESSOR, not to suffer any holes to be made or drilled in the outside stone or brick work, nor to suffer any signs to be placed upon the building except such as the LESSOR shall in writing approve.

(j) [Not to Assign.] Not to assign, underlet, or part with the possession of the whole or any part of the demised premises without first obtaining the written consent of the LESSOR.

(k) [To Permit Lessor to Enter.] That the LESSOR at all reasonable times may enter to view the premises and to make repairs which the LESSOR may see fit to make, or to show the premises to persons who wish to lease or buy, and that during three (3) months next preceding the expiration of the term of the lease he will permit the LESSOR to place and keep upon the front of the building a notice that the premises are for rent or sale.

(l) [To Yield up Premises.] That at the expiration of the said term, the LESSEE will peaceably yield up to the LESSOR or those having his estate therein the premises and all erections and additions made upon the same, in good repair in all respects, reasonable wear and damage by fire and other unavoidable casualties excepted, as the same now are or may be put in by the LESSOR.

(m) [Property and Persons on Premises at Lessee's Risk.] That all property of any kind that may be on the premises during the continuance of this lease shall be at the sole risk of the LESSEE, and that the LESSOR shall not be liable to the lessee or any other person for injury, loss, or damage to property or to any person on the premises, unless the LESSOR is negligent.

(n) [Assent Not Waiver of Future Breach of Covenants.] That no assent, express or implied, by the LESSOR to any breach of any of the LESSEE's covenants, shall be deemed to be a waiver of any succeeding breach of the same covenant.

(o) [Use of the Premises.] The LESSEE shall use the premises only for the purpose of office and/or retail use.

5. [Lessor's Covenant for Quiet Enjoyment.] The LESSOR warrants and covenants that the premises may be used for the purposes herein contemplated throughout the term of this lease and any extensions thereof. The LESSEE shall quietly enjoy the premises for the full term herein granted and for all extensions herein provided for.

6. [Termination of Demise or Suspension of Rent in Case of Fire, etc.] Provided, also, that in case the demised premises or any part thereof shall at any time during the said term be destroyed or damaged by fire or other unavoidable casualty so as to be unfit for occupancy and use, and so that the premises cannot be rebuilt or restored by the LESSOR within 120 days thereafter, then and in that case this demise shall determine; but if the premises can be rebuilt or restored within 120 days, the LESSOR will at his own expense and with due diligence so rebuild or restore the premises, and a just and proportionate part of the rents hereby reserved shall be paid by the LESSEE until the premises shall have been so rebuilt or restored.

7. [Termination of Demise or Suspension of Rent in Case of Taking by Eminent Domain.] Provided, also, that in case the whole or part of the premises demised shall be taken by the Town of _____ or the Commonwealth of Massachusetts or other public authority for any public use, then this demise shall determine (if only a part is taken, at the election of the LESSEE) from the time when possession of the whole or of the part so take shall be required for such public use, and the rents, properly apportioned, shall be paid up to that time; and the LESSEE (whether he elects that this demise shall so determine or not) shall not claim or be entitled to any part of the award to be made for damages for such taking for public use; and such taking shall not be deemed a breach of the LESSOR's covenant for quiet enjoyment hereinbefore contained: (Provided, further, that if the LESSEE shall not so elect that this demise shall determine, the obligations and liabilities of the LESSEE upon his covenants hereinbefore contained shall continue in all respects notwithstanding such taking for public use.)

8. [Default and Bankruptcy.] In the event that:

(a) the LESSEE shall default in the payment of any installment of rent or other sum herein specified and such default shall continue for ten (10) days after written notice thereof; or

(b) the LESSEE shall default in the observance or performance of any other of the LESSEE's covenants, agreements, or obligations hereunder and such default shall not be corrected within ten (10) days after written notice thereof; or

(c) the LESSEE shall be declared bankrupt or insolvent according to the law, or, if any assignment shall be made or LESSEE's property for the benefit of creditors then the LESSOR shall have the right thereafter, while such default continues, to re-enter and take complete possession of the leased premises, to declare the term of this lease ended, and remove the LESSEE's effects, without prejudice to any remedies which might be otherwise used for arrears of rent or other default, as well as receive LESSEE's indemnification for its reasonable attorney's fees.

9. [Surrender.] The LESSEE shall at the expiration or other termination of this lease remove all LESSEE's goods and effects from the leased premises, (including, without hereby limiting the generality of the foregoing, all signs and lettering affixed or painted by the LESSEE, either inside or outside the leased premises). LESSEE shall deliver to LESSOR the leased premises and all keys, locks thereto, and other fixtures connected therewith and all alterations and additions made to or upon the leased premises, in the same condition as they were put in during the term hereof, reasonable wear and tear and damage by fire or other casualty only excepted. In the event of the LESSEE's failure to remove any of LESSEE's property from the premises, LESSOR is hereby authorized, without liability to LESSEE for loss or damage thereto, and at the sole risk of LESSEE, to remove and store any of the property at LESSEE's expense, or to retain same under LESSOR's control or to sell at public or private sale, without notice any and all of the property not so removed and to apply the net proceeds of such sale to the payment of any sum due hereunder, or to destroy such property.

10. [Lessee's Option to Purchase.] Provided, further that the LESSEE shall have, and the LESSOR hereby grants to the LESSEE, the exclusive right at his option, to purchase the premises at the end of the lease period at a price that must be agreed upon by the parties or this provision shall be rendered void. The price shall be the fair market value as agreed upon by the parties, with the LESSOR's consent to such an agreement being an essential provision of this agreement. If both parties cannot agree on a purchase price, then the LESSEE shall waive this option to purchase provision. If such a price is agreed upon, such option to purchase shall be exercised by the LESSEE by written notice to the LESSOR not less than 120 days before the end of the lease period. If such option is exercised, the LESSOR and LESSEE shall, within 10 days after such exercise, execute and acknowledge in duplicate the contract of sale.

11. [Lessee's Right of First Refusal.] Should the LESSOR, during the lease term, or any extension thereof, after six months elect to sell all or any portion of the leased premises, whether separately or as part of the larger parcel, the LESSEE shall have the right of first refusal to meet any bonafide offer of sale on the same terms and conditions of such offer. Upon the LESSEE's refusal to meet such bonafide offer within 7 days of notice thereof from the LESSOR, the LESSOR shall be free to sell the premises or portion thereof to such third person in accordance with the terms and conditions of his offer.

IN WITNESS WHEREOF, the parties hereto have set their hands and seals as of this _____ day of _____, _____.

WITNESS: LESSOR:

_____   _____

_____

                                                 LESSEE:

                                                 _____

AMENDMENT TO LEASE/RENTAL AGREEMENT

The undersigned parties to that certain agreement dated _____,

_____ on the premises known as _____,

hereby agree to amend said agreement as follows:

WITNESS the hands and seals of the parties hereto this ____ day of _____,

_____.

Landlord: Tenant:

_____   _____

_____   _____

This page intentionally left blank.

NOTICE OF INTENT TO ENTER

Date:

To:

It will be necessary to enter your dwelling unit for the purpose of _____

_____

_____. If possible we would like

access on _____ at ____o'clock ___.M.

In the event this is not convenient, please call to arrange another time.

Sincerely,

_____

Address:

Phone:

This page intentionally left blank.

Notice to Quit/Rental Increase

Date: _____

_____
_____
_____

Dear _____,

Notice is hereby given you to quit and deliver up the premises now occupied by you as a Tenant at Will at a rental of $_____ per month at the expiration of the next rental period (the last day of _____) of your tenancy, beginning after this notice.

The premises are described as followed:

_____
_____
_____

PLEASE NOTE: Any monies tendered by the tenant and accepted by the landlord after receipt of this notice in an amount less that ($____) (the new rental amount) are accepted for use and occupation only and not as rent and without in any way waiving any and all rights under this notice or under any subsequent summary process proceeding. The Landlord reserves the right to accept monies reestablishing any new tenancy.

If you wish to enter into a new tenancy, your rent commencing on _____ will be $_____ per month, payable in advance.

Very truly yours,

_____

This page intentionally left blank.

RESERVATION OF RIGHTS LETTER

Date:_____

_____

_____

_____

Dear_____,

As you are aware, I am your landlord at _____
_____.

Please be advised that any money tendered to you today or hereafter is received and accepted as use and occupation only or toward arrears only and is not to be deemed as rent for said premises. I am reserving my rights with regard to pursuing court action for this eviction matter. Please be advised that I an not renewing your tenancy at will. Therefore, you must vacate the premises in accordance with the notice to quit or I will proceed with a court action to evict you and for all rent and related matters.

I anticipate your kind cooperation.

Very truly yours,

_____

This page intentionally left blank.

48 Hour Notice to Quit

Date: _____

_____

_____

_____

Dear _____,

    Notice is hereby given you to quit and deliver up the premises now occupied by you as a tenant at sufferance at the expiration of forty-eight (48) hours from receipt of this notice the premises now being held by you as my tenant namely:

_____

    HEREOF FAIL NOT, or I shall take due course of law to eject you from the same.

    PLEASE NOTE: Any monies tendered by the tenant and accepted by the landlord or his agent after _____ and after receipt of this notice are accepted for use and occupation only and not as rent and without in any way waiving any and all rights under this notice or under any subsequent summary process proceeding. The landlord hereby reserves the right to accept monies re-establishing any new tenancy.

    You are notified to produce at the trial of any subsequent summary process action or at any continuance thereof the original of this notice.

                          Very truly yours,

                       _____

This page intentionally left blank.

30 Day No Fault Notice to Quit

Date:_____

_____

_____

_____

Dear _____,

    Notice is hereby given you to quit and deliver up the premises now occupied by you as a Tenant at Will at a rental of $_____ per month at the expiration of the next rental period (the last day of _____) of your tenancy, beginning after this notice.

    The premises are described as follows:

_____

_____

PLEASE NOTE: Any monies tendered by the tenant and accepted by the landlord or their agent after receipt of this notice are accepted for use and occupation only and not as rent and without in any way waiving any and all rights under this notice or under any subsequent summary process proceeding. The landlord hereby reserves the right to accept monies re-establishing any new tenancy.

    Very truly yours,

_____

This page intentionally left blank.

14 Day Notice to Quit for nonpayment (Tenancy-at-Will)

Date:_____

_____

_____

_____

Dear _____,

    Notice is hereby given you to quit and deliver up the premises now occupied by you as a tenant at will at a rental of $_____/month at the expiration of fourteen (14) days from receipt of this notice the premises now being held by you as my tenant namely:

_____

    HEREOF FAIL NOT, or I shall take due course of law to eject you from the same.

    PLEASE NOTE: Any monies tendered by the tenant and accepted by the landlord or their agent after receipt of this notice are accepted for use and occupation only and not as rent and without in any way waiving any and all rights under this notice under any subsequent summary process proceeding. The landlord hereby reserves the right to accept monies re-establishing any new tenancy.

    If you are a tenant under will and you have not received a Notice to Quit for NonPayment of Rent within the last (12) months, you have a right to prevent the termination of your tenancy by paying or tendering to the above the full amount of rent due within ten (10) days after your receipt of this notice.

    AMOUNT DUE:

    You are notified to produce at the trial of any subsequent summary process action or at any continuance thereof the original of this notice.

Very truly yours,

_____

This page intentionally left blank.

14 Day Notice to Quit for Nonpayment (Lease)

Date: _____

_____

_____

_____

Dear _____,

    Your rent being in arrears, you are hereby notified to quit and deliver up in fourteen (14) days from receipt of this notice the above-described premises now held by you as my tenant. This notice of termination is pursuant to paragraph number _____ of your written lease.

    Amount Due: _____

_____

_____

    If you fail to so vacate, I shall employ the due course of law to evict you.

    Please be advised that any money paid to the landlord after your receipt of this notice is accepted without waiving any right to re-acquire possession of the premises, and without any intention of reinstating your tenancy or establishing a new tenancy.

    Very truly yours,

_____

This page intentionally left blank.

7 Day Notice to Quit for Cause (Lease)

Date:_____

_____

_____

_____

Dear _____,

    In accordance with paragraph number _____ of your written lease, you are hereby given notice to quit and deliver up the premises now occupied by you as my tenant at the expiration of seven (7) days from receipt of this notice.

    The premises are described as follows:

_____

    The reason for this notice is your failure to comply with covenants in the written lease, namely your failure _____ in accordance with paragraph number _____ of the lease and _____ in violation of paragraph number _____ of the written lease. Said violations of the lease have continued despite prior oral and written warnings.

    Please be advised that any money paid to the landlord after your receipt of this notice is accepted without waiving any right to re-acquire possession of the premises, and without any intention of reinstating your tenancy or establishing a new tenancy.

                        Very truly yours,

                        _____

This page intentionally left blank.

VIA FIRST CLASS AND CERTIFIED MAIL

Date:_____

To: _____

_____

_____

Re: **<u>DEMAND FOR PAYMENT OF DISHONORED CHECK</u>**

WARNING: YOU MAY BE SUED 30 DAYS AFTER THE DATE OF THIS NOTICE IF YOU DO NOT MAKE PAYMENT

Dear:_____:

Be notified that your check in the amount of $_____ dated, _____, made payable to the order of _____, has been dishonored by the _____(bank), upon which it was drawn because of _____(reason it was dishonored).

Pursuant to Massachusetts General Law C. 93 § 40A, be advised that if you do not make payment within 30 days of the date of this letter you can be sued to recover payment. If a judgement is rendered against you in court, it will include not only the original face amount of the check, but also additional liquidation damages of not less than one hundred dollars ($100.00) nor more than five hundred dollars ($500.00).

Please make payment in the form of a bank check or money order, in the amount of $_____ to _____ and forward it to my address at: _____.

Very truly yours,

_____

This page intentionally left blank.

COMMONWEALTH OF MASSACHUSETTS

_____, SS

—

NO._____

_____,
                    Plaintiff/Landlord

v.

_____,
                    Defendant/Tenant

_____

_____

SUMMARY PROCESS
C.A.

AGREEMENT FOR JUDGMENT

THE PARTIES IN THE ABOVE-CAPTIONED ACTION HEREBY STIPULATE AND AGREE TO THE FOLLOWING:

1. Judgment for the plaintiff for possession shall enter this day.

2. Execution for possession shall be issued today but shall not be effective until _____.

3. Judgment for the plaintiff for damages in the amount of _____. Execution for money damages is to be stayed until and unless an Execution is requested pursuant to paragraph four hereof.

4. If the tenant/defendant fails to comply with or make payment in accordance with the agreement set forth below, the landlord/plaintiff may request an execution for money damages plus costs and statutory interest by filing a motion which shall indicate what covenants or payment shave not been complied with and the balance owed. A copy of the motion must be provided to the tenant/defendant or his/her attorney.

5. The parties hereby agree that the following are each material terms of the Agreement and further agree that any one violation of a term on any occasion shall be considered a material provision of this Agreement:

_____

_____

_____

_____

Money damages in the amount of _____ are to be paid by the defendant to the plaintiff according to the following payment schedule and plan:

Monthly payments of _____ are to be paid to the plaintiff by mail to: _____
_____ on or by the first day of each month beginning on or by _____ and continuing until the entire balance is paid in full (_____ monthly payments).

6. The tenant/defendant hereby waives and releases unto the plaintiff any and all claims he/she has or may have had arising out of his/her occupancy on the premises from the beginning of the world to date of this Agreement.

7. The parties waive all rights to appeal. The tenant/defendant waives his/her right to move for any stay of execution.

8. The parties hereby acknowledge that they have read this Agreement for Judgment, that it contains all the terms of their agreement and that they have executed it as their free act and deed.

9. Any and all payments received hereunder are on account of use and occupancy and/or arrearages only, and are received with a full reservation of all the rights of the plaintiff in this action. No tenancy shall be created.

10. The defendant hereby allows the plaintiff or his/her agent to enter the premises to inspect, to make repairs thereto, or to show the same to a prospective tenant, purchaser, mortgagee or its agents.

THE ABOVE STIPULATIONS ARE AN AGREEMENT WHICH PLACES THE PARTIES UNDER THE RESTRAINT OF A DIRECT ORDER OF THE COURT, THAT THEY DO OR REFRAIN FROM DOING THE PARTICULAR ACTS STATED HEREIN. ANY VIOLATION OF THIS AGREEMENT CAN RESULT IN CONTEMPT AS THE DOCUMENT IN QUESTION IS INTENDED TO OPERATE AS AN INJUNCTION.

_____   _____
Plaintiff's signature   Defendant's signature
dated: dated:

SO ORDERED:

_____
Justice
dated:

COMMONWEALTH OF MASSACHUSETTS

_____, SS   TRIAL COURT OF THE COMMONWEALTH

DISTRICT COURT DEPARTMENT

_____ DIVISION

CIVIL ACTION NO._____\

_____
(Plaintiff)

VS.

AFFIDAVIT RE: NONPAYMENT OF RENT; NONMILITARY AFFIDAVIT AND COMPETENCY

_____
(Defendant)

TO THE CLERK OF THE ABOVE-NAMED COURT

I, _____, hereby certify that the defendant(s)_____
         (plaintiff/plaintiff's attorney)

_____, has made payments in the amount of $_____, and is currently indebted to the plaintiff(s) in the amount of $_____, for rent of the premises as set forth in the plaintiff's complaint.

The defendant(s) is not infant or incompetent person.

The defendant is not in the military service of the United States or its allies, as defined in the Soldier's and Sailor's Civil Relief Act of 1940, as amended but is present at

_____

_____

Signed under the pains and penalties of perjury.

Date: _____   _____
                                 (signature)

                                 _____
                                 (printed name)

( ) Execution for Possession   _____
      and Rent Requested
                                 _____
                                 (address)

                                 _____
                                 (telephone)

INDEX

SPHINX® PUBLISHING ORDER FORM

<table>
<tr><td colspan="2">BILL TO:</td><td colspan="2">SHIP TO:</td></tr>
<tr><td colspan="2"></td><td colspan="2"></td></tr>
<tr><td colspan="2"></td><td colspan="2"></td></tr>
<tr><td>Phone #</td><td>Terms</td><td>F.O.B. Chicago, IL</td><td>Ship Date</td></tr>
</table>

Charge my: ☐ VISA ☐ MasterCard ☐ American Express

☐ **Money Order or Personal Check**

Credit Card Number

Expiration Date

Qty	ISBN	Title	Retail	Ext.		Qty	ISBN	Title	Retail	Ext.
		SPHINX PUBLISHING NATIONAL TITLES					1-57071-333-2	Jurors' Rights (2E)	$12.95	
	1-57248-363-6	101 Complaint Letters That Get Results	$18.95				1-57248-374-1	Law School 101	$16.95	
	1-57248-361-X	The 529 College Savings Plan (2E)	$18.95				1-57248-377-6	The Law (In Plain English)® for Small Business	$19.95	
	1-57248-349-0	The Antique and Art Collector's Legal Guide	$24.95				1-57248-223-0	Legal Research Made Easy (3E)	$21.95	
	1-57248-347-4	Attorney Responsibilities & Client Rights	$19.95				1-57248-165-X	Living Trusts and Other Ways to Avoid Probate (3E)	$24.95	
	1-57248-148-X	Cómo Hacer su Propio Testamento	$16.95				1-57248-186-2	Manual de Beneficios para el Seguro Social	$18.95	
	1-57248-226-5	Cómo Restablecer su propio Crédito y Renegociar sus Deudas	$21.95				1-57248-220-6	Mastering the MBE	$16.95	
	1-57248-147-1	Cómo Solicitar su Propio Divorcio	$24.95				1-57248-167-6	Most Val. Business Legal Forms You'll Ever Need (3E)	$21.95	
	1-57248-166-8	The Complete Book of Corporate Forms	$24.95				1-57248-360-1	Most Val. Personal Legal Forms You'll Ever Need (2E)	$26.95	
	1-57248-353-9	The Complete Kit to Selling Your Own Home	$18.95							
	1-57248-229-X	The Complete Legal Guide to Senior Care	$21.95				1-57248-098-X	The Nanny and Domestic Help Legal Kit	$22.95	
	1-57248-391-1	The Complete Partnership Book	$24.95				1-57248-089-0	Neighbor v. Neighbor (2E)	$16.95	
	1-57248-201-X	The Complete Patent Book	$26.95				1-57248-388-1	The Power of Attorney Handbook (5E)	$22.95	
	1-57248-369-5	Credit Smart	$18.95				1-57248-332-6	Profit from Intellectual Property	$28.95	
	1-57248-163-3	Crime Victim's Guide to Justice (2E)	$21.95				1-57248-329-6	Protect Your Patent	$24.95	
	1-57248-367-9	Employees' Rights	$18.95				1-57248-385-7	Quick Cash	$14.95	
	1-57248-365-2	Employer's Rights	$24.95				1-57248-344-X	Repair Your Own Credit and Deal with Debt (2E)	$18.95	
	1-57248-251-6	The Entrepreneur's Internet Handbook	$21.95				1-57248-350-4	El Seguro Social Preguntas y Respuestas	$14.95	
	1-57248-235-4	The Entrepreneur's Legal Guide	$26.95				1-57248-217-6	Sexual Harassment: Your Guide to Legal Action	$18.95	
	1-57248-346-6	Essential Guide to Real Estate Contracts (2E)	$18.95				1-57248-219-2	The Small Business Owner's Guide to Bankruptcy	$21.95	
	1-57248-160-9	Essential Guide to Real Estate Leases	$18.95				1-57248-168-4	The Social Security Benefits Handbook (3E)	$18.95	
	1-57248-254-0	Family Limited Partnership	$26.95				1-57248-216-8	Social Security Q&A	$12.95	
	1-57248-331-8	Gay & Lesbian Rights	$26.95				1-57248-221-4	Teen Rights	$22.95	
	1-57248-139-0	Grandparents' Rights (3E)	$24.95				1-57248-366-0	Tax Smarts for Small Business	$21.95	
	1-57248-188-9	Guía de Inmigración a Estados Unidos (3E)	$24.95				1-57248-335-0	Traveler's Rights	$21.95	
	1-57248-187-0	Guía de Justicia para Víctimas del Crimen	$21.95				1-57248-236-2	Unmarried Parents' Rights (2E)	$19.95	
	1-57248-253-2	Guía Esencial para los Contratos de Arrendamiento de Bienes Raices	$22.95				1-57248-362-8	U.S. Immigration and Citizenship Q&A	$16.95	
	1-57248-103-X	Help Your Lawyer Win Your Case (2E)	$14.95				1-57248-387-3	U.S. Immigration Step by Step (2E)	$24.95	
	1-57248-334-2	Homeowner's Rights	$21.95				1-57248-392-X	U.S.A. Immigration Guide (5E)	$26.95	
	1-57248-164-1	How to Buy a Condominium or Townhome (2E)	$19.95				1-57248-192-7	The Visitation Handbook	$18.95	
	1-57248-328-8	How to Buy Your First Home	$18.95				1-57248-225-7	Win Your Unemployment Compensation Claim (2E)	$21.95	
	1-57248-191-9	How to File Your Own Bankruptcy (5E)	$21.95							
	1-57248-343-1	How to File Your Own Divorce (5E)	$26.95				1-57248-330-X	The Wills, Estate Planning and Trusts Legal Kit	&26.95	
	1-57248-222-2	How to Form a Limited Liability Company (2E)	$24.95				1-57248-138-2	Winning Your Personal Injury Claim (2E)	$24.95	
	1-57248-231-1	How to Form a Nonprofit Corporation (2E)	$24.95				1-57248-333-4	Working with Your Homeowners Association	$19.95	
	1-57248-345-8	How to Form Your Own Corporation (4E)	$26.95				1-57248-380-6	Your Right to Child Custody, Visitation and Support (3E)	$24.95	
	1-57248-232-X	How to Make Your Own Simple Will (3E)	$18.95							
	1-57248-379-2	How to Register Your Own Copyright (5E)	$24.95				1-57248-157-9	Your Rights When You Owe Too Much	$16.95	
	1-57248-104-8	How to Register Your Own Trademark (3E)	$21.95					**CALIFORNIA TITLES**		
	1-57248-394-6	How to Write Your Own Living Will (4E)	$18.95				1-57248-150-1	CA Power of Attorney Handbook (2E)	$18.95	
	1-57248-156-0	How to Write Your Own Premarital Agreement (3E)	$24.95				1-57248-337-7	How to File for Divorce in CA (4E)	$26.95	
							1-57248-145-5	How to Probate and Settle an Estate in CA	$26.95	
	1-57248-230-3	Incorporate in Delaware from Any State	$26.95				1-57248-336-9	How to Start a Business in CA (2E)	$21.95	
	1-57248-158-7	Incorporate in Nevada from Any State	$24.95				1-57248-194-3	How to Win in Small Claims Court in CA (2E)	$18.95	
	1-57248-250-8	Inmigración a los EE.UU. Paso a Paso	$22.95				1-57248-246-X	Make Your Own CA Will	$18.95	
	1-57248-400-4	Inmigración y Ciudadanía en los EE.UU. Preguntas y Respuestas	$16.95				1-57248-397-0	The Landlord's Legal Guide in CA (2E)	$24.95	
							1-57248-241-9	Tenants' Rights in CA	$21.95	
								Form Continued on Following Page	**SubTotal**	

To order, call Sourcebooks at 1-800-432-7444 or FAX (630) 961-2168 (Bookstores, libraries, wholesalers—please call for discount)

Prices are subject to change without notice.

Find more legal information at: **www.SphinxLegal.com**

SPHINX® PUBLISHING ORDER FORM

Qty	ISBN	Title	Retail	Ext.
		FLORIDA TITLES		
____	1-57071-363-4	Florida Power of Attorney Handbook (2E)	$16.95	_____
____	1-57248-396-2	How to File for Divorce in FL (8E)	$28.95	_____
____	1-57248-356-3	How to Form a Corporation in FL (6E)	$24.95	_____
____	1-57248-203-6	How to Form a Limited Liability Co. in FL (2E)	$24.95	_____
____	1-57071-401-0	How to Form a Partnership in FL	$22.95	_____
____	1-57248-113-7	How to Make a FL Will (6E)	$16.95	_____
____	1-57248-088-2	How to Modify Your FL Divorce Judgment (4E)	$24.95	_____
____	1-57248-354-7	How to Probate and Settle an Estate in FL (5E)	$26.95	_____
____	1-57248-339-3	How to Start a Business in FL (7E)	$21.95	_____
____	1-57248-204-4	How to Win in Small Claims Court in FL (7E)	$18.95	_____
____	1-57248-381-4	Land Trusts in Florida (7E)	$29.95	_____
____	1-57248-338-5	Landlords' Rights and Duties in FL (9E)	$22.95	_____
		GEORGIA TITLES		
____	1-57248-340-7	How to File for Divorce in GA (5E)	$21.95	_____
____	1-57248-180-3	How to Make a GA Will (4E)	$21.95	_____
____	1-57248-341-5	How to Start a Business in Georgia (3E)	$21.95	_____
		ILLINOIS TITLES		
____	1-57248-244-3	Child Custody, Visitation, and Support in IL	$24.95	_____
____	1-57248-206-0	How to File for Divorce in IL (3E)	$24.95	_____
____	1-57248-170-6	How to Make an IL Will (3E)	$16.95	_____
____	1-57248-247-8	How to Start a Business in IL (3E)	$21.95	_____
____	1-57248-252-4	The Landlord's Legal Guide in IL	$24.95	_____
		MARYLAND, VIRGINIA AND THE DISTRICT OF COLUMBIA		
____	1-57248-240-0	How to File for Divorce in MD, VA and DC	$28.95	_____
____	1-57248-359-8	How to Start a Business in MD, VA or DC	$21.95	_____
		MASSACHUSETTS TITLES		
____	1-57248-128-5	How to File for Divorce in MA (3E)	$24.95	_____
____	1-57248-115-3	How to Form a Corporation in MA	$24.95	_____
____	1-57248-108-0	How to Make a MA Will (2E)	$16.95	_____
____	1-57248-248-6	How to Start a Business in MA (3E)	$21.95	_____
____	1-57248-209-5	The Landlord's Legal Guide in MA	$24.95	_____
		MICHIGAN TITLES		
____	1-57248-215-X	How to File for Divorce in MI (3E)	$24.95	_____
____	1-57248-182-X	How to Make a MI Will (3E)	$16.95	_____
____	1-57248-183-8	How to Start a Business in MI (3E)	$18.95	_____
		MINNESOTA TITLES		
____	1-57248-142-0	How to File for Divorce in MN	$21.95	_____
____	1-57248-179-X	How to Form a Corporation in MN	$24.95	_____
____	1-57248-178-1	How to Make a MN Will (2E)	$16.95	_____
		NEW JERSEY TITLES		
____	1-57248-239-7	How to File for Divorce in NJ	$24.95	_____
		NEW YORK TITLES		
____	1-57248-193-5	Child Custody, Visitation and Support in NY	$26.95	_____
____	1-57248-351-2	File for Divorce in NY	$26.95	_____
____	1-57248-249-4	How to Form a Corporation in NY (2E)	$24.95	_____
____	1-57248-401-2	How to Make a NY Will (3E)	$16.95	_____
____	1-57248-199-4	How to Start a Business in NY (2E)	$18.95	_____
____	1-57248-198-6	How to Win in Small Claims Court in NY (2E)	$18.95	_____
____	1-57248-197-8	Landlords' Legal Guide in NY	$24.95	_____
____	1-57071-188-7	New York Power of Attorney Handbook	$19.95	_____
____	1-57248-122-6	Tenants' Rights in NY	$21.95	_____

Qty	ISBN	Title	Retail	Ext.
		NORTH CAROLINA TITLES		
____	1-57248-185-4	How to File for Divorce in NC (3E)	$22.95	_____
____	1-57248-129-3	How to Make a NC Will (3E)	$16.95	_____
____	1-57248-184-6	How to Start a Business in NC (3E)	$18.95	_____
____	1-57248-091-2	Landlords' Rights & Duties in NC	$21.95	_____
		NORTH CAROLINA AND SOUTH CAROLINA TITLES		
____	1-57248-371-7	How to Start a Business in NC or SC	$24.95	_____
		OHIO TITLES		
____	1-57248-190-0	How to File for Divorce in OH (2E)	$24.95	_____
____	1-57248-174-9	How to Form a Corporation in OH	$24.95	_____
____	1-57248-173-0	How to Make an OH Will	$16.95	_____
		PENNSYLVANIA TITLES		
____	1-57248-242-7	Child Custody, Visitation and Support in PA	$26.95	_____
____	1-57248-211-7	How to File for Divorce in PA (3E)	$26.95	_____
____	1-57248-358-X	How to Form a Corporation in PA	$24.95	_____
____	1-57248-094-7	How to Make a PA Will (2E)	$16.95	_____
____	1-57248-357-1	How to Start a Business in PA (3E)	$21.95	_____
____	1-57248-245-1	The Landlord's Legal Guide in PA	$24.95	_____
		TEXAS TITLES		
____	1-57248-171-4	Child Custody, Visitation, and Support in TX	$22.95	_____
____	1-57248-399-7	How to File for Divorce in TX (4E)	$24.95	_____
____	1-57248-114-5	How to Form a Corporation in TX (2E)	$24.95	_____
____	1-57248-255-9	How to Make a TX Will (3E)	$16.95	_____
____	1-57248-214-1	How to Probate and Settle an Estate in TX (3E)	$26.95	_____
____	1-57248-228-1	How to Start a Business in TX (3E)	$18.95	_____
____	1-57248-111-0	How to Win in Small Claims Court in TX (2E)	$16.95	_____
____	1-57248-355-5	The Landlord's Legal Guide in TX	$24.95	_____

SubTotal This page _____

SubTotal previous page _____

Shipping — $5.00 for 1st book, $1.00 each additional _____

Illinois residents add 6.75% sales tax _____

Connecticut residents add 6.00% sales tax _____

Total_ _____

To order, call Sourcebooks at 1-800-432-7444 or FAX (630) 961-2168 (Bookstores, libraries, wholesalers—please call for discount)

Prices are subject to change without notice.

Find more legal information at: **www.SphinxLegal.com**